# MISCHIEF
# IN GREENLAND

H. W. TILMAN

First anchorage off glacier in Evighedsfjord

# MISCHIEF IN GREENLAND

H. W. TILMAN

TILMAN

First published 1964 by Hollis & Carter
This edition published 2016 by Tilman Books
www.tilmanbooks.com
a joint venture by
Lodestar Books www.lodestarbooks.com
and Vertebrate Publishing www.v-publishing.co.uk

Original text copyright © Simon Heyworth Davis 1964
Additional material copyright © the contributors 2016

Cover design by Jane Beagley
Vertebrate Graphics Ltd. www.v-graphics.co.uk

Lodestar Books has asserted their right
to be identified as the Editor of this Work

Series editor Dick Wynne
Series researcher Bob Comlay

The publisher has made reasonable effort to locate
the holders of copyright in the illustrations in this book,
and will be pleased to hear from them regarding
correct attribution in future editions

All rights reserved

A CIP catalogue record for this book
is available from the British Library

ISBN 978-1-909461-24-6

Typeset in Baskerville from Storm Type Foundry
Printed and bound by Pulsio, Bulgaria
All papers used by Tilman Books are sourced responsibly

# Contents

| | | |
|---|---|---|
| | Foreword: | |
| | Tilman's Influence – *Colin Putt* | 9 |
| | **PART ONE** | |
| I | The Objective and the Crew | 17 |
| II | Fitting-out | 29 |
| III | To Belfast | 39 |
| IV | The Atlantic | 47 |
| V | To Godthaab | 57 |
| VI | Northwards to Igdlorssuit | 69 |
| VII | At Igdlorssuit | 81 |
| VIII | Among the Mountains | 90 |
| IX | Homeward Bound | 103 |
| | **PART TWO** | |
| X | A New Objective | 115 |
| XI | To Cape Farewell | 127 |
| XII | To Godthaab and Evighedsfjord | 137 |
| XIII | Climbing in Evighedsfjord | 149 |
| XIV | First Attempt on Exeter Sound | 163 |
| XV | Mount Raleigh | 175 |
| XVI | Homeward Bound | 188 |
| | John Davis | 196 |
| | Bird Migration in the North Atlantic | 202 |
| | Zoology in the Arctic | 205 |
| | Afterword: | |
| | Bill Tilman: An Inspiration – *Annie Hill* | 211 |

# Photographs

| | |
|---|---|
| First anchorage off glacier in Evighedsfjord | 2 |
| *Mischief* alongside the quay at Godthaab | 65 |
| Godthaab—Church and Hans Egede monument | 65 |
| Iceberg in the Vaigat | 78 |
| Igdlorssuit Eskimos or Greenlanders | 83 |
| Igdlorssuit—church and rack of shark meat | 83 |
| Doryman under sail | 86 |
| Igdlorssuit—weighing shark liver | 86 |
| Anchorage at Upernivik glacier | 93 |
| Summit ridge of peak climbed on Upernivik | 93 |
| Glacier on Upernivik | 100 |
| In Inukaavsait between Qiope and Upernivik Island | 100 |
| Entrance to Kangerdkuarssuk | 107 |
| Iceberg in the Vaigat | 107 |
| Evighedsfjord—at the first bend | 143 |
| Kangamiut | 146 |
| Among loose floes | 146 |
| Evighedsfjord—crossing the ice-fall | 151 |
| Evighedsfjord from halfway up first peak | 154 |
| Evighedsfjord—on shore at the first anchorage | 159 |
| Mountains in Evighedsfjord | 159 |
| Iceberg in Exeter Sound | 168 |
| Camp below Mt. Raleigh | 179 |
| Mt. Raleigh from Totnes Roads, Exeter Sound | 179 |
| Approaching the anchorage in Exeter Sound | 184 |
| Cliffs of Mt. Raleigh from cliffs of 'false' Raleigh | 184 |
| Pilot whales off Cape Farewell | 191 |
| Holsteinborg—original Moravian church *circa* 1732 | 191 |

# Maps

| | | |
|---|---|---|
| 1 | *Mischief*'s Track in 1961 | 16 |
| 2 | *Mischief*'s Track in 1962 | 114 |

# Mischief

Bristol Channel Pilot Cutter built at Cardiff 1906 by Thos. Baker, East Canal Wharf. Length 45 feet. Beam 13 feet. Draught 7 feet 6 inches. Net tons 13.78. T.M. 29 tons.

| | | |
|---|---|---|
| 1906–1919 | Working pilot boat owned by William Morgan or 'Billy the Mischief' | |
| 1920 | Sold for £450 to a Mr Unna who sailed her to Takoradi | |
| 1927 | First appears in the Yacht Register and had subsequently in 27 years ten different owners | |
| 1954 | Bought at Malta by Ernle Bradford who sailed her to Palma, Mallorca and sold her to her last owner, H.W. Tilman | |
| 1954 | Palma—Gibraltar—Oporto—Lymington | 2000 m. |
| 1955–56 | Las Palmas—Monte Video—Magellan Straits—Valparaiso—Callao-Panama—Bermuda—Lymington (*Mischief in Patagonia*, 1957) | 20,000 m. |
| 1957–58 | Las Palmas—Bahia Blanca—C. Town—Durban—Beira—Comoro Is.—Aldabra—Aden—Port Said—Malta—Gibraltar—Lymington (*Mischief Goes South*, 1968) | 21,000 m. |
| 1959–60 | Las Palmas—C. Town—lies Crozet—Kerguelen—C. Town—St Helena—Lymington (*Mischief among the Penguins*, 1961) | 20,000 m. |
| 1961 | West Greenland. Godthaab—Umanak Fjord—Godthaab—Lymington (*Mischief in Greenland*, 1964) | 7500 m. |
| 1962 | West Greenland. Godthaab—Evighedsfjord—Holsteinborg—Exeter Sound (Baffin Is.)—Lymington (*Mischief in Greenland*, 1964) | 6500 m. |
| 1963 | Baffin Bay. Godthaab—Godhaven—Upernivik—Lancaster Sound—Bylot Is.—Pond Inlet—Godthaab—Lymington (*Mostly Mischief*, 1966) | 6500 m. |

Surveyed Dec. 1963 and reported no longer fit for long voyages. Two mountains and a cape have officially been named after her—Mont du Mischief, by the French, on Île de la Possession, Îles Crozet; Cap Mischief, also by the French, on Île de Kerguelen; Mount Mischief, by the Canadian Survey, Exeter Sound, Baffin Is. near to Mt. Raleigh.

FOREWORD

# Tilman's Influence

## *Colin Putt*

I LEFT SCHOOL IN 1943 to work as a surveyor's assistant in the field, making ordnance maps of previously uncharted country in New Zealand. This led naturally to an interest in exploring difficult country and in mountaineering as a means to that end. The leading New Zealand mountaineer Danny Bryant, a member of the 1935 Everest reconnaissance expedition with Eric Shipton and Bill Tilman, provided my introduction to their books. To us in New Zealand, Shipton and Tilman were the perfect exemplars, their small low-cost expeditions to explore unknown mountain country, climbing virgin peaks as a secondary objective, seemed a perfect fit to our own situation and ambitions.

Then at the end of the 1950s, a French report on Antarctic activities and achievements described how Tilman had more recently adopted a seaborne approach to the problem of accessing remote mountains. From his more recent books, it became clear that he had quickly become a leading authority on sailing very small ships in high latitudes.

In 1964 I was involved in preparations for a joint mountaineering and scientific expedition to Heard Island, a remote Australian Antarctic Territory with unclimbed peaks and a challenging lack of safe anchorages. A ship, crew, finances and supplies had been acquired but we were lacking that most important item of all, a sailing master. Warwick Deacock, our expedition leader was a firm believer in always going straight to the top of any organisation, always asking for the best available. So, as expedition secretary I was instructed to write to Tilman as the best man for the job, inviting him to take command of our ship, the schooner *Patanela*. He accepted, writing that he had long viewed Heard Island as a worthy destination but that *Mischief* was too small to carry both the shore party and the sailing crew necessary to take the ship off to the nearest sheltered anchorage at Kerguelen some 200 miles to windward*.

Arriving straight from the airport in Sydney, he reviewed our state of preparation, at once saw what was needed, asked for a marline spike and set about splicing wire ropes. He lived on board and quietly assumed control of the final fitting out, loading and departure. Here was a man who really knew what he was about, one from whom you could learn all about small sailing ships, yet one who stuck closely to his doctrine of the minimum which had been so successful in the mountains. His practical seamanship went far beyond the conventional knowledge found in yachting books and magazines into areas I had not previously recognised; fundamentally he was a Victorian master mariner rather than a mid-twentieth century yachtsman.

Tilman's choice of route from Sydney to Heard Island went of necessity westward against the prevailing wind across the Great Australian Bight using *Patanela*'s engine. At Cape Leeuwin on the South-East corner of Australia he stopped the engine and reached North up the West Australian coast into the variable winds of the horse latitudes. He used the variables expertly to sail West toward South Africa until we were past the longitude of Kerguelen, then went reaching down across the Roaring Forties and Furious Fifties to Kerguelen, running back before them to Heard Island. 'Only a fool will sail to windward on a passage' he remarked, 'you go where the wind is going your way.'

From time to time in the variables we were headed by the wind. If the wind was moderate Tilman would sail close hauled on whichever tack placed our course closer to the chosen direction. In this way we might make slow progress but we didn't lose any ground. If the contrary wind became strong enough to make the ship pitch violently and slam into waves he would heave to on the more favourable tack. If ever she heeled far enough for water to run up on to the lee deck he would come up on deck, take a good look at the situation and call all hands to shorten sail. He never cracked on in a way which would subject the ship or the crew to an excessive beating but he never slowed her down more than was necessary. He had a simple rule that if in a

---

\*   *Mostly Mischief* – Published by Tilman Books, June 2016

# TILMAN'S INFLUENCE

light wind our speed fell to less than three knots we could start the engine and bring the speed up to no more than a fuel-efficient seven knots. He made clear to us the duties of the watch on deck and gently but firmly corrected any neglect of those duties. He explained what he did, usually in the course of conversation at mealtimes, and those who wished could learn a tremendous amount about sailing as distinct from yachting.

The Heard Island expedition was successful in every way; it taught me more than I had known there was to learn. On our return to Sydney, I went back to my work in the heavy chemical industry and the Skipper, as we had come to call him, returned to England to take *Mischief* to sea on her next West Greenland voyage.

Four years later, I heard that *Mischief* had been lost, had been replaced by *Sea Breeze*, and that her first voyage toward Scoresby Sund had been ruined by a 'polite mutiny'. Feeling that I had earned a holiday, I wrote to the Skipper offering my services to *Sea Breeze* on her next voyage, offering to help put down any mutiny that might arise. Tilman accepted my offer, my benevolent employer gave me leave with pay and my long-suffering wife gave me leave of absence.

The 1970 voyage was to the west coast of Greenland, between Cape Farvel and the Arctic Circle where there are continuous ranges of mountains within easy distance of the coast. In that year, 1970, the heavy *storis** pack-ice coming out of the Arctic ocean down the East coast of Greenland, round Cape Farvel and up the west coast was much denser than usual and prevented us from getting to the coast at all for much of the time. We did comparatively little climbing but learned a great deal about sea ice. On our first attempt to get through the *storis* to the clear water inshore, the engine failed just as the wind changed and closed up the ice; we stayed there beset for ten days while icebergs came ploughing through the *storis* like icebreakers, tossing thousand-ton floes aside like autumn leaves and compressing the ice ahead of them so as to nip us and make the hull creak, pop and groan.

Beset in the *storis* and watching for icebergs which might be bearing down on us, the Skipper's chief worry seemed to be that somebody might see us and forcibly rescue us against our will. He was opposed to

---

\*    A floating mass of closely crowded icebergs and floes

the prospect of rescue believing that 'Every herring should hang by its own tail'; we should be prepared and able to rescue ourselves should the need arise. The rest of us, weaker mortals, were more concerned about the risk of the ship being crushed by the ice; I even raised the subject of putting aside a grab-bag of essentials to take with us if we had to abandon ship in a hurry. The Skipper's view was more considered, 'When a ship is crushed it takes a while for her to sink and in our situation there is ice alongside to step off on to.'

I had long known that the Skipper was a brilliant survivor, he had fought right through the First World War at the front in France and survived where thousands didn't; he had escaped to Dunkirk from behind the advancing Panzers, then fought right through WW-II in the real shooting areas, much of the time behind the enemy lines. Between the wars and after WW-II he had explored and made notable ascents in the world's highest mountains, then sailed worldwide to the most remote and difficult seas in a little, old unstrengthened pilot cutter. On the 1970 Greenland voyage I began to learn how he did it.

On the way home across the North Atlantic some of the latent damage to the hull turned into a serious leak, the gaff broke so that the ship could no longer work to windward off the lee shore of Ireland and we had three small fires on board. All these incidents were dealt with suitably and we returned to England safe and happy*.

Tilman never panicked, remaining calm in seemingly desperate situations, always thinking things through to a rational conclusion, making his decision and announcing what was to be done, clearly and completely. He had been well and truly battle-hardened in two world wars and this, together with his very high intelligence and abundant common sense allowed him to take the best action in any situation. It dawned upon me that the worst thing you could do for your own survival in a sticky situation would be to doubt and oppose him. To be reasonably sure of surviving you must place complete faith in him, obey, help and support him.

Before heading back to Sydney after the 1970 Greenland trip, I paid a productive visit to my employer's London headquarters. Within a year, I was back in the UK with my family and spent the next three

---

\* *In Mischief's Wake* – Published by Tilman Books, December 2016 years working within easy reach of Lymington, the home port for the Skipper's pilot cutters. My weekends were often spent climbing in North Wales and the Peak District, dinghy sailing in the Channel and, during the winter lay-up months, working weekends on *Sea Breeze* and her successor, *Baroque*. These weekend sessions started as visits by myself alone but grew into social occasions with my children and their friends, crew from former voyages such as Bob Comlay and Simon Richardson, and last but not least Sandy Lee of Lymington, the most skilled master of many crafts I've ever known.

The Skipper, always the perfect gentleman, was also the perfect host at these working bees. Where was the fabled misogynist recluse? I never met such a person. Certainly Tilman didn't always suffer fools gladly, male or female. Sometimes he failed to notice uncomfortable conditions which others saw as hardships, but in congenial company he could be the life and soul of the party and he was always concerned and caring to his friends, although a little shy with strangers. He did have a horror of commercialisation of adventure, any attempt to involve him in such would turn him away, so would any suggestion that his volunteer crews should be paid or that he should install a two-way radio with which to cry for help and rescue. People who had tried to open these ideas with him may well have left with an impression of a laconic recluse, for he was too polite to enter into argument with them.

Tilman not only learned to sail, navigate and command late in life, but he was also largely self-taught. When he did get himself into trouble at sea he was remarkably good at fighting his way out of it and, like Shackleton, never lost a crew member through any fault of his own. He was not unlike the Polynesian sailors on this side of the world, of whom David Lewis was one, rushing into disaster and then surviving through superhuman strength and endurance. We should remember too that the expectation that a small sailing ship's master will do everything perfectly and that the crew will be perfectly safe is a very recent phenomenon. When I first went to sea in working sailing vessels seventy years ago, the smaller ones, and the yachts of the time, had no bulwarks or guard rails, just a toe rail. The big ketch *Lena* had good solid bulwarks but we had to climb along on the outside of them to get past the deck cargo of horned cattle.

For me, Tilman stands at the head of the list of great men whom I have been privileged to know and have tried, humbly, to make my exemplars, with Heinrich Harrer, David Lewis, Trevor Kletz, Warren Bonython and Sir Geoff Allen.

Colin Putt
*6 March 2015*

# PART ONE

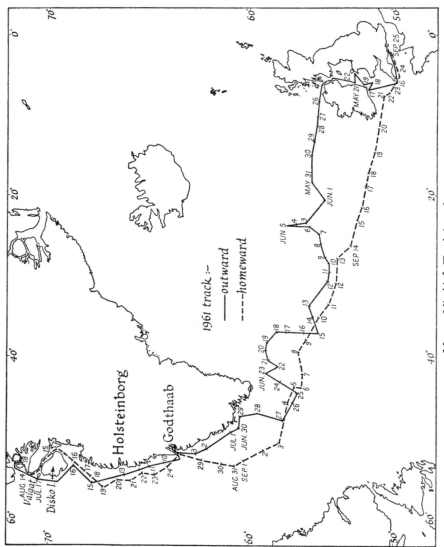

Map 1: *Mischief's* Track in 1961

CHAPTER I

# THE OBJECTIVE AND THE CREW

THIS THIRD BOOK ABOUT MY OLD PILOT-CUTTER *Mischief* is a description of two successive voyages to Greenland and Baffin Island in search of mountains. All that is needed by way of introduction is to state the reasons for choosing those particular objectives. To give reasons for wishing to sail or climb, though often attempted, is difficult and in my opinion is best left alone. If pressed to give reasons for doing such things, perhaps the best answer is found in Stevenson's words: 'In the joy of the actors lies the sense of any action. That is the explanation, that the excuse.'

In the long night watches at sea, or when lying tediously becalmed, even a man whose mind is generally a blank is more or less obliged to think of something. In such circumstances, when homeward bound from Cape Town, with the Crozet Isles and Kerguelen behind us and over 6000 miles of ocean ahead, it occurred to me that there might be cruising grounds equally exciting but far less distant than the southern ocean. In northern waters, for example. So far *Mischief*'s three voyages, each of about a year's duration and each covering some 20,000 miles, had all been to the Southern Hemisphere. A cruise in that direction has several points in its favour. One enjoys, for instance, three summers in a row, leaving England in August, arriving in the south at the beginning of the southern spring, and reaching home in time for the fag-end of yet another northern summer. Then the course followed by a sailing ship bound south by way of the Atlantic ensures having for the most part favourable winds, reducing to a minimum the unprofitable and uncomfortable business of beating against head winds. Furthermore, until the vessel reaches the latitudes of the Forties, the crew can count on soaking themselves in sunshine. Starved of sun as we are in England this is no small thing and no doubt accounts for the fact that almost every yachtsman contemplating a long cruise confines his choice to the Mediterranean, the

17

West Indies, or the South Sea Islands, places of sun and warmth, blue seas and skies, palm trees and hula-hula girls. And since these voyages are supposed to be pleasure cruises, the fact that one can drink wine almost throughout the voyage is not to be overlooked. One may stock up in the first place at the Canaries or the Azores, and replenish in Brazil or Chile if bound west, or at Cape Town if bound eastwards. True, the wine will be cheap and will not much benefit by keeping or by being well shaken up every day. But, as they say in Spain, cursed bad wine is better than holy water.

Still, even when accompanied by fair winds, sunshine, wine, flying fish, and all the other blessings of tropical seas, 20,000 miles is a long way to go for the sake of a month or so spent climbing some obscure mountains, the more so, if, as had happened on that last voyage, mountains reputed to be 5000 feet high prove to be only 3000 feet high. To misquote Prince Hal, this had seemed to me an intolerable deal of sea to one half-pennyworth of mountains. But, it may be asked, what have mountains to do with long sea voyages? Well, in my opinion, a voyage is the better for having some other objective beyond that of crossing an ocean or making a landfall on another continent, and what better objective could a man have than a mountain? This is not to underrate the satisfaction they yield or to belittle the difficulties or even dangers of voyages in small boats. In these respects a cruise in home waters may chance to provide challenge enough. But when crossing oceans or sailing in remote, lonely seas, or on unlit coasts, a man accepts the fact that no help will be at hand. The hazards of being overwhelmed by a storm or of stranding must be faced by himself and his crew alone. If overwhelmed by a storm that is the end of the matter. The consequences of running aground might be worse in some respects, for in such case one would have leisure to reflect upon the loss of one's ship and the carelessness or negligence which had brought about the loss. The amateur sailor, or haphazard navigator, should ponder a remark of the editor of the new edition of Lecky's *Wrinkles*, 'There is nothing more distressing than running ashore, unless it be a doubt as to which continent that shore belongs.'

Provided, however, that the voyage is planned with due regard to seasons, carried through with seamanlike prudence, and attended by a reasonable amount of luck, the risks are small and the voyage comes

## THE OBJECTIVE AND THE CREW

19

to be regarded as merely a step towards the final objective. The latter, I feel sure, is an added incentive to the crew, takes their minds off the voyage, and finally gives them a sense of achievement. Moreover, it helps the amateur sailor to adopt a more professional attitude towards the sea and his ship, regarding them as means to an end rather than ends in themselves. There are, indeed, many amateurs who have such an affection for ships and the sea that for them it is enough to be afloat, even if they never go out of sight of land. Whether they are amateur or professional, I suppose all sailors begin their sea careers because of a love for the sea and ships, and the romance of a sea-life. No doubt the professional's first love may soon dwindle into respect, as a sweetheart may dwindle into a wife, while the amateur is rarely at sea often enough or long enough for his ardour to cool.

But to hark back to mountains. The sole object of the three long voyages I had made in *Mischief* had been to combine sailing with climbing, the obvious solution for a man who liked both and was reluctant to give up either. To wish to follow two such enjoyable pursuits at the same time may lay one open to the charge of being too greedy of pleasure, almost gluttonous. Sydney Smith's notion of bliss, his acme of pleasure, was the eating of *paté de foie gras* to the sound of trumpets. Sailing and climbing are not, of course, comparable with that, but pleasures they must be called, if of a robust kind. To combine the two pursuits might appear to be impossible, just as it is proverbially difficult to blow and swallow at the same time. True, the great mountain ranges, the Alps, the Himalayas, the Andes, are remote enough from the sea, but there are lesser mountains that are almost washed by the sea or closely linked to it and readily accessible by the glaciers they send down into the sea. For example, some of the New Zealand Alps, the Patagonian Andes, mountains in Tierra del Fuego, and several mountainous islands in the Antarctic or sub-Antarctic such as South Georgia, the South Shetlands, Heard Island, or the Crozet and Kerguelen that we had already visited. Some of these places can be reached only by sea. They are all in the Southern Hemisphere, possessed of rude, cold climates, and are remote and not easily accessible.

Though remoteness and inaccessibility are to my mind desirable features they are scarcely compatible with short voyages. One can't have everything. Voyages in the Northern Hemisphere are obviously

20                    MISCHIEF IN GREENLAND

going to be shorter, for the mountains that can be reached by sea in a small boat lie in Spitsbergen, on both coasts of Greenland, and on the Canadian side of Davis Strait. One might add the coast range of Alaska were it not almost as distant by sea as the Southern Hemisphere; for owing to adverse winds and currents a vessel might have to sail far out into the Pacific before turning north. The hurricane season, too, would have to be considered; in avoiding it one might be bogged down in the Lotus Land of the West Indies and lose one's crew.

Nowadays Greenland can easily be reached by air, but only a man in the devil of a hurry would wish to fly to his mountains, forgoing the lingering pleasure and mounting excitement of a slow, arduous approach under his own exertions. In fact the approach to these sort of places by sea in a small boat will take up most of the time available, will probably be more exacting than the mountaineering itself, and may be the more rewarding part of the enterprise. But a voyage to northern waters, unlike one southwards, has little to offer in the way of pleasure to a yachtsman beyond a bracing climate and spectacular scenery—icebergs, ice floes, ice mountains. There is no care-free Trade Wind sailing to be enjoyed. On the outward voyage at any rate head winds are likely to be the rule rather than the exception. Sunshine, too, may well be less than that of an average English summer, for the North Atlantic on the whole is a region of cloud. Instead of the crew delighting in the freedom of shorts and a shirt, or complete nudity, they may be pent up in winter woollies. As for basking on deck, only the helmsman will spend any time there and he will be wrapped up in sweaters and oilskins.

But a man need not be an ascetic, devoted to hair shirts, to relish a voyage under the moderately adverse conditions that prevail in the North Atlantic, or even in the Arctic, in summer. We amateur sailors are of necessity summer sailors, taking our punishment in mild doses, seldom or never likely to experience what professional seafarers, particularly trawlermen, have to contend against when the sea is in its savage winter moods. Men who go to sea or climb mountains for fun derive some of their satisfaction—a lot of it retrospective—in facing and overcoming rough weather and rough terrain, cold, fatigue, and occasionally fright. When undergoing these self-inflicted minor hardships, feeling cold and frightened, eating biscuit and pemmican, they

THE OBJECTIVE AND THE CREW 21

may comfort themselves with the thought that while many non-participants will write them down as asses, there are others to whom their modest sufferings will afford a little vicarious pleasure. A favourite moral reflection of Mr Pecksniff was that if everyone were warm and well fed we should lose the satisfaction of admiring the fortitude with which others bear cold and hunger.

Of the several possible cruising grounds in the north I felt inclined first towards Spitsbergen or its near neighbour Northeastland. I was soon put off by a letter from Roger Tufft, one of the crew who had sailed with me to the Crozet, and who within ten days of our return had joined a party in Spitsbergen. He told me that there were no less than eleven other expeditions in the field. Owing to its being so far north (N. lat. 80°) and at the same time easily accessible from Norway, over the past thirty years Spitsbergen has been overrun with expeditions, mainly from the universities. Northeastland and Edge Island, lying close to Spitsbergen, are less easily approachable on account of ice, but from a mountaineering point of view they are of no interest. Although there may be little left for a climber to do in Spitsbergen, an ambitious sailor might undertake to sail round it. This difficult feat was accomplished by Commander Worsley, one of those who made the famous boat journey with Shackleton from Elephant Island to South Georgia. In 1925, in the auxiliary bark *Island* of about 100 tons, strengthened against ice, with an amateur crew of twelve, he succeeded in sailing anti-clockwise round Spitsbergen in spite of damage to both rudder and propeller from the pack-ice.

Instead of Spitsbergen I began thinking of Greenland. I may be wrong, but I suspect that an average man's knowledge of it begins and ends with the well-known hymn, 'From Greenland's icy mountains'. Supposing him to be a man who has forgotten, like Falstaff, what the inside of a church looks like or who in youth was not addicted to 'hollaing and singing of anthems', he may not know that much. A brief outline of it may therefore be welcome. If we except the continent of Australia, Greenland is the largest island in the world. Geologists, by the way, darkening counsel as they sometimes do, now say it may be two islands.

They think that at one point beneath the ice-cap there is a trough which is below sea-level. Assuming, however, that it is one island it is so

22                    MISCHIEF IN GREENLAND

large that if plunked down over Europe it would extend from the north of Scotland to the Sahara and from the Bay of Biscay to the Po valley. The whole is covered with an ice-cap thousands of feet thick except along the coasts where there is a strip of ice-free country varying in width from one mile to one hundred miles. The ice-cap covers more than nine-tenths of the land and at one point rises to a height of 10,000 feet. In 1950 the population of Greenlanders was about 22,000, confined to small towns and settlements along the coastal strip, mainly on the west coast. They are of mixed European and Eskimo descent. The country belongs to Denmark, and there are neither roads nor railways.

For mountaineers the east coast of Greenland, where the mountains are higher and less known, is the more attractive. In recent years an increasing number of climbing expeditions have gone there. But in a small boat, unstrengthened for working among ice, this coast is virtually unapproachable. According to the American Pilot Chart:

> East Greenland has much more pack-ice than West Greenland, and no ship should attempt to navigate in its waters unless it is specially designed. The East Greenland ice is usually broken and rafted into heavy floes of various sizes often with a thickness of 20 to 30 feet. It is too great to cut with the prow of a ship. The ice belt is traversed by seeking out the leads of open water, thus the course is tortuous, the ship twisting and turning, worming its way between the floes and fields. A high premium is placed on short turning circles and the manoeuvrability of vessels such as the Norwegian seal-hunter type. Experienced navigators on meeting the ice edge off north-east Greenland are said to insist on clear weather and a steady barometer before attempting passage to the coast.

On the other hand, West Greenland, according to the same authority, is not regarded as requiring a vessel built especially strong to withstand ice, except possibly so far north as Melville Bay and the approaches to Thule. In West Greenland there are three principal mountain regions. In the south in the vicinity of Cape Farewell (N. lat. 60°); half-way up the coast round about N. lat. 66°; and in the Umanak fjord region in N. lat. 71°. Although it is 800 miles north of Cape Farewell and inside the Arctic Circle I was strongly advised to go to the Umanak region by a

THE OBJECTIVE AND THE CREW 23

friend, Dr H. I. Drever of St Andrew's University. He had himself been there twice and had been completely captivated by it. In his opinion half-measures were a waste of time. I must go the whole hog and sail really far north where the scenery was grander, the icebergs bigger and better, and where the sparse inhabitants still followed to some extent the Eskimo way of life.

Dr Drever, I may as well admit, is a geologist. Many geologists are mountaineers, either of necessity because their studies have obliged them to visit mountainous regions, or because as budding mountaineers they have chosen a profession that seemed likely to furnish excuses for visiting mountains. In one or two earlier books about climbing I may have made some disparaging remarks about geologists and no doubt these were heartily reciprocated. Before the war, and indeed today, parties of climbers intent on visiting far distant ranges such as the Himalayas liked to clothe their more or less frivolous aims with a thin mantle of science. The small party of friends then became an expedition, acquired some standing, and with luck might acquire some cash assistance—a slight token of approval sometimes accorded by various learned societies to those who appear eager to enter what Goethe called the 'charnel-house of science'. For such a party the obvious scientific cloak to assume was the study of geology because it was generally easy to include in the party a man well qualified to geologize as well as climb.

On rare occasions, as might have been foreseen, this dual role led to a conflict of interests or involved the leader in a difficulty such as the following. It happened on the way back from Everest through Tibet where in those days (the 'twenties and 'thirties) one of the conditions of travel, clearly stated in the official pass, was that no stones should be turned over or bits chipped off living rock lest thereby some evil spirit might be released. It was futile to think of our geologist, a single-minded chap like N.E.O., complying with that sort of rule, so I had to shut my eyes and ultimately to pay out of expedition funds for a yak or a mule to carry homewards the fruits of two or three months' diligent chipping. One night the box of specimens (which N.E.O. used as an anchor for the guy of his tent) disappeared, the thieves no doubt judging from its weight that it could hardly contain anything but rupees. That put me in a fix. If I complained to the local headman that a box

24 MISCHIEF IN GREENLAND

of rock specimens had been stolen we should be confessedly guilty of having broken the rules; while if I said that rupees had been stolen the search might be pressed with such vigour that the box would be found and no doubt opened, proving us to be liars as well as breakers of rules. So I did nothing, thereby convincing N.E.O. that I was both conniving at theft and an enemy to science.

Dr Drever (whose name has provoked these geological reminiscences) put me in touch with a Commander Stamphøj of the Danish navy who gave me charts as well as welcome advice. The next thing was to find a crew. I needed five men and simple though this may sound the finding of a crew is the stumbling block upon which such ventures are likely to come to grief. And even though the crew problem is finally solved the solution often remains doubtful to within a few days before sailing. The long time involved is one great hindrance and for that reason it is easier to find a crew for a voyage of only five months than for one of twelve. There are probably hundreds of men knocking about who would welcome such a chance and who might be suitable; the difficulty lies in making the project known to them. There are also hundreds of sailing clubs and associations a few of whose members might be interested, but an individual like myself can make his wants known only to two or three. So far I have not had any volunteers from the yachting fraternity as represented by clubs. This in no way indicates a lack of enterprise. Such men have their own boats or crew regularly in friends' boats; most are probably interested in racing rather than cruising; long voyages do not appeal to all yachtsmen, and, as I have said, a voyage is more likely to appeal if it is in search of sun and warmth, of exotic faces and places, instead of to cold, barren, uninhabited regions. So in the end one may have to advertise, and those who reply, though they will certainly be keen on the sea and sailing, may know little about it. They may be too young to have settled down; or men who have settled down and found it a mistake; or possibly those who will never settle down—the cankers, as it were, of a calm world and a long peace.

A crew of six all told may seem large for a boat like *Mischief*. As a working boat, a pilot-cutter, the pilot who owned her would have had with him two men, or a man and an apprentice, and after the pilot had boarded the ship that needed his services the two of them would have sailed her home. This was in the years before the First World War when there were still numbers of real sailors about. In 1956 when returning from South America four of us sailed her home from Colón via Bermuda without feeling overworked; and with only four aboard there is plenty of room and more comfort below. The point of having six is that when the climbing party of two goes ashore enough are left on board to handle the boat. She might, for example, have to clear out of an anchorage in a hurry on account of wind or drifting icebergs. With six the work is easy, but ease has to be paid for by having less elbow-room below, stricter rationing of water, and the cost of extra food.

When preparing for this voyage in the autumn of 1960 I had a stroke of luck in hearing from two eager volunteers almost before I had decided where to go. Most people would think that the B.B.C. programme 'Down Your Way', which at that time was going strong, would be heard by only local listeners. They would be wrong. Barmouth, where I live, had a visit from Mr Franklin Engelmann, the maker of that programme. Although merely an English settler and no representative of the Principality, I had to utter a few vocables. I said something about the Crozet Islands voyage and the trouble I had had in finding a crew and as a result had letters from two men, one living in Birmingham and the other in Norwich, offering their services. If this method of making one's wants known were normally available the crew problem would soon be solved.

One of these letters came from David Hodge, a tanker officer on shore temporarily on sick leave. It is not often that among a yacht's crew there is a man with a First Mate's Ticket. David Hodge was about to sit for his and passed the examination before we sailed. He knew nothing of sailing boats but with his sea training he was soon at home on board *Mischief.* I appreciated having with me an adept at navigation, someone who would check my results, keep me up to the mark, and repress any leanings towards carelessness. At the end of the voyage David confessed that on the whole he preferred a 20,000-ton tanker, but I have no doubt that he enjoyed the voyage as much as we enjoyed his company.

David was a Norfolk man and so was the second volunteer letter-writer. Terence Ward was an electrician by trade, keen on sailing, unmarried, and therefore ready to take time off for the sake of

26 MISCHIEF IN GREENLAND

making a long voyage. His Broads sailing included experience in the last of the Norfolk wherries so that he was accustomed to handling heavy gear and heavy boats. He knew something about photography and undertook the making of a film with a cine-camera I had on loan from the Royal Geographical Society. As the Bulgarian proverb says: 'A man can go nowhere without money, not even to church.' It had occurred to me that part of the outlay on this voyage might be recovered if we made a successful film. Like many other apparently bright ideas this one proved to be laughably false. There are films and films, and between those made by the amateur and the professional there is a gulf. An amateur film may be judged by friends, or by fellow climbers and yachtsmen, who see it for nothing, to be highly pleasing, and the same film seen by professionals, who are expected to buy it, will be damned as worthless. It will be either technically a mess or lacking in general interest. On the whole I think that to make a successful film of an expedition one must regard the making of it as the main end and not as a by-product.

The third victim I hooked was Major E. H. Marriott, who had sailed in *Mischief* to Patagonia in 1955–6. Knowing him better than the others I can give him fuller notice. Despite a liking for leaving the ship at intervals to become a tourist, Charles Marriott, as he is generally known, had done well on that venture, especially on our crossing of the Patagonia ice-cap. On the crossing his feet had suffered so much damage that he had had to leave us at Valparaiso to come home by steamer. He is one of the 'make-do-and-mend' or 'do-it-yourself' school, both from preference and because, like John Gilpin, he has a frugal mind. On this occasion he had made out of old sailcloth his own wind-proof jacket. He had not made his own boots, though from the state they were in I thought he might well have done and therein, I suspect, lay partly the cause of his foot troubles.

When he joined us on that voyage he had had more sailing experience than I had. He even went to the length of wearing a yachting cap. In a yacht bound for New Zealand he had got as far as the Canaries where he had been marooned and had had to live on bananas until he could raise the wind for a passage home. In another yacht bound for Vancouver he had got as far as Vigo before the owner decided not to proceed and sailed home. On yet another occasion, when in some

Spanish port in a yacht, he had sustained a concussion of the head (not in the bullring) and had spent several weeks there in hospital. As a result of this he can focus only one eye at a time, a severe handicap (as will later appear) when on a mountain.

He was a regular soldier who before the last war made the grave mistake of taking the two-year course at the Military College of Science, with the effect that when war broke out he was a marked man and was given the unsoldierly job of inspecting fuses and generally seeing that munitions contractors fulfilled their contracts. However, there is crust and crumb in every loaf. At the Military College of Nonsense, as Charles called it, they had taught him the theory of navigation and the Astronomer Royal himself would be astonished at some of the things Charles could tell him about the solar, stellar, and planetary systems. As a result of this theoretical teaching he became so addicted to logarithms and haversines that a computing machine would have had difficulty in digesting the data Charles assembled when working a sight. But on that occasion he had come in the capacity of climber rather than navigator and I was glad to have him for he is an experienced mountaineer—so experienced that his movements on a mountain are now, like my own, deliberate. For the present voyage, I had hinted he might have to cook as well as climb. He could not join us before we sailed from Lymington, so, making what turned out to be an unlucky choice of rendezvous, I agreed to pick him up at Belfast.

A fourth volunteer was Dr J. B. Joyce, who in the event, at the last moment, decided reluctantly that he was not fit enough to make the voyage. He came with us only to Belfast. He was a climber, too, but was to have doubled the role of cook and doctor—a suitable arrangement because in the old sailing ships the cook was known as the 'doctor'. I hoped that though none of the crew would offer any scope for Joyce's particular line in medicine—he was an obstetrician—his general medical knowledge would cover the more likely emergencies. In none of my crews had we had a doctor and I suppose we had been lucky in never needing one. On this occasion, when we just missed having one, we did at one time feel the need.

When, some three days before sailing, we finally decided that Joyce could not come, it looked as if we must sail short-handed. But in that time I had the luck to find a substitute in young Michael Taylor-Jones

28        MISCHIEF IN GREENLAND

who, after a brief telephone conversation, boldly took a chance and came down from Cumberland to join us. He had just left Oundle and was due to go up to Cambridge to study physics in October. We soon learnt that Charles, too, had been at Oundle. So from the start, although separated by a generation or two, he and Michael were on the old-boy network. Charles displayed such a recent knowledge of the school, acquired apparently from frequent visits, that I suspected he regretted having ever left.

Lastly there was John Wayman whom I got in touch with through a friend. He was a Rugby stalwart and looked the part, a useful man, I thought, to have around in time of need. He captained, we learnt, one of the lowlier teams fielded by the Wasps. In my eyes he seemed young enough but since he had dropped to that Club's eighth or ninth team he was evidently old for Rugby. He was a cotton salesman and a keen yachtsman in his spare time, sailing every summer holiday in chartered yachts with a crew of fellow Rugby hearties. In the nature of things chartered yachts are not likely to be as well found or as well looked after as privately owned boats. In due time we heard something of these holiday adventures across the Channel, adventures that made my hair stand on end. *Mischief*'s voyages may be long but for the most part they are sedately safe.

CHAPTER II

# FITTING-OUT

B Y WAY OF INTRODUCING a dull chapter I might take the liberty of transposing the lines of an old couplet:

> To furnish a wife will cost you much trouble,
> But to fit-out a ship the expenses are double.

On the way home from Cape Town on the previous voyage the charging engine had behaved badly and had finally succumbed to the treatment it received at the hands of our hardhitting mechanic. The battery therefore could not be charged and in order to preserve what life there was left in it we gave up using it to start the main engine. As a result of this long spell of idleness and neglect the main engine, when we reached home, had been condemned as beyond repair. Its interior looked like something dredged up from one of the wrecks of the Armada. So that one big job that had to be done before this Greenland voyage was to install a new Perkins 4/99 diesel engine. The removal alone of the old engine was something of a feat. To the casual eye it appeared that it must either have been installed piece by piece or the boat must have been built round it. Then months elapsed before the new engine was delivered and the installing of it took a lot of time and money. Diesel engines are reputedly more reliable than petrol engines and in a small boat they have the immense advantage of lessening the fire risk. The presence on board of anything up to seventy gallons of petrol had always been to me a source of anxiety, an anxiety that none of the amateur engineers who had sailed with me on earlier voyages had done anything to diminish. They had all been cigarette addicts and generally liked to work over the engine with a cigarette dangling from their lips, their hands being too oily to remove it. Watching them at work, turning over in one's mind the stories of disastrous fires at sea, one felt that at any moment one might become an actor in another such story.

30                    MISCHIEF IN GREENLAND

During the winter I visited Lymington several times to work on board and to take back more homework. The cabin and galley needed painting, a job that cannot well be left for the crew to do when they are living on board a week or so before sailing. The daily use of paraffin stoves for months on end has a remarkable effect on white paintwork. The whole of the galley assumes a rich umber tone like the inside of a Tibetan house, while the deckhead immediately above the stoves becomes black as soot. The cabin paint is less affected but it too assumes a faint yellow tinge. Since washing is not very effective the only thing to do—short of stripping the paint and starting afresh—is to cover the dingy surface with more white paint.

Homework implied taking home for cleaning, overhaul, and possibly renewal, most of the wire standing rigging, the guardrails, and all the blocks and purchases of the running rigging. This is time well spent because when it starts to blow at sea a boat-owner can have no peace of mind unless he is satisfied that so far as he can tell the rigging will stand. At the cost of making *Mischief* look a little 'bald-headed' I saved myself having to work on the topmast rigging by deciding not to send up the topmast on this voyage.

Some critics have remarked that in their opinion *Mischief*'s mast, in the words of Mr Chucks the bosun, is 'precarious and not at all permanent'; and although it is staunchly stayed with shrouds of two-and-a-half-inch wire there have been times when I agreed with them. The extra strain of a heavy topmast aloft—twenty feet of it above the cap— as well as the windage of it and its five supporting wire stays, is hardly offset by the small advantage of being able to set a topsail. The more so on a North Atlantic voyage where we might expect some rough weather and where a topsail could not often be set. The big reaching jib which normally hanks on to the topmast forestay can equally be hanked to a stay running from the top of the mainmast. On voyages southwards we carried the topmast as far as a South American port or Cape Town before housing it and later sent it up again for the homeward passage. Real sailors, I suppose, would think nothing of reefing or sending up the topmast when at sea, a feat we have not yet dared to attempt. To lower or raise the spar is easy enough but before it can be passed through the cap of the mast the five wire stays have to be shackled or unshackled. After a long spell at sea shackles become hard

FITTING-OUT

to undo, however well greased they may have been, much too hard for a man working aloft in a seaway who will need one of his hands, if not both, with which to hang on.

'Damn description', said Byron, 'it is always disgusting.' However that may be many novelists devote more space to description than to action and the writers of crime stories usually invite us to study in detail the lay-out of the house or the library where the murder took place. On these grounds, though no one on board was murdered, I think a description of *Mischief*'s lay-out is permissible. Starting from forward below deck there is the forepeak with the chain-locker holding forty-five fathoms of ⅝-inch chain on the port side and a rack for sails on the other. Stowed there also are a sixty-pound CQR anchor, a small kedge anchor, grapnel, navigation lamps, and lead-lines.

Aft of the forepeak bulkhead is the galley. It is unfortunate that the place upon which the well-being of the crew so largely depends is in the fore part of the boat where the motion is most felt and where the amount of ventilation that can be obtained depends upon the prevailing weather. The fore-hatch is the only source of ventilation and if the boat is on the wind this has to be kept closed. Air in moderation is all to the good but the man working in the galley naturally prefers it unmixed with salt water. Three gimballed Primus stoves and the sink are on the port side with a number of lockers underneath, and on the other side are more lockers and a large open bin in which the spare mainsail is generally stowed. Over this bin is a canvas pipe-cot. No one ever sleeps there and it is used for stowing sails which are passed down from the foredeck through the hatch. The movable ladder leading up to the hatch comes in handy as a chock for the cook's back when he is attending to the stoves. On the bulkhead between the galley and the cabin is a hand wash-basin with a mirror above so that in the rare event of anyone wanting to shave or wash while at sea the facilities are there. Water for the galley is drawn from the main tank under the cabin table by means of a pump and there is also a pump for pumping dirty water out of the sink and the wash-basin. Thus, except that there is no way for the cook to draw the sea-water he requires but by a bucket over the side, the galley arrangements are almost on a par with the most modern kitchen. Sea-water is used whenever possible for cooking and always for washing-up. A pump for drawing it would

32                    MISCHIEF IN GREENLAND

mean yet another hole in the ship's side and such holes should be kept to a minimum.

There used to be a door in the bulkhead between galley and cabin but this has long since been abolished as an unnecessary nuisance. It might have served a purpose in shutting out smells but personally I think a good sniff of what is brewing in the galley is no bad thing, even if it is only a warning of things to come. And with no barrier between them the crew can partake of the feelings of the cook, hear him cursing vehemently if he and his pots are being thrown about or singing cheerfully if things are going well. In the fore part of the cabin there are three bunks. Of the two on the port side, one above the other, the upper has the advantage of a deck-light which allows enough light for reading. Against that it is farther to fall if one is thrown out. The proprietors of the port-side bunks have around them ample stowage space for their gear, while the man in the starboard bunk has a part share in a narrow though elegant chest of drawers standing against the bulkhead. All three occupants of these bunks are really in clover because this is the warm part of the cabin. Just abaft the foot of the mast is a small stove which burns diesel oil. It is convenient not to have to carry coal, coke or such like fuel for heating and even in a seaway the stove burns reasonably well. It is safe enough if care is used, though on one occasion when I was on board alone at Lymington the stove touched off a holocaust in the cabin. It was my fault for not noticing the thing was leaking and that the drip-tray beneath was half full of oil. A fire extinguisher from the galley when brought into play merely fed the flames and filled the cabin with noxious fumes. I got out in time, grabbing another extinguisher from the engine-room as I fled, and this one when brought into action through the cabin skylight saved the day. Still, he who would have eggs must bear with cackling; a man can't expect to enjoy warmth without experiencing the occasional rubs that its generation may entail.

As I have said, the occupants of the three forward berths are pretty snug when the stove is lit, whereas those in the three berths in the after part of the cabin, of which mine is one, derive far less benefit from it. I see no way of remedying this. Here also there are two bunks on the port side and one, the skipper's, to starboard. This is the beamiest part of the boat. The centre space is occupied by the main water

FITTING-OUT

33

tank holding 100 gallons and between the tank and the bunks on each side there is room for a wide settee. No cushions are provided for these but some sybarites bring their own. The table fitted with fiddles sits on top of the water tank. Thus, when the crew are gathered round the table three aside, their knees and feet are more or less in contact with the water tank which in cold weather is the equivalent of a block of ice. Possibly the sort of jacket one fits round hot-water tanks to keep the heat in would in this case be equally effective in preventing the cold from getting out. The table is immediately under the raised skylight which admits to the cabin plenty of light and sometimes plenty of water. There is headroom immediately under the skylight, elsewhere in the cabin the head must be carried bent. On the bulkhead at the after end of the cabin are lockers and shelves, one of the latter holding the small wireless receiving set and the other a barograph where it can be seen by the skipper reclining in his bunk. Beneath bunks and settees there is more stowage space for stores. There is no space for stores under the cabin sole where the inside ballast, four tons or more of iron pigs, lies tightly wedged. Even so we can carry enough stores for three or four months. About the middle of the cabin there is on each side a locker containing a thirty-gallon water tank; these are filled from on deck. The total water capacity of 200 gallons is made up by a forty-gallon tank on deck above the after part of the cabin; a pipe from it leads from the deck into the cabin.

A sliding door at the after end of the cabin opens to a narrow passage which gives access to the companion-way up to the cockpit and the deck. The main engine and charging engine are on the port side of the passage and on the other is the 'heads'. Here, besides the lavatory, there is the seventy-gallon fuel tank, hanging space for oilskins, a rack for boots, and a big locker where the Aldis lamp, hand-bearing compass, safety belts, and several other things live. The engine is boxed in and since it is seldom in use at sea the top of the box serves as a chart table. As well as the engines there is room on the port side for yet another thirty-gallon tank and shelves for tools, bosun's stores, blocks, shackles, cordage and small stuff. This tank was used originally for water but we now use it for paraffin. I still cherish the hope that on some future voyage, perhaps to the Islands of the Blest, it will be filled with wine. Lurking under the companion-way ladder are the two twelve-volt batteries, one for the wireless and an electric lighting system which is not much used, and the other for starting the main engine. This cannot be started by hand; if the battery is flat the engine has, so to speak, had it. Aft of the batteries is a dark cavern, the space beneath the cockpit floor and the counter, which is used for stowing warps, spare rope, and odd bits of wood.

The well of the bilge lies at the forward end of the engine-room passage-way where it is conveniently sited for catching pencils, dividers, india-rubbers, pipes, and even stop-watches, when they fall off the chart table. Having dropped two stopwatches into this well, thereby stopping them for good, I have long since given up using them. For counting the minutes or seconds that elapse between the taking of a sight and going below to read Greenwich time on the chronometer watch one can either count in one's head or use a wrist-watch. No less than three pumps can suck at this well. The main stand-by is an old-fashioned barrel-pump on deck by the cockpit which does the job handsomely with a minimum of effort. There is a rotary pump inside the 'heads' which is hard to turn, often out of order, and has a nasty trick of siphoning back. More than once, having emptied the bilge with this pump, we have been startled to find it full to overflowing a few minutes later. The third is a pump worked off the charging engine, fitted by me in a misguided moment. It can deliver only a piddle at best, and the futility of fitting such a pump is evident when one considers that at sea charging engines are fickle things, and in conditions when an extra pump might be badly needed, with a lot of water coming below, the charging engine would almost certainly have been put out of action. What a lot of money owners of small boats waste on mechanical devices that cannot always be depended upon and which anyway save only a few minutes' labour!

So much for *Mischief* below deck. From the stemhead on deck the bowsprit sticks out about twelve feet and there are some eight feet of it inboard reaching back to the bitts. Slung between the bowsprit shrouds which support it laterally is a rope net, useful for arresting sails or crew on their way into the sea. In calm weather it has been used as a hammock. The jib goes out along the bowsprit on a traveller and is set flying. The only time a man, or sometimes two men, have to go out on the bowsprit is for hanking the big reaching jib to the stay. It is

FITTING-OUT

therefore wise to get this sail in early if the wind freshens. The anchor chain leads out on the port side of the stem, passing first through a chain-stopper, the anchor winch being set back level with the bitts. These are two massive pieces of oak standing three feet above the deck. The fisherman-type anchor weighing about 100 lbs is lashed on deck near the winch, and on the other side of the foredeck, near the bitts, is carried a nine-foot dinghy. This is launched by hoisting it over the rail by means of the jib halyards. There used to be three ventilators let into the foredeck, but their copper cowls have been demolished so frequently either by the sea or rough usage that we have now plugged up the holes. Ventilators on the deck of a small boat are bound to let in as much water as air unless they are high, cumbersome affairs with water-traps, or can be mounted above the deck on the coach-house roof.

The mast is stepped well forward, about one-third of the overall length of the boat (forty-five feet) from the stem. Mounted on it are two winches for setting up the last bit of the throat and peak halyards. As I have said earlier, the mast has been thought hardly man enough for the job. It is a solid spar only seven-and-a-half inches in diameter and may well be the original mast. All the other spars that were in the boat when I took her over in 1954 have at one time or another been renewed. The only time I have misgivings about the mast, when the possibility that it may be precarious and not very permanent looks menacing, is in a rough sea with insufficient wind to keep the gaff from swinging about. In those circumstances the upper part of the mast looks as if it were being wrung or twisted like a dishcloth. But one should speak well of the bridge that carries one over; what bends will not break; and judging by the number of modern masts that are broken every summer round our coasts I believe it is not as frail as it looks.

By the bulwarks at the foot of the shrouds are two wood kevels each holding half a dozen iron belaying pins. The pins are fitted with a home-made device consisting of a wooden roller round which ropes render easily when swigged on. The wooden rollers are kinder to rope than are iron pins and cause less wear. About five feet up the shrouds the screens for the navigation lights are wired on; and just below the screens a sheer-pole, too, is fixed to the shrouds having attached to it a couple of long pegs for holding the coiled halyards. Between the mast and the cabin skylight there is space for a small deck locker used

36 MISCHIEF IN GREENLAND

for stowing the numerous short lengths of rope required frequently for lashings, as well as the handles for both the reefing gear and the mast winches. The reefing gear is the Appledore type and is probably the original fitting. The cabin stove-pipe emerges inside this locker so the lid has to be trimmed to the wind as if it were a ventilator cowl.

The cabin skylight, mounted on a foot-high coaming, is offset from centre so that the port-side deck is at this point wider by a couple of feet than the starboard. The reason for this is that when she was a pilot-cutter, the punt, as the pilots called the dinghy, used to be carried on the port side. By means of a tackle on the mast with its fall led to the cockpit, the man at the helm could raise the punt clear of the bulwarks for his mate to launch her off. The six panes of the skylight, by the way, are of half-inch plate glass; even so we once had one of these broken by a wave in the Red Sea of all places.

The twin staysail booms, dinghy oars, boathooks, and harpoon are lashed on one side of the skylight, and on the other, when it is not set up, the topmast. This would come in useful as a spare spar in case of accidents, and it has been used as a sheer-leg when through mischance or mismanagement we have gone aground on a falling tide—as may happen at times to the most prudent mariners.

Aft of the skylight is the forty-gallon water tank covered by a wood grating and on this is lashed an oak water-breaker holding about six gallons and a box for holding chafing gear. This consists of rags, bits of canvas, and ropeyarn to make up the 'Scotsmen' to wrap round ropes where they are liable to chafe. Rags may be scarce at the start of a voyage but as it progresses discarded shirts and trousers become increasingly available. Aft of the water tank is the sliding hatch covering the companion-way and between the two is space to lash jerry-cans of petrol for the charging engine and a five-gallon drum of fish-oil for calming troubled waters. The staysail sheet winches are on deck alongside the cockpit coaming.

Inside the nine-inch-high coaming the cockpit is roomy enough, measuring about five feet by six feet by two feet deep. It has seats on both sides, their main use being to provide a stepping-stone to the deck. If the weather is fine enough the crew prefer to spend their leisure hours lying about the deck rather than sitting in the cockpit. The helmsman, too, manages best by standing up as he can thus see farther

FITTING-OUT

and has more control of the long brass tiller. Usually there is one among the crew who insists on sitting down throughout his watch, or even lying stretched out on one of the benches, a position from which he can see nothing but the sky and can barely watch the compass. This is mounted on a small binnacle in the middle of the cockpit floor and can be illuminated at night by a wandering lead from the chart-room. Often in the course of a voyage, owing to trouble with the charging engine or shortage of petrol, we have to forgo this lighting and rely upon the self-luminous compass card.

All round the inside of the cockpit are capacious lockers, one reserved for paint and the others for spare sheets, bosun's chair, handy-billy, and the weather-boards for closing the entrance to the companion-way. The cockpit is self-draining in so far as it has two outlet pipes. They are of small bore, full of bends, easily blocked and difficult to clear; and the amount of debris that collects under the cockpit grating and finds its way into the pipes is really astonishing—matches, blanket fluff, broken biscuit, sweet and chocolate wrappings, and so on. But no hairpins! The pipes drain slowly even when clear, but should the cockpit happen to be half-full of water this rapidly drains into the lockers, thence into the engine-room, and so to the bilge where it can be easily cleared.

Abaft the cockpit stands the gallows for the boom to rest on when the mainsail is down; it is a piece of six inches by six inches oak resting on substantial iron stanchions. The boom is a massive spar some twenty-six feet long and nearly as thick as the mast so that it is heavy enough by itself; when resting on the gallows it has on top of it the gaff and the mainsail, the canvas probably soaking wet and double its normal weight. Altogether, therefore, when the boom is lashed down to the gallows and the boat is rolling, the stanchions are under a heavy strain. On one voyage we began to fear that they would be torn out of the deck, so that now I have had two iron cross-stays fitted as braces to keep the whole thing rigid.

Finally, between the gallows and the taffrail is the iron horse and buffer for the big main-sheet block, the single-ended main-sheet being made fast to one of two massive samson posts, one on each side of the cockpit. Bulwarks about a foot high enclose the whole of the deck and two feet above the bulwarks a wire guard-rail is supported by iron stanchions. I am told that when she was a working boat there was no guardrail as this would have hindered the launching of the punt and the hoisting of it on board. Wide though the decks are, I should say that without a guard-rail it would be easy enough to lose a man overboard. Without it the crew would feel naked and unprotected, and for my part, if there were any sort of sea running, I should be inclined to go about the deck on all fours. The rail comes in handy, too, for leaning against when taking sights at times when, perhaps, owing to the sails being in the way, one cannot see the sun from the safest and steadiest position—braced against the gallows with one leg curled lovingly round a stanchion.

*Mischief*'s dimensions, by the way, are forty-five feet long overall, thirteen-foot beam, and she draws about seven feet six inches aft. Her T.M. tonnage is twenty-nine tons, and deadweight about thirty-five tons. She was built at Cardiff in 1906.

CHAPTER III

# TO BELFAST

THIS FIRST VOYAGE TO GREENLAND seemed to me a less momentous undertaking than the three voyages southwards. The time involved did not amount to more than a long summer cruise, nor did so many ominous question-marks hang over the enterprise as they had, for example, over the voyage to the Crozet Islands—how we should fare in the Roaring Forties, whether we should find our islands, or whether the crew would see through to the end so long a voyage. On the other hand I was not happy about the Atlantic crossing and the expected head winds to which I was unaccustomed. By taking thought the ocean voyager can usually plot a course that ensures avoiding long periods of head winds. If bound for America, for instance, most yachts, unless they are racing, sail south to the Azores or Canaries whence the North-east Trades will quickly blow them westwards. That would be too roundabout for sailing to Greenland. We should have to go direct and make the best we could of the prevailing westerlies. In Davis Strait, too, we might expect trouble with fog and icebergs. Unknown perils loom the larger. I had never seen an iceberg; my experience of ice was limited to the small floes we had encountered in the Patagonian fjords.

Having agreed to call at Belfast for Charles—a matter of five or six days as I fondly imagined—I wanted to leave Lymington about the middle of May. The earlier the better, because in spring there is more chance of having some easterly or northerly winds on this side of the Atlantic. David Hodge and Terry Ward therefore joined the boat early in May. We had enough to do. All the running rigging and some of the standing rigging had to be rove, the deck and deck-fittings to be painted, the anchor chain turned and marked, sails bent, and all the gear and stores to be stowed. For shipping the bowsprit we pulled the boat's head into the quay so that having got the spar in place we could shackle on the bobstay and the shrouds from a firm base instead of

39

40 MISCHIEF IN GREENLAND

from the dinghy. For some obscure reason we did not shackle on the masthead stay, the bowsprit's main support, but left it until the boat was back in her usual position alongside the quay with the bowsprit overhanging the water. I then climbed out on it to shackle the stay. Off the Berthon boatyard at fitting-out time there is much coming and going of yachts, some to marvel at, some to admire. In this busy, narrow river one's own experience leads one to expect that one of these craft may by chance hit something or stick on the mud. A day-boat that I watched did not seem in the least likely to fulfil my expectations; she looked so smart and was so smartly handled that I shouted to David to draw his attention to it. Misunderstanding me, and thinking that I wanted a hand at the end of the bowsprit, he started to climb out to join me. Whereupon, with a resounding crack, the bowsprit, the shrouds, the net, and David and I all found ourselves tangled up in the water together. Luckily it was high water. At low water we should have landed in bottomless mud.

Even if unstayed the bowsprit is stout enough to bear two men. The trouble was that it had broken before off Cape Town where we had put back to have it scarfed, and the scarf had now come unstuck, having been made too short in the first place. When it had been repaired we put it back, this time taking care to make all fast before venturing out on it. On the whole the gremlin that lurked in this unlucky spar behaved considerately. It had broken in the first place when we were close enough to Cape Town to put back, and now it had broken while we were still in harbour.

We were to have one other small misadventure before sailing day. The new Perkins engine had yet to be tried out, so one afternoon with the Yard engineer on board we cast off. In a few minutes, in the narrowest part of the fairway, with expensive yachts moored to piles on either hand and the Yarmouth ferry about to sail, we found that the cooling system was not working. Before the Yard launch arrived to tow us home we had some panic-stricken moments, wondering which yacht we should hit and how much it would cost, or whether the ferry boat would hit us first. After a fresh start the engine behaved perfectly and out in the Solent we even went backwards. I never much care for going backwards in *Mischief*. The propeller is on the port side and whichever way one puts the tiller she seems to go in an unexpected direction. I think on this occasion we may have been covered against third-party risks, for I like to insure against that while in home waters. Outside this, for the sort of voyage that *Mischief* undertakes, the premium is excessive, running into hundreds of pounds. So, like the flies on the mouthful of meat about to be devoured by the old-timer, 'I guess, she just has to take her chance.'

John Wayman joined a few days before sailing, followed by Joyce who then broke the news that he could not make the whole voyage. He was to come only as far as Belfast. I then got in touch with Michael Taylor-Jones who joined us with only a day to spare. Food and stores were to be brought over from Southampton the day before sailing in order that the confusion normally prevailing on sailing day should be to some extent reduced. Bonded stores—drink, tobacco, cigarettes— are brought with the food stores and are accompanied by a Customs officer to see fair play. The Southampton officials must by now be almost reconciled to *Mischief*'s, departures and arrivals, each of which they are obliged to witness, clearing the ship in and out with a minimum of formality. Yachts under forty tons have to apply in the first place to H.M. Customs, London, for permission to carry bonded stores. Whether in fact or in fiction, brandy, rum, tobacco, have come to be associated with life at sea. And the Finns, who are a nation of seafarers, go so far as to say: 'If tobacco and brandy cannot help a man, death is at hand.' Consumption of these things in *Mischief* is usually small. We take enough spirits for us to have a drink on Saturday nights, on rare occasions of stress, or to celebrate landfalls and birthdays. One needs a few bottles in hand, too, for presents or to return hospitality. This time Charles had asked me to bring six bottles for his own private behoof, and since it now seemed almost certain that he would have to cook, I felt this to be a wise provision. As for tobacco, while at home I smoke a pipe moderately, and at sea immoderately, on the principle of making hay while the sun shines. It seems a mistake not to smoke all one can while one can at so moderate a cost. Joyce smoked fairly furiously but he would not be with us long enough to count. David Hodge got through a lot of cigarettes, supporting with equanimity the superior attitude of the rest of the crew who were all non-smokers.

Some slight confusion arose when it came to stowing the bonded stores. On other occasions less rigidly-minded Customs officers had not insisted on sealing the stores but had left them in the cabin where the local Customs man could see that they were still intact just before we sailed. But this time the stores must be put in a locker and sealed up, all the lockers being already full to bursting. There was nothing for it but to take out some forty tins of biscuit and dump them on the cabin floor where there was still some room.

Meeting as they do with all sorts and conditions of men, Customs officers must be in the habit of sizing up people quickly. I wondered what they made of their brief meeting with the odd collection gathered in the cabin. The Master of *Mischief*, as he signed himself on the numerous documents thrust before him, at which he peered through spectacles earnestly but un-intelligently, sucking at a pipe in the endeavour to look like a hard-bitten sailor, silent as becomes both an eminent mountaineer and a man who has really nothing to say. David Hodge, officially the mate, but not a bit like the bucko mate all sailing ships should have; slightly built and thin, as well he might be after the complication of diseases that had put him ashore. Dr Joyce, plethoric if you thought of him as a possible climber, but as a ship's doctor merely becomingly stout; perspiring perceptibly in the crowded cabin, and drawing nervously at a cigarette as he hungrily eyed the several thousand that were about to be sealed up. Terry Ward, small, fair, cherubic, like a schoolboy on holiday, though past the thirty mark. John Wayman, also fair and inclining to fat, too fat for a Wasp, I thought, though in mid-May even the Wasps must begin to relax. And Michael, our young physicist, tall and frail, too young to have started shaving seriously and with a long lock of hair which every minute he had to throw back with a disgustingly girlish toss of his head. A gentlemanly-looking lot, the Customs officer might think, with the exception of one or two; but not men to go into the jungle with, if that was his criterion, and certainly not to sea.

On May 14th, watched by a modest crowd of well-wishers, we cast off and motored down the river, preceded by the Yard launch with Ted the bosun who likes to see us safely off the premises. The slightest deviation on *Mischief*'s part from the winding, narrow fairway, a mere nervous shrinking from colliding with an oncoming Yarmouth ferryboat, will infallibly put her on the mud. At the mouth of the river, after a warm handshake from Ted, we hoisted sail and headed for the

Needles Channel. It was a pleasure to have for once a crew who knew the ropes. With the exception of Dr Joyce and David, all were familiar with sailing boats, and David with his sea background very quickly got the hang of things. I think what most impressed our steamboat officer was that a sailing boat could not always be pointed in the direction you wanted to go. Outside the Needles the wind freshened and headed us. We had not been butting into it long before we noticed that a seam near the throat of the mainsail was beginning to go. Both the mainsails we carried had seen long service and seam trouble might be expected, though not quite so early as this. As the tide was on the point of turning against us, we headed for Swanage Bay where we anchored off the town to spend a quiet evening repairing the sail. After supper when we got the anchor and were under way we were hailed by the owner of a motor launch drifting down on us who wanted us to tow him in, his engine having failed. As the evening was fine and no danger threatened his appeal fell on deaf ears. I felt a bit of a cad but the pangs of remorse were stilled when presently we heard his engine start. If I were the owner of a motor boat with a broken-down engine, I think I would pretend to be fishing or enjoying a few moments of engine-less peace rather than ask a sailing boat for a tow. As the Persians say: 'The wise man sits on the hole in his carpet.'

At the end of a pleasant day sailing close-hauled all along West Bay we went about to clear Start Point. That night the south-east wind freshened so much that we reefed and by morning, the sea having got up, the crew, except for David and myself, were far from well. To make things easy for us we handed the main and ran under stays'l alone till at tea-time we passed the Wolf Rock. There are no off-lying dangers here so we sailed close to watch the seas breaking furiously at the foot of the lighthouse. At the same time the nuclear submarine *Nautilus* passed, her square conning tower standing up like a house. Meantime the galley to which we looked for aid and comfort had become merely a source of distress. Michael had long since had to give up, Joyce battled with breakfast and lunch, while David came to the rescue for supper. This was no sort of way to run the galley and I hoped for a fast run to Belfast where Charles might take over and put things on a proper footing. But Belfast lay many days away. This wind was the last fair wind we were to have, almost the last wind of any kind.

44                    MISCHIEF IN GREENLAND

Instead of laying the course for the Smalls we got pushed steadily west as the wind backed to north. Late on the evening of the 17th we sighted land. Undoubtedly Ireland, but why no glimmer of light from the Tuskar Rock lighthouse near its south-east corner? We were not lost but uncertain of our position. Finally the near presence of a small rocky islet obliged us to go about and at the same time we sighted the Coningsbeg light-vessel twenty miles west of Tuskar! This part of the Irish coast, sprinkled with wonderfully vivid names such as the Brandies, the Barrels, the Bore, the Saltees, held yet another surprise in store. Sailing eastwards towards the Tuskar we presently spotted a red flashing light where according to both the chart and the Pilot book there should have been only the white flashing light of the Barrels buoy. A feverish search through the list of lights in the current *Brown's Nautical Almanac* revealed that a light-vessel with a red flashing light had replaced the Barrels buoy. That my chart and Pilot book had not been kept up to date shocked our professional sailor. He disliked such slipshod methods, though he admitted that while poking around at four knots in a thirty-tonner one had more time to correct these little mistakes than when proceeding at eighteen knots in a 20,000-ton ship; always provided, of course, that the elementary rule of keeping a good look-out was observed. The professional sailor regularly receives his *Notices to Mariners* and sees to it that his charts are corrected up to date before every voyage. Few amateurs, I suspect, are as careful as that. They buy or borrow their Pilot books and charts, regardless of the edition, leave them uncorrected, assuming them to be as the law of the Medes and Persians which altereth not. The stoutly bound Pilot books will last his lifetime, while the charts need be replaced only when most of their important detail has been obscured by pencil marks, cocoa stains, oil, sea-water, and perhaps pigeon droppings. I mention the last because we were frequently boarded by lost homing pigeons which took up their quarters in the chart-room and turned it into a guano island.

We duly sighted the Tuskar, a light for which I have kindly feelings. When I had last seen it, sailing over from Barmouth in a friend's four-tonner, they had made the signal 'U', meaning 'you are standing into danger', as indeed we were. This time after sighting it we sailed all night on the port tack and fetched up off the South Bishop off the Pembrokeshire coast, having lost ground to the south. The tides in St George's Channel run strongly. The characteristic of this light had also been changed from flashing every twenty seconds to flashing every five seconds. On the next tack between Wales and Ireland we did better but not as well as we expected. The next light which ought to have been Arklow turned out to be the Blackwater fifteen miles to the south. The weather was lovely and the sea calm. We took the opportunity to go aloft to unreeve the jib halyard in order to stretch it and take out the turns.

Having motored up to the Arklow light-vessel in a flat calm we picked up a northerly breeze and set off to have another look at Wales. Early on the morning of the 20th Anglesey showed up more or less where expected. Our navigation seemed to be improving with practice. Back we went again towards Ireland where we fetched up at the Codling light-vessel having made no northing whatsoever. We were suffering on the rack of bliss. As one flawless spring day of sun and warmth succeeded another, the water ruffled fitfully by light northerly winds, life became more and more tedious. I wondered why Charles and I had been such fools as to pick on Belfast as a rendezvous. But at least we avoided crossing the Irish sea again. Four times was enough. It would be tiresome to relate how we drifted, motored, and sometimes sailed up the Irish coast until at last on Monday, May 22nd, we rounded Mew Island and entered Belfast Lough. At last we had some wind, enabling us to sail in style into Ballyholm Bay, west of Bangor, where we anchored. A passing yacht, taking part in a race, hailed us to say that there was a better anchorage round the corner in Bangor Bay. I could not see much difference myself as both bays are wide open in every direction except south. Bowing to local knowledge we moved, and as we anchored for the second time I noticed a familiar figure, with yachting cap and beard, gesticulating from the beach.

Charles with his dunnage soon came on board; the crew, I think, being notably impressed with his maritime appearance. He had for the moment discarded his gum-boots, likewise the black patch he used to wear over one eye, but otherwise he fully lived up to the picture I had drawn. It relieved me to learn he had no qualms about taking over the galley, indeed he had come prepared by bringing a private store of spices and a recipe book. As I told him, we had not had a square meal

46          MISCHIEF IN GREENLAND

since leaving Lymington nine days before. The crew in turns had done their best but none showed much talent for cooking except perhaps Michael who had a deft hand with pancakes. It is best if possible to have one man in the galley, for if everyone takes a hand things are left dirty, nothing is put back in its place, and the stores and cooking gear become hopelessly jumbled. In fact it is a case of what's everybody's business is nobody's business—the reason offered by an Irishman at the time of the 'Troubles' when asked why a local magnate, much disliked by both sides, had not been shot.

The Royal Ulster Yacht Club, housed in a Victorian mansion overlooking the Lough, is noted for hospitality. We lost no time in making our number there and that evening, having first prepared our stomachs with libations of draught stout, we made good the deficiencies of the voyage. We spent two days at Bangor, replenishing fresh stores and doing odd jobs on board. One of the jib halyard sheaves had worn so much as to fray the halyard, so we hung a block on the mast instead of using the sheaves. This worked in so far as the rope rendered without getting frayed or twisted but the luff of the jib could not be hauled really tight. We sailed at six on the morning of the 25th to catch the north-going tide. The voyage to Greenland had begun.

CHAPTER IV

# THE ATLANTIC

THE NORTHERLY WINDS that might have sent us far on our way had we passed south of Ireland still persisted. But at sea as on land, the truth of the Spanish proverb, that whichever way you go there is a league of bad road, is generally borne out. At sea one must accept whatever winds blow, for it is not often possible to cheat the wind like a 'vile politician seeking to circumvent God'. Readers of *Typhoon* may recollect that a similar view was held by that sturdy seaman Captain MacWhirr, a man who 'as if unable to grasp what is due to the difference of latitudes, always wore, at home or in the Tropics, a brown bowler hat and black boots'. He had a contempt even for the laws of storms and thus expressed it to his mate at a moment when his ship was about to be all but overwhelmed by a typhoon: 'All these rules for dodging breezes and circumventing the winds of heaven, Mr Jukes, seem to me the maddest thing.'

When the tide turned against us as well as the wind we could make no progress so we ran into Red Bay where we anchored. There is little shelter from northerly winds in this deserted bay but at any rate we were out of the tide. In the evening the wind veered so that we could steer north and with the tide now under us we went like a scalded cat. The tides in the North Channel run at three knots. At midnight, northwest of Rathlin Island, I came on deck to find her moving backwards, the sails all aback and the tiller lifeless, the sea around seething as if about to boil. We were in the tail of a race, probably in the vicinity of Shamrock Pinnacle. In order to get steerage way we had to start the engine.

Having at last rounded the corner of Ireland we had the wind free and could steer west. By eight o'clock next morning, a big sea then running, we had Inishtrahull Island abeam three miles away. We did not lose sight of the Irish mountains for another two days, but we were now in the open ocean with nothing between us and America two

48                    MISCHIEF IN GREENLAND

thousand miles away. When presently the wind again headed us we
had trouble persuading *Mischief* to go about, the sea being so rough.
At the second attempt we got her round but not before the flogging
jib had shaken one of the sheet blocks out of its strop. When the wind
dropped at midnight we rolled about with the boom slamming wildly.
In such circumstances the question is whether to call all hands to get
the sails off or to leave things as they are in the hope that the wind will
soon come again. Experience teaches that leaving the sails up seldom
pays but hope generally triumphs over experience, as Dr Johnson
remarked of a man marrying for the second time. Although we stead-
ied the boom to some extent by bowsing it down with the handy-billy,
by 2 a.m. a large rent had appeared in the sail so down it had to come.
I had hoped that this sail, the weaker of the two we carried, would have
taken us across. It had already given so much trouble that we decided
to change it, a decision easier to make than to carry out on the deck
of a small boat in a rough sea with no sail to steady her. Having first
prised the second sail out of its bin in the galley we pushed it by main
force into the cabin and on to the deck through the skylight. There
are about 700 square feet of canvas in the sail, a lot of canvas to unroll
while trying to sort out the head and the foot, the tack and the clew.
Having bent it on and hoisted, we bundled up the old sail as best we
could and stuffed it below, wet as it was.

On May 30th we had our first good day's run when we logged
120 miles, and on the following day we did ninety-four miles. We felt
we were getting somewhere, for Cape Farewell, the southern tip of
Greenland, was less than 1500 miles away. We began making absurd
calculations, little thinking that another thirty days would elapse
before we rounded that noted cape. Cape Farewell is 59° 46′ north
and 43° 53′ west, but the mariner is advised not to go north of 58° 30′
when passing it on account of the ice which accumulates off the cape.
This meant for us roughly a course of west-north-west, a course that
we could seldom lay, the wind blowing most often from somewhere
between north-west and south-west. We sailed on the tack that allowed
us to point nearest to west-north-west and changed to the other tack
when that looked the most profitable. If both tacks were equally bad
we chose the port tack whereby we got farther north where degrees of
longitude measure fewer miles. In the Northern Hemisphere the Great

THE ATLANTIC                                                    49

Circle course, which is the shortest possible, lies to the north of the rhumb line course—the course that looks the shortest on a Mercator chart but in fact is not. Sailing thus, generally well off our course, we might log a hundred miles and yet make good less than half that in the direction of Cape Farewell, or even nothing at all.

Meantime the jib halyard continued to be troublesome. The sea being reasonably smooth, I went aloft and changed the block. Later we reverted to using the sheaves on the mast, and finally to the block again. It was unsatisfactory but by using the winch on the mast we could set the halyard up taut, twists and all. I must have been feeling energetic because after that I showed Charles how to make a cake, a task well within the capacity of a man who had spent two years at the Military College of Science. In fact he was already doing well and even beginning to reach out for the higher branches of his present profession. He is blessed with a cast-iron stomach. If the boat is knocking about a lot, as it was the next day, one does not expect anything but the simplest fare for supper. Defying the weather, Charles produced a rich stew with dumplings the size of cricket balls floating in it. I was about to add 'like half-tide rocks', a phrase that might have cast doubts on the wholesomeness of Charles's dumplings. We still had some fresh bread left. Ordinary bread keeps for about ten days at sea before sprouting a green mould. I suppose sliced bread wrapped in cellophane might keep longer but such bread, even without a green mould, is hardly worth eating. Having finished the fresh bread we go on to what I call 'twice-baked', thick slices of bread or rolls that have been in the oven a second time. This seems to keep indefinitely, only its bulk prevents one from carrying enough for the whole voyage. Baking bread at sea for a crew of six on paraffin stoves is not feasible on account of the time, labour, and paraffin oil needed.

Nothing could be more different from Trade Wind sailing than sailing in the Atlantic in the latitudes of the fifties. No two days are alike, and for that matter the night that follows the day will generally see a change of some sort in the weather. However peaceful the sky may appear as the sun sets, it is a rash gamble to leave the Genoa up if one wants to pass an undisturbed night.

Sunshine and rain, winds and calms, reefing and unreefing, followed each other incessantly and at brief intervals. Happily in summer the worst conditions seldom last long. What moderate gales we had were generally over in twenty-four hours, and it was rare for a calm to last more than a few hours. Such is the impression I had of our weather and when writing this I expected to have it confirmed by referring to the log we kept. Log-books are normally couched in terse, seamanlike language, but I find that our log-book is terse to the point of dumbness. When the helmsman is relieved he enters in the appropriate columns the course steered, the wind direction, and the reading of the patent log. The space left for general remarks or for noting—as should be done—anything of the slightest interest seen, is too often a blank. If a ship or a whale has been seen there is usually a remark, but on the whole it is difficult to tell from our log-book whether the sun shone or the rain fell, or whether the wind was of gale force or a light breeze.

A log-book entry which causes difficulty is that of the wind direction. When a ship is sailing it is not always easy to say within a point where the wind is from; the truest indication is probably the direction of the waves. But confusion chiefly arises from the magnetic variation, for the wind direction entered in the log should be the true direction after the variation has been added or deducted. In the Atlantic variation increases rapidly westwards, rising to 36° west, or more than three points, off Cape Farewell. Half way up Davis Strait it is as much as 55° west and increases as the Magnetic Pole is approached. Some find the converting of magnetic bearings into true, and vice versa, puzzling in spite of all the supposedly fool-proof rule-of-thumb rhymes. Any doubts there may be are best resolved by drawing a little diagram. One or two of the crew failed to master the problem and when estimating the wind direction before entering it in the log-book either ignored the variation or applied it the wrong way. In consequence, when looking over the log-book, one is startled by the erratic way in which the wind appears to have behaved. Sometimes, on the change of watch, an entry suggests that the wind shifted four points without apparently affecting the course steered or the set of the sails. When deciding on which tack to sail the large magnetic variation had, of course, to be allowed for. We might, for instance, be steering north-by-east by compass and yet making good two or three points of westing, whereas, on the other tack, perhaps steering west of south, we should have been heading for the Bay of Biscay.

# THE ATLANTIC 51

Even in the Atlantic, in the month of June one feels entitled to some warm, sunny days. We experienced on the whole grey, lowering weather with more rain and drizzle than sunshine. On one such dirty, drizzling day, when we were close-reefed and close-hauled in a strong westerly wind the *Empress of Britain* passed close. A little later the *Southern Prince* of the Prince Line overtook us. In spite of the sea running David called her up with the Aldis lamp and asked her to report us at Lloyds. As her freeboard is less than three feet communication by lamp from *Mischief*'s deck when a sea is running is intermittent, the lamp often being obscured in the middle of a letter. Nevertheless the message was read and in due course reached my home.

Sailing to windward in a rough sea is generally wasted effort. For two days we steered NW by N making little or no westing, so we hove-to and had a quiet night. When we let draw we tried her on the starboard tack and in the course of another two days lost about forty miles to the east. I found this discouraging. Besides the lack of progress I was worried by the wear and tear caused by prolonged beating in rough weather. On previous voyages we had generally managed to make ground in the required direction however hard the wind blew. The crew did not seem to mind. Having had no experience of long spells of down-wind sailing they took our slow, arduous progress as a matter of course. But they felt cold, cold accentuated by the general wetness, for there was usually spray flying or rain falling, or both. For the two-hour spell at the helm they adopted the unseamanlike practice of wearing gloves. Woollen gloves were so soon saturated that they devised ingenious waterproof mitts from plastic bags or pieces of canvas. Under these conditions none of us looked forward to a spell in the cockpit holding the brass tiller or the equally cold, wet tiller line. How fast the time passes on watch depends much on how the boat is sailing. When close-hauled in a lumpy sea—which means in effect that she is going up and down in the same hole—the hours seem interminable, whereas if she is going fast in the right direction with the log spinning merrily they pass like a flash. Perhaps the watch passes most quickly when one has to really concentrate on steering her, when running with the wind dead aft and the imminent threat of a Chinese gybe hanging over one.

On this passage we seldom had any inducement to sit about on deck and in the North Atlantic there is seldom much to see except a waste of grey water devoid of life or ships. We were now north of the northernmost steamer track used by ships bound for Scandinavian ports round the north of Scotland. The last ship sighted, an ore carrier called the *Afghanistan*, had altered course to have a look at us and gave us three friendly blasts on her siren by way of encouragement. We returned the compliment with three dismal squeals from our hand fog-horn. The few birds seen, we wrote off as gulls, for we knew no better and had on board no keen bird-watchers such as we had on the later voyage. Most of the way across Terry Ward trolled a line—not, perhaps, such a hopeless gesture as it may sound, for on the way home, in fine, warm weather, I saw some tunny leaping. When there was no work on deck most of the time had to be spent below, usually flat on one's back reading or sleeping. I am told that in a steamer, where there are rivets in the deckhead, an alternative occupation is to count them.

No doubt we had our meals to look forward to and discuss. In that respect we might have been likened to Carlyle's pot-bellied Jutes and Angles, men who 'watched the sun rise with no other hope than that they should fill their bellies before it set'. It is a commonplace that men are more interested in their food than are women (who has ever heard of a female gourmet?), presumably because men are seldom put to the trouble of buying or cooking their food. Yet while women are (or used to be) *ipso facto* cooks, they never become chefs. No woman, I suppose, would be seen dead in a chef's cap, but apart from that objection they lack the inventive genius and poetic fire of a chef. The fact that there are no women poets of great note is perhaps significant. I suspect, too, that the naturally frugal mind of a woman would boggle at the scale upon which a chef conducts operations. For example, Alexis Soyer, that Napoleon of the kitchen, to celebrate the ending of the Crimea war, served up a dish which he called a Culinary Emblem of Peace, containing among many other ingredients twelve boxes of lobsters and two hundred eggs.

Charles would be the first to admit that he is no poet and sometimes we had to stimulate his imagination. I was surprised to hear David of all people urging the claims of currant duff as a wholesome, seamanlike sweet. At Lymington, where we used to have supper ashore, he had consistently turned down delicious steamed puddings in favour of cheese on the grounds that when at sea he had eaten enough duff to

THE ATLANTIC

last his lifetime. Between making a cake, which Charles soon perfected, and making a duff, the difference is barely perceptible. Thus duffs, varying in hue and texture, and sometimes in taste, were included in our homely repertoire of sweets—stewed apple rings, stewed prunes, rice, and (all too rarely) pancakes. Potatoes, and rice, too, figure daily in the main course, yet in spite of all this carbohydrate, much sleeping, little exercise, and lack of worry, no one put on weight. Stews, curries, rissoles, sausages, spaghetti and macaroni dishes, were about the extent of our resources, the meat for these dishes having to be always bully beef or spam. In the matter of carbohydrates, we now at last had to start eating biscuits. We hoped that the particular kind we started on would soon be finished. I had bought two large tins of them in Cape Town, had thought little of them then, and less now, but could not bear to throw them away. 'Remainder biscuit' has an ominous ring. 'Dry as the remainder biscuit after a voyage' suggests weevils as well as dryness. These were at least free from weevils and they served well enough as a means of conveying to the mouth large quantities of butter and jam. It is on this account, in order to moderate the consumption of butter and jam, that the 'Lifeboat' biscuits we normally use have to be rationed. These biscuits might have been specially packed for a crew of six. There are ninety-six to a tin and at sixteen a man we get through a tin a day.

The fight that we had to get westwards and to round Cape Farewell can best be understood from the brief entries I made in a diary for the latter half of the passage. All bearings, by the way, are true. My hopes and fears are not set down, for I have generally found that in the event these are made to look damn silly.

> Tuesday, June 13th. Steering north yesterday till wind backed in the evening. Early this morning wind backed farther to south-west and glass fell to 28.9. Reefed before breakfast when we were doing 6½ knots. A sight at 9 a.m. put us in Long. 33° 14′ west. A new canvas bucket washed overboard. Glass down to 28.7 and a flat calm since 5 p.m. Handed sails and hoisted again at 8 p.m. when wind came in hard from north. Reefed. Had to run off to south-west owing to wind. Reefed again and handed jib. Blew hard all night.

# MISCHIEF IN GREENLAND

June 14th. Sea rough and fresh head wind. Steering south-west. Gybed later and steered north.

June 15th. Wind fell light in night. Lowered main for repair at 4 a.m. and at 6 a.m. hoisted with all reefs out. Wind south, steering west-north-west, steady rain and glass down to 28.7. No sun, no sights for last twenty-four hours. Very cold on watch. My feet always cold. 4 p.m. glass down to 28.4. Wind backed to south-east, rain stopped, and sun came out. Wind fell light, violent rolling, handed sails. Hoisted in the night with wind from west. Barometer flattened out.

June 16th. Very fresh wind. Took reef out of main but soon had to reef again. Strong wind all afternoon and evening with barometer rising. Overcast. Steering north.

June 17th. Same dull windy weather. Went about in the evening and then about again to steer north-west. 10 p.m. wind freshening, reefed. Midnight reefed again and hove-to.

June 18th. Sunny morning but wind about Force 8. Weather sheet of backed fores'l parted. Got sail down with difficulty and hoisted storm jib in lieu. Nut came off starboard shroud shackle bolt. Now about N. lat. 58°.

June 19th. Blew hard all day but some sun. Wind moderated by evening when barometer rose and rain set in.

June 20th. Reached N. lat. 59° 05′. Went about in the afternoon but by night on port tack again steering north-west. Wind from west-south-west has hardly varied a point since Saturday. Now about 150 miles west of Farewell. All complain of cold.

June 22nd. Still beating against WSW wind. Sunny until afternoon when some fog came up with a harder wind. Mains'l down for stitching. Went about steering south. Small Danish ship *Nancie S.* bound east stopped while we hove-to to speak them. Asked them to report us but don't think they heard as we had no megaphone. The wind has been at WSW for five days. We sail north-west up to Lat. 59° and then go about again. No sign of any ice but still 100 miles west of cape.

THE ATLANTIC                                                    55

June 22nd. Still beating but did better steering west by north until heavy rain started and wind headed us. Now about 70 miles southeast of Cape. Glass falling at night so reefed and dropped jib to slow down. We may be farther north than we think.

June 23rd. All plain sail steering north-west. Noon sight disappointing, not so near cape as we thought. Lat. 58° 58′ Long. 42° 10′. Went about steering south-west. Strong wind and rough sea, twice failed to stay and had to gybe her round. Strop of jib halyard block on mast parted. Too rough to do anything so now are without jib. 6 p.m. sighted first iceberg ½ a mile on port bow. About 30 ft. high. My seaboots filled with water when getting jib in.

June 24th. Wind freshened yesterday evening. Reefed. About 11 p.m. a tear in leach of mainsail opened so had to get sail down. Quite a job. Under stays'l only, so can only steer south. Same hard, cold wind all day. Mains'l sodden but repaired with herring-bone stitching a long rub caused by the topping lift. Tear in leach still to do. Had trysail up and steered south-west, but a snap sight this evening showed we had lost 13 miles to east. Poor outlook.

June 25th. Same wind all night. Very cold on watch. Some sun today. Got sail patched and hoisted by midday. Renewed stays'l hanks which were all worn through. Now down to Lat. 57° again and evening sight put us 43° 10′ west. Wear and tear continues. Jib outhaul stranded, ditto halyard, also stays'l sheet and wire of port topping life. Not happy about the mainsail.

This was about the nadir of our fortunes. From a position not far from Cape Farewell, in three days we had been blown a hundred miles or so to the south. Whatever the crew may have thought about it, certainly at this time the breeze of anxiety began to ruffle my brow. We had about three weeks' water left, and Godthaab, the port for which we were aiming, was still nearly 500 miles away. At this comparatively early season the more southern ports of Greenland are difficult to approach on account of ice—the ice that is drifted round Cape Farewell and up the west coast by the Greenland current. We might surely expect more favourable weather in Davis Strait but we were not there yet; in my gloomier moments I even saw us having to run for Iceland

56 MISCHIEF IN GREENLAND

to refresh—almost as far away as Ireland. I was worried by the wear and tear occasioned by constant beating and the wet conditions. Wet, sodden rope, with never a chance to dry, seems to fray much more readily, and wet, sodden canvas is hell to repair. The last job on the mainsail had cost David and me several hours work. Such troubles were not serious except that cumulatively they tended to slow us down still more. Happily the crew remained unperturbed, though I warned them that with only three weeks' water left there was a limit to the time we could spend beating about off Cape Farewell. But better things were now in store for us. Cape Farewell had exacted its tribute. We had paid our footing.

CHAPTER V

# TO GODTHAAB

O N THAT SAME SUNDAY EVENING the wind moderated and went round to south. We hoisted the jib on the Genoa halyard. On this halyard there is no purchase, so that the luff of the sail sagged disgracefully. But it was better than having no jib. All that night we ran west by north until in the morning the wind failed. Much to our surprise and pleasure the sea fell calm, too, as it had not been for a long time. After motoring for an hour we had to stop. Having lost a pipe and begun looking for it in the bilge as the most likely place, I discovered a lot of oil. The overflow pipe, passing under the floor-boards between the engine and the 'heads', had broken, and Terry Ward had to solder in two new pieces. Rain fell throughout the day and we got no sights, but by dead reckoning we put outselves in Long. 46°, well to the west of Cape Farewell. To be west of this cape had for a long time been the summit of our hopes so that night we celebrated the event by lacing our cocoa liberally with rum.

For yet another night we continued to sail west and a morning sight put us in Long. 47°, several miles west of where we expected to be. Evidently we had been feeling the benefit of the East Greenland current which sweeps round Cape Farewell. For a hundred miles beyond the cape the coast trends only a little north of west, so that after rounding the cape the current is west-going. A noon sight gave us a latitude of 58° N., a long way south of Farewell, but we were now rapidly closing the land, steering north with a fine breeze from west-north-west. Two days before, when we were fighting to make westing, such a wind would hardly have been designated a 'fine breeze'. We began meeting large icebergs and found them more of an encouragement than a menace. Their presence meant that we were in the East Greenland current and they were no menace because in that latitude at that time of year there is practically no darkness. In the middle of the night, of course, it is not exactly as bright as day, and when fog

## MISCHIEF IN GREENLAND

comes down, as it did that evening, the visibility is poor. I had just come to the conclusion that it would be prudent to have a look-out posted in the bows when the fog cleared away and disclosed a large iceberg close ahead.

On June 29th—a red-letter day for us—fog prevailed almost throughout the day. Although the sun shone brightly overhead we could get no sights, our horizon extending to no more than 200 yards. The clammy fog made it perishing cold despite the sun and despite the cabin stove which we had long since been lighting daily. As we sailed on through the mist it became obvious that we were in a situation that the prudent mariner does his best to avoid. We had little idea how near we were to some unknown part of a rock-bound and probably ice-bound coast towards which we were sailing in fog, surrounded by scattered icebergs. If we went about, as caution advised, we could steer only south. So we carried on and at four o'clock that afternoon our boldness or rashness had its unmerited reward. A vast berg looming up ahead obliged us to alter course to clear it and at that moment the fog rolled away. After a month at sea the dullest coast looks exciting, but a more dramatic landfall than the one we now made, both as to its suddenness and its striking appearance, could scarcely be imagined. Two or three miles ahead, stretching away on either hand, lay a rocky coast thickly fringed with stranded icebergs and backed by high, barren mountains. Beyond the mountains and over-topping them was the faintly glistening band of the Greenland ice-cap. To identify any particular part of this strange, wild coast was hardly possible, but we guessed that a bold cape a few miles westwards might be Cape Desolation at the western end of Julianehaab Bight. An evening sight for longitude confirmed this. But on our making towards the cape the fog closed in again and we stood out to sea. Fog or no fog, the novelty of sailing in smooth water, the luck of our landfall, its magnificent aspect, all combined to give us a feeling of elation. From a hidden source Charles dug out a Christmas pudding and took elaborate pains over concocting a rum sauce to help it down—pains that are wasted on this kind of sauce for they merely serve to adulterate the main ingredient.

By a happy chance we had first sighted Greenland at almost the same spot as John Davis had in 1585 and in similar foggy conditions. This great Elizabethan seaman and explorer, whom we remember by

TO GODTHAAB

the name of his Strait, was the discoverer of Greenland. It is more correct to say that he rediscovered it because Greenland had been settled
by Norsemen from as early as the tenth century and it was not until
the fifteenth century that their communication with Norway ceased.*
On July 20th, 1585, John Davis's two ships *Sunneshine* of fifty tons and
*Mooneshine* of thirty-five tons were a month out from the Scillies:

> 'The 20th as we sayled along the coast the fogge brake up. and
> we discovered the land which was the most deformed, rockie, and
> mountainous that ever we saw. The first sight whereof did shew as if
> it had bene in the form of a sugar-loafe, standing to our sight above
> the cloudes, for that it did shew over the fogge like a white liste in
> the skie, the tops altogether covered with snow, and the shoare beset
> with yce a league off into the sea making such yrksome noise so that
> it seemed to be the true pattern of desolation, and after the same our
> Captaine named it, the land of Desolation.'

Scattered about the world are many capes, islands, bays, and harbours
of refuge whose names betray the disgust, despair, relief, or hope of
the daring seaman who first saw and named them. In these parts alone
there are for example, the Bay of God's Mercy in Hudson Strait, Cape
Mercy off Baffin Island, Refuge Harbour, Cape Providence, and Sanderson's Hope. Desolation, too, was the name given to the island discovered in 1772 by Kerguelen-Trémarac and subsequently named after
him. As patterns of desolation there was not much to choose between
Kerguelen and the coast of Greenland. Desolate though it might be,
we viewed the coast with emotions very different to those of John Davis
and his men. As well we might. Ice mountains were probably the last
thing they had wished to see whereas we had come in search of them.
And we were secure in the knowledge that there were ports at hand
where we could refit and replenish our stores as easily as if at home.

---

\* The last vessel from Greenland returned to Norway in 1410. The evidence
found in excavations of Norse burial grounds suggests that they died out
either by excessive intermarriage or adverse conditions. There is no indication
of absorption by the Eskimo race or of destruction at the hands of Eskimos.

60    MISCHIEF IN GREENLAND

In Davis Strait the weather is less boisterous than in the Atlantic. Winds are mainly from southerly or northerly quarters and in summer rarely attain much strength. Force 6, or possibly on one occasion Force 7, was the most we experienced and on the whole we suffered more from lack of wind than too much. In the summer months fog is a great nuisance. If it were coupled with dark nights the icebergs would be a serious menace. Moving slowly, as we were, we could see bergs in time to avoid them even when visibility was down to 200 yards or less. All the icebergs sighted on this part of the coast break off from the glaciers of East Greenland and are brought here by the current. After rounding Farewell the current fans out and presently divides, part of it going west across the Strait to join the Labrador current and part continuing north up the coast. The flow of bergs is mainly from April to August though some are found in any month of the year. None of these bergs reach Newfoundland waters. They end by melting south of Farewell or in the middle of Davis Strait where in summer the water is relatively warm.

Unlike pack-ice, which moves generally with the wind, the movement of bergs is affected almost entirely by currents because of the far greater proportion of ice below water than above. The amount submerged varies with the type of berg. A solid block-like berg with sheer sides floats with only about one fifth above the surface, while a so-called 'picturesque' berg, pinnacled and ridged like a miniature mountain, might have one third or even as much as a half above water. We saw some great blocks of bergs 100 feet high and covering an acre or more of sea in the waters west of Cape Farewell. They became fewer as we went north and disappeared entirely before Godthaab was reached. On this voyage, unlike that of the following year, we saw no pack-ice. The bergs which appear off the Newfoundland banks in spring derive mainly from some twenty huge West Greenland glaciers northwards of Disko Island. It is estimated that 7500 break off these twenty glaciers each year. An average of 396 drift south of Newfoundland and approximately thirty-five as far south as Lat. 43° N., that is south of the Grand Banks where the Titanic was sunk. After circling the head of Baffin Bay they are carried by the Labrador current down the Canadian coast. A berg calved in summer may reach the Hudson Strait region by autumn where it becomes fixed in the pack-ice, to be released and appear off Newfoundland in the spring.

We never tired of looking at bergs. At first we counted and logged all those in sight but north of Disko Island they became too numerous to count. If some particularly vast or grotesquely-shaped monster hove in sight we sometimes went out of our way to have a closer look at him. According to the light their colour varied from an opaque dazzling white to the loveliest blues and greens. Some had caves or even a hole clean through them in which the blue colour was intense and translucent. When passing a berg it is best to keep on the windward side on account of the number of bergy bits or growlers which break away and litter the sea to leeward. In fog or at night, in waters where there is no reason to expect ice floes, the presence of these bits of ice would indicate a berg in the vicinity. If it is rough waves may be sometimes heard breaking against the berg, but no reliance can be placed upon detecting changes of air or sea temperature in its vicinity or of receiving echoes from it from a fog-horn. Radar would pick up a large berg but would probably fail to show a 'growler' quite big enough to sink a ship. The only certain method is to see it. That a good lookout all round even in daylight is essential was impressed on me the day after we made our landfall. The wind had dropped and there was nothing in sight, no land, no ice. We handed the sails and motored for some eight hours, for most of the time in fog. When the boom and mainsail are resting on the gallows the helmsman's vision is obscured on one side unless he stands up on the cockpit seat and steers with his foot, or has a line round the tiller. For one reason or another I was standing in the cockpit, peering intently ahead into the fog. Happening to bend down and glance under the boom to the port side I was startled by the sight of the large, luminous mass of an iceberg less than fifty yards away.

We had more to look at than icebergs. In clear weather we could see the bold, mountainous coast and there were several ships about. A small coaster passed inside us and we saw for the first time some of the three- and four-masted schooners of the Portuguese fishing fleet. Off this coast there are a number of banks rich in cod and halibut, the resort of Norwegian, German, and British trawlers as well as these Portuguese schooners which, after fishing the Grand Banks in May and June, come north to the Davis Strait banks to complete their catch. They fish from dories with hand lines and later we sailed by some of

62                    MISCHIEF IN GREENLAND

their dories in action. The schooners we now saw were fishing on the Danas bank, north of the big Frederikshaab glacier. Other important banks are Fiskernaes, the Fyllas off Godthaab, and the Great and Little Hellefiske banks farther north.

When we arrived off Godthaab fjord on the morning of July 4th the weather was fortunately clear, for it is not an easy place to find or to enter. A submerged reef reaches out from the north shore of the entrance and the fairway lies between the tail end of this reef and a dense cluster of islets, possibly some fifty in number. On one of the outer islets there is a small beacon and on the islet directly opposite the tail of the reef there is a concrete pillar, with a light. The pillar which is only about ten feet high, is not readily seen from the offing, and in summer when it is never really dark the light is not much help. On this our first approach we acted with the utmost caution. Having closed the outer beacon we met a small fishing boat whom we consulted as to our next move. To ask, as they say in Spain, is no disgrace. We could not talk to them but they pointed out the way and soon we were passing the lit beacon, noting with interest some white water on the port hand marking the reef. It is safe to pass within a stone's throw of the islet for the water is deep.

The town and harbour lie about fifteen miles up the fjord from the outer islet, though the fjord, with many branches, runs inland for a good fifty miles. The tides run strongly but the navigation as far as the harbour entrance is straightforward. On this lovely summer day we had a magnificent sail up the calm, blue fjord, the black, barren shores close on either hand and in the distance some startling rock peaks over 3000 feet high, their gullies still streaked with snow. Off the town we handed the sails, started the engine, and began nosing round looking for the harbour entrance. It was extremely puzzling. The entrance is narrow with two right-angle bends in it, so that from seaward one appears to be steering straight for the unbroken shore of the inlet. Presently we spotted the leading marks, small beacons with flashing lights, and gradually the way unfolded. Some of us had a strong impression that out of regard for the natives Greenland was 'dry'. However, on rounding the last bend, bringing in view the quay and the warehouse, we saw a beautiful sight, a twenty-foot-high stack of cases of Carlsberg lager. So we were reassured on one point. Our enthusiasm equalled that of the Rev. Dr Folliot, a man with an interminable swallow, who summed up the well-stocked cellars of Crotchet Castle with the remark: 'A thousand dozen of old wine—a beautiful spectacle, I assure you, and a model of arrangement.'

Entering a strange harbour, especially if it is small and full of ships, is to me as much of a nervous strain as entering a room full of strangers. One has no clear idea what to do or where to go. There is more than a likelihood of making a fool of oneself by anchoring in some prohibited area or, goaded to desperation, smack in the fairway. On this occasion we managed remarkably well. Giving the quay a wide berth we headed for a high rock wall on the far side of the harbour. Sounding our way along by the wall we anchored in five fathoms between it and a small Danish naval vessel. This rock wall, by the way, has painted on it in enormous letters the names of various visiting ships. Had we had enough paint we would have added another. The *Mallemuken*, as this naval vessel was called, had a dual role of fishery protection and coastal survey. She was steel-built, whereas all the other survey vessels we met were wood. In Belfast we had met an elderly couple whose daughter was married to a Danish naval officer. Oddly enough the commander of the *Mallemuken*, who presently came on board, proved to be the man. Speaking excellent English he invited us on board *Mallemuken* for beer and shower-baths, both of which we needed. I thought it my duty to wait on board until the harbour authorities and the police had interviewed us and given us permission to land. At five o'clock, when we were still apparently of no interest to anyone, I rowed ashore to find the harbour-master. As befits a harbour-master he was a big, cheerful man, and spoke fairly fluent American. He said he had seen us arrive and since where we were lying was in nobody's way we might stay there as long as we liked. What about coming ashore, I asked. Why not? Having come so far it would be a pity not to land, and provided none of the crew had venereal disease there could be no possible objection. And there the formalities ended. No bother, no police, no Customs, no Immigration, and no health officials to harry us. Would it were everywhere thus!

The harbour has a deep-water quay where ships of several thousand tons can lie and a fish-quay and fish-curing factory were in course of construction. At the shallow end of this landlocked harbour is a

64 MISCHIEF IN GREENLAND

slipway and mooring buoys for the Catalina seaplanes which daily arrive and depart for places up and down the coast. The only links between the harbours and settlements along the coast are by sea and air. There are no roads in Greenland. Godthaab (or Good Hope) is the capital of West Greenland, and although founded as long ago as 1721 by Hans Egede, the Lutheran missionary, it has all the appearance of a raw, thriving pioneer town, so extensive is the work in progress. A rough, unsurfaced road about a mile long leads from the harbour to the town itself which is scattered about over a small peninsula of solid rock interspersed with boggy hollows. As a result of this unpromising site all foundations have to be blasted out, all telephone lines and power cables are carried overhead on forests of poles, there is no underground drainage system, and water is laid on to standpipes by the roadside. Except for the stone-built house that had belonged to Hans Egede himself, the buildings and houses are of wood or prefabricated material; the houses are painted in lively colours—green, red, yellow, blue—but the public buildings have a more sober aspect. When we returned in 1962 large blocks of three-storey flats were either finished or nearly ready for occupation. Besides the stores for the necessities, such as provisions, hardware, clothing, and a bakery, there are photographic shops, a bookshop, and another for radio sets and electrical appliances. In fact one can buy there pretty well everything one is likely to need at much the same price as in Europe. One peculiarity is that for successful shopping a local guide is needed. The shops are scattered about, often without any window displays, and are not easily found or identified. Some of them might be mistaken for a private house or a public building. There are many independent traders but the bigger shops are controlled by the Royal Greenland Trading Company which in former days had a monopoly of all Greenland trade. As the result of a Commission appointed soon after the last war the whole set-up has been transformed and the Danish Government and the Trading Company between them are now actively engaged in the development of Greenland, so far as this is possible; and in all aspects of the Greenlanders' life, educational, medical, administrative, and economic, in the hope that in time the country will be run by the Greenlanders themselves and stand upon its own feet. All this will cost and is costing vast sums of money with no prospect of any quick return. The

*Mischief* alongside the quay at Godthaab

Godthaab—Church and Hans Egede monument

66        MISCHIEF IN GREENLAND

main hope rests upon a rapid development of inshore fishing by helping the Greenlanders to equip themselves with boats and by building
and improving harbours, wharves, and fish-curing factories. The trade
in sealskins, formerly of the first importance, is now secondary to fishing. A copper mine on the east coast and a cryolite mine at Ivigtut in
the south-west are also sources of revenue, cryolite being a rare mineral
of importance to the aluminium industry.* No doubt behind all this
expenditure there is the hope that other valuable and workable mineral deposits will be found as they have been in the Canadian Arctic.
Meantime the Greenlanders have their education, technical training,
medical care, law, order, and government provided for them by the
Danish tax-payer.

In 1944 the total population was about 20,000 and has probably
since increased. The population of Godthaab was about 3000 of whom
500 were Danes. Having been in contact with Europeans for so long
nearly all the so-called Eskimos are of mixed descent; and partly as
a result of the way they are being cared for they have moved far away
from the primitive Eskimo stage and are now a sophisticated people
fully aware of the blessings of civilization. They have long had the
use of firearms and marine engines and they are now familiar with
the cinema, wireless sets, tape-recorders, juke boxes, and jive. There
are two houses of entertainment in Godthaab, one patronized almost
entirely by Greenlanders—the lower orders, as it were—and the other
by both Danes and Greenlanders of substance. The Danish customers
were all technicians or workmen resident only for the short summer
working season; the more permanent residents, officials and such like,
seemed to hold themselves aloof. We usually went to the last, the Kristinemut, where, provided one ordered in advance, an evening meal
could be had—eggs, chips, salmon steaks, whale steaks, beef steaks,
or smörgenbrod. In both establishments the juke boxes were worked
overtime by youthful Greenlanders, so that in that respect there was

---

\*    A complete list of Greenland exports would have to include shark liver,
cod liver, their oils, train oil, sperm oil, eiderdown, blue-fox furs, bearskins,
sealskins, walrus hides, various salt fish, canned shrimps, smoked salmon,
mutton and wool — these last from the Julianehaab region where sheep-farming is carried on.

## TO GODTHAAB 67

little to choose. But at the Kristinemut beer was the main attraction and bottled lager was consumed in large quantities. Godthaab's main export at the present must surely be empty bottles, for as yet little fishing is done there.

Most of the crew of the *Mallemuken* resorted in the evening to the Kristinemut where we became friendly with them. There were about a dozen in the crew, nearly all young National Service men, who seemed happy enough to be doing their two years' service in Greenland. As might be expected in a small vessel, well beyond the reach of any Danish naval 'top-brass', duties were light and the discipline far from severe. Their commander, too, had a pleasant life, living mostly ashore with his wife in a convenient house overlooking the harbour. He and his wife were the only contact we made with the upper strata of Godthaab society. A representative from the only newspaper in the world that is published in the Eskimo language, the Atuagagdliutit, paid us a visit and subsequently an article about us and some photographs appeared. It may have been as a result of this that we had no other visitors. I was surprised at the lack of interest; many Danes are boat-minded, as it were; no other yachts that I have heard of have visited Greenland waters; and in other foreign ports *Mischief* has usually attracted a lot of attention. One explanation we heard was that the Dane is shy and dislikes intruding upon strangers. Those Danes in Godthaab employed on constructional work were probably far too busy—they worked a twelve-hour day—while the rest were mostly officials who, as a class, stick to their own kind and shrink from compromising themselves with outsiders, particularly with foreign outsiders. Elsewhere in Greenland it was different. We had the kindest reception from the Danes we met, official or unofficial.

We did not want to spend more than a few days in Godthaab. We had still 400 miles to go and were in a hurry to get on, the outward passage of forty days having taken longer than we expected. The day after our arrival was a blank day for it rained incessantly, but the day after that we went alongside the quay for water and fuel oil. The *Umanak*, a large passenger-cargo ship, which runs monthly from Copenhagen, had just arrived and was unloading. She takes eight or nine days from Copenhagen and until recently the monthly sailing was maintained throughout the year. Three years ago, a new ship on her maiden voyage

68 MISCHIEF IN GREENLAND

disappeared one stormy January night off Cape Farewell leaving no survivors. The voyages in January and February have since been discontinued, the darkness of those months, and the ice, making it altogether too hazardous.

Having warped our way round the stern of *Umanak*, fouling her ensign staff with our mast in the process, we got alongside, filled up with water from a water-cart, and had a forty-gallon oil drum put on deck. In siphoning the oil into our tank we spilt some on deck. Next morning, when we should have sailed, I slipped on this oil and in falling heavily against one of the sheet winches cracked a rib. We had to postpone our departure for two days till July 9th while I lay prone feeling very sore.

Before leaving we filled up with fresh food such as potatoes, onions, and bread. In a country like Greenland everything that a European needs, except fish, coal, and perhaps mutton, has to be imported. Coal of a poor quality is mined on Disko Island and sheep-farming, as I have said, is carried on in the south. Whether things like potatoes, onions, fruit, are available in the shops depends upon the recent arrival of a ship from Denmark. One or two of the residents, I noticed, had attempted the growing of vegetables like cabbage and radishes, while several houses had small built-in conservatories in which flowers were successfully grown. Our bread, by the way, had some remarkable features. It was rye bread—dark, heavy loaves about a foot and a half long and six inches square. This, of course, is baked in Godthaab but it would have been neither fresher nor staler had it been imported, for it has an immutable quality, as unchanging as the leopard's spots or the Ethiopian's skin. Perhaps in the course of weeks it becomes a shade harder, otherwise it remains as good as ever for an indefinite period. We took a lot on board and before it was finished some of us were looking forward to the day when biscuits would once more have to be eaten. Unless one had the jaws and teeth of a shark the slices had to be cut very thin, a feat which demanded a bread knife of exceptional strength that would neither buckle nor break. But perhaps the most impressive feature of this bread was that until one got used to it—and that took an awful long time—it had the effect of a strong aperient.

CHAPTER VI

# NORTHWARDS TO IGDLORSSUIT

FOUR DAYS IN GODTHAAB, or for that matter in most ports, is long enough, and if the appointed sailing day is deferred the morale of the crew suffers. I should have liked to have put it off a little longer on my own account and because, too, the day was foggy. But we got our anchor and motored out and after chugging away for six hours against wind and tide passed Agtorssuit, the last of the islands. Outside we hoisted sail and squared away, the stays'l boomed out one side and the mainsail the other, with the wind dead aft.

On clear days it is tempting to sail close to the Greenland coast so that the mountains and glaciers that comprise a great part of it can be fully admired. However, the stranger upon that coast does well not to be too free with it, fringed as it is with islets, skerries, and submerged rocks, some of them extending several miles from the shore. In addition, the absence of sea-marks or anything on shore that is readily identifiable makes it difficult to tell what part of the shore one is looking at. It is therefore wise to refrain from hugging the coast and to secure a good offing, but having done that the problem of defining one's precise whereabouts has still to be solved, and all too often solved without the help of sights. Ships navigating this coast rely very much on radar. As might have been guessed, these remarks are preparatory to explaining, if not excusing, how we found ourselves astray the very next day.

After making good progress in the night and part of next day we were later obliged to go about and stand in towards the land. The sea was smooth, absolutely flat, and we obtained sights both at noon and in the evening, for the fog lay only in patches. The sights agreed pretty well with our dead reckoning and at 6 p.m. when we were motoring, there being no wind, we thought we were about fifteen miles off the land. An hour later some islets loomed out of the mist only about half a mile away. Moreover, on looking over the side we could see through the dark, still water to the bottom. In the words of George Robey's

69

70         MISCHIEF IN GREENLAND

song, we stopped, and we looked, and we listened. Terry Ward seized the opportunity to drop a bright, spoon-shaped spinner over the side and to our surprise and delight caught a five-pound cod. Two more were caught in quick succession. As we found later a spinner is superfluous; anything, a bit of rag, or even a bare hook will do the business. Cod are bottom feeders, so one just keeps the sinker on the bottom and jigs it up and down with the wrist—jigging for cod, as it is called. In that sea classic *Sailing Alone Round the World*, Slocum recalls an old Banks fisherman who from force of habit would, 'while listening to a sermon in the little church on the hill, reach out his hand over the pew and "jig" for imaginary cod in the aisle.'

When the mist lifted we saw before us a wide landscape—high mountains, glaciers, and on the shore what looked like a small settlement. To identify it was another matter. By our reckoning we should have been off Sukkertoppen, a region of many high mountains. But now the *Arctic Pilot* came to our aid. Describing the entrance to Sondre Stromfjord, about twenty-five miles farther north, it mentioned an easily identified mountain with a horned summit and a black strip of basalt running down its face. With the aid of glasses we could make out such a mountain so that it looked as if we were a long way out of our reckoning. Sondre Stromfjord, by the way, is one of the longest of West Greenland fjords, about 100 miles long, and at its head is a big airfield built during the war by the Americans and then known as 'Bluie West 8'. It is now used by Scandinavian Airways, among others, as a stopping place en route to the Pacific coast of America. Passengers and mail for Greenland are landed here and distributed thence by Catalina seaplanes.

That we were badly out in our reckoning was confirmed by a sight at noon next day which put us fifteen miles farther north than we should have been according to the sights of the previous day. Errors are to be expected if sights are taken with fog about, even though it appears to be only slight fog. If anxious to get a sight one too readily believes the horizon is good enough, but such sights are unreliable. The fog played some maddening tricks. Often the horizon would be perfectly clear in every direction except the one required, immediately below the sun. Lecky, the redoubtable author of Lecky's *Wrinkles*, had a way of overcoming the difficulty of taking sights in fog:

NORTHWARDS TO IGDLORSSUIT

By sitting in the bottom of a small boat in smooth water, or on the lowest step of the accommodation ladder, the eye will be about two feet above the sea-level, at which height the horizon is little more than a mile and a quarter distant, so that unless the fog is very dense, serviceable observations are quite possible. The writer, on three different occasions, when at anchor off the River Plate during fog, has been able to ascertain the ship's position in the way described, and after verifying it by the lead, has proceeded up to Montevideo without seeing land.

But Lecky, both as a navigator and as a teacher of navigation, was in a class by himself. He was a hydrographer, as well as a master mariner, who has left his name on various charts, particularly those of the Patagonia channels where there are many reminders of his indefatigable zeal—'Lecky's Retreat', 'Lecky's Monument', 'Lecky's Look-out'.

Another source of error and trouble for the navigator in Davis Strait is mirage. This is common and when it is present some abnormal refraction of the horizon must also be present. Rocks, islands, icebergs, ships, none of which can be identified for what they really are, appear floating in the air, sometimes upside down. According to the text-book this is occasioned thus:

When the sea surface is relatively cold (and the wind very light) so that the density of the air decreases for a short distance above the surface, light rays from objects low down near the horizon are bent down, the same way, in fact as are usually the rays of the sun when entering the earth's atmosphere at a low altitude. The effect is to render visible objects which are normally below the horizon. A further occasional effect is produced when the air is appreciably warmer than the sea when an inverted image is seen over the object. This "superior image" is most often seen in high latitudes and wherever the sea surface temperature is abnormally low.

Having mentioned Lecky I am tempted to repeat here a story which he tells with evident relish and which shows him as a man eager to instruct, but always in a practical and genial way:

# 72                    MISCHIEF IN GREENLAND

As an instance of ignorance of some of the commonest truths of nature, the writer cannot refrain from introducing the following anecdote. One evening he was pacing the deck with his chief officer and, seeing the sun's lower limb touching the horizon, told his companion that at that moment the whole of the sun's disc was really below it, although from the effects of refraction it was still visible. This the officer could not and would not believe. He aptly quoted the saying "seeing is believing, and feeling is the naked truth". However he was convinced some few minutes later by a very familiar experiment. Being firmly seated in front of an empty wash-hand basin, so that the brass plug at the bottom was quite invisible, the basin was about half-filled with water, when, without moving his head, he at once, to his great astonishment, saw the plug.

After this long and not unlearned digression concerning mirage and refraction, it is time to return to *Mischief*, now stealing very gently away from the coast. We moved that night but only just. The air no more than breathed. It was so still that not a block creaked and even when sailing we made no ripple in the water. Early next morning, smooth though the sea was, I noticed a patch of white water over a submerged rock not a cable's length away. Evidently we were still too close inshore, for this probably was the Pandora reef which the Pilot mentions and locates not over precisely as 'consisting of a ridge of scattered rocks, on which the sea breaks, reported to lie from three to six miles westward of the western extremity of Simiutak'—Simiutak is an island at the mouth of Sondre Stromfjord. The wind now came in strong from SSE so we stood out to the north-west and later gybed to north, the wind being too nearly dead aft to be comfortable. Sure enough before evening we had the father and mother of a crashing gybe which brought me on deck at the run to see if the mast had gone overboard. The hook on the boom guy, a wire rigged to prevent such mishaps, stretching from the end of the boom to the anchor winch, had straightened out leaving the boom free to crash over the moment the wind got behind the sail. Hooks are things which one buys without much thought provided they look man enough for their job, but it would be prudent to buy only those tested or guaranteed as when buying anchor chain. None of the rigging had suffered damage.

*Mischief's* gear is strong, as well it needs to be in view of the strains to which it is at times subjected by some of her crews. My cracked rib, I think, sustained more damage from this gybe than did anything else. In leaping for the deck, galvanized into violent motion by the crash of the boom, I felt it grate. So David cocooned me in yards of sticking plaster, and on account of the pain its removal would inflict I left it on long after the need for it had passed.

The fair wind bustling us northwards did not last long. According to the fickle and variable habit of the wind in those regions it soon died away before coming in light from the north. However, we had crossed the Arctic Circle (N. 66° 30´) and had we been so minded might have awarded ourselves a Polar Diploma such as are given to passengers in ships cruising to the North Cape. On July 14th we were off the coast opposite Holsteinborg and among a great many trawlers and a few Portuguese schooners fishing the Hellefiske Bank. Hellefiske, by the way, which at first sight I translated mentally as 'Hellish good fishing', is in fact the Danish name for a fish not unlike halibut. We sailed close to several dories, either scudding back to the parent schooner under jib and lugsail with a full load of cod, or moored to their long line with the doryman busily starting to haul it in. One man triumphantly waved a big cod which he had just taken off the hook. The dories are flat-bottomed and about fourteen feet long, without buoyancy tanks, without even a fitted thwart, centre-board, or rudder. The absence of inside fittings makes it possible to stow them on the deck of the schooner in nests of six, some sixty dories to a schooner. The mast is stepped for sailing from or back to the schooner and is unstepped while fishing. Those we saw had bright green and yellow sails. The bait used is frozen herring cut up small, or frozen squid, sardines, or caplin. The 3000-foot-long line has about 500 hooks suspended from it by short lengths of line called snoods. As we sailed by these men we ourselves were suffering no hardships and we could have but a faint idea of what they faced every day, handling such a line with half-frozen hands, tossing up and down in a dinghy in Davis Strait, apart from the task of baiting the 500 hooks, and worse still, removing the hooks from the mouths of heavy, cold, slimy, flapping fish. The doryman stays out until his dory is so full of fish as to leave only a few inches freeboard, before sailing back to the schooner. There, standing up in the heaving dory, he has to gaff

74                    MISCHIEF IN GREENLAND

his catch one by one on to the schooner's deck. What thorough boatmen and seamen these dorymen must be, and how strong and valuable
the tradition that ensures a supply of men eager and proud to follow
so hard a calling! None but a doryman could picture with truth the
long intervening period spent plying his lone hand far from the parent
ship. Alan Villiers, who made a voyage in one of these schooners, thus
describes the launching of the dories and their return:

> And now here was a vessel which cheerfully put out an anchor upon
> banks in the open sea, miles from the sight of any land (an anchorage
> to me had always been at the least a partly-sheltered roadstead) and
> then proceeded to send away her crew in fragile little boats, without
> as much as a life-jacket between them or an air-tight tank in any of
> the boats.
>
> It was wretchedly cold, and raining. The cold sea swept across
> the schooner's low decks. The one-man dories were neither particu-
> larly strong nor especially seaworthy for the work they had to do.
> They were already laden with tubs of baited line, buckets of bait,
> light masts and oiled sails, oars, bailers, anchors and sisal lines, and
> each held its occupant's personal container, made of wood, brightly
> painted, and holding his tobacco, a flask of water and a small loaf
> of bread, a few olives and perhaps a piece of Portuguese ham sau-
> sage, and a watch, if he were rich enough to own one. This was gener-
> ally tied up in old newspaper, where it kept company with a whistle,
> or a conch to blow in fog. Knives, boat compass, sinkers, jiggers, a
> honing stone, and grapnels for the long line, completed the dory's
> cargo. When the doryman himself jumped in, in his heavy woollen
> clothing and oilskins, and giant leather boots with wooden soles an
> inch or more thick, the dory had quite a load before it began to look
> for fish. "Out dories" was the order, and out they went with a will and
> a rush. There was a tot of brandy for each man who wanted it, and
> the brandy was dispensed with more generosity than the bait. The
> cabin-boy poured out the brandy from a kettle. It was traditional for
> the ship to offer a tot to each doryman before he set out on the day's
> fishing, just as it was traditional that life-saving gear should never be
> used. If a man's dory could not save him, nothing could.

## NORTHWARDS TO IGDLORSSUIT

The ship was rolling so much, her four yellow masts swinging like pendulums against the grey, wet sky, that I feared some of the dories must be smashed. But these men were experts at getting boats away and a perfect drill had been worked out, probably centuries earlier. The schooner's low sides and low freeboard were a help. The dories were plucked from the nests by overhead hooks which fitted into the protruding grommets spliced into bow and stern. These hooks were manipulated by simple tackles led aloft, with the hauling part by the rail, so that a man or two on each tackle could swing a dory easily from the nest to the rail. Here its doryman hurriedly adjusted its thwarts, saw that the plug was in, climbed the rail and jumped in himself. As the ship rolled towards that side, the tackles were let go at just the right moment and down went the dory with a rush and a thwack upon the sea. Immediately the iron hooks disengaged themselves, alert mariners hauled them back inboard, the doryman shoved off from the side for his life, and dropped astern. Once clear of the ship's side, his little dory seemed smaller than ever, and dancing and leaping in the sea, he rigged his mast and little oiled sail, and away he skimmed towards the horizon, to choose a place to lay out his lines. In a few moments the grey sea all around was covered with the little dories, skimming away like dinghies jockeying for the start at some stormy regatta. But this was no regatta. The shelterless dories looked like an invitation to frostbite, and the black sea was restless and heaving, contorting itself without rhythm as it frequently does on shallow banks. Within a few minutes less than a dozen of our fifty could be seen. Not an accident, not a shout, not a swamped dory, nor a lost piece of gear.

... The recall went up at five. Within fifteen minutes the first dory was back loaded to the gunwales. Every few minutes the doryman had to bale furiously to keep himself afloat. For the next two hours we were picking up our dories. Captain Adolfo entered his estimate of each man's catch in the little black book kept for the purpose. The fish were not weighed or measured in any way, but no doryman gaffed up any cod until he had seen the dark countenance of the captain peering down over the rail at his dory. A cold wind came up from the north with a sting of ice in it; nobody worried about it, though the water was lapping at the counters and along the low sides

76          MISCHIEF IN GREENLAND

of half the dories. As each came alongside and its catch was recorded, the doryman was handed down a gaff by the deck-boy, and he began at once to heave his fish up and over the rail into the pounds. This in itself was a labour of difficulty, for the cod were big and the schooner's sides high to a dory. The roll of the ship sent the dories jerking in all directions, though they were supposed to be held in position by the deck-boys. There were often four dories discharging along each side, and a dozen others waiting off to take their places. As each dory was discharged it was moved quickly along the ship's side aft, where it was at once hoisted inboard and nested. As each doryman came aboard he joined the hoisting teams, without any time off for a hot drink or a bite to eat, though there was coffee waiting in the galley. No one ate until all the dorymen were back, the fish all in the pounds, and the dories nested and lashed down.

The next time we closed the land we found ourselves at the mouth of Disko Bay. Disko is a large island separated from the mainland by a strait called the Vaigat which extends about sixty miles north-westwards and has a least width of six miles. To go north by way of the Vaigat was longer than by the open sea but we preferred the longer way on account of the scenery, both sides of the strait being mountainous. Moreover Disko Bay and the strait are famous for huge icebergs, some of them up to 300 feet high, calved from the great glaciers of Christianshaab, Jakobshaven, and Ritenbank. These glaciers descend from the ice-cap itself which from here northwards reaches right down to the coast. All along the coast south of Disko there is a strip of ice-free country varying in width from one mile to one hundred miles. The widest part lies inland from Holsteinborg and is of some value as a breeding ground for reindeer.

The mouth of Disko Bay was as far as we got on our passage to the Vaigat. For the best part of a fine, sunny morning we beat up and down across the wide mouth without making any progress. The blue, iceberg-strewn waters of the bay were flecked with white horses by a fierce wind whistling out of the Vaigat. Bowing to superior force we eased the sheets, pointed her head north-west, and went out to sea like a train. The more northing we made the better the weather became. Clammy fog and cold rain were forgotten as one clear, sparkling day

NORTHWARDS TO IGDLORSSUIT

followed another, the sun shining perpetually from a cloudless sky. At this time of year, north of Lat. 690, the sun never set. After sinking towards the west, he hesitated as if in thought, before beginning once more to climb—very strangely to our unaccustomed eyes. We found this phenomenon extremely agreeable. It made the night watches as pleasant as those by day, caused no alteration in our daily life, and abated not a jot our ability to sleep. The brilliant weather we now enjoyed, and continued to enjoy more or less unbroken throughout our stay in these northern parts, seemed to have set in when the sun first remained above the horizon all night, as if before his unceasing vigil the malign spirits of fog and rain dare not show themselves.

The one drawback to these halcyon days was the absence of wind. That north-easterly blow in Disko Bay was the last we were to have. For the rest of the way to Igdlorssuit, a small Eskimo settlement sixty miles north of Disko, we drifted and motored. In these circumstances we had no qualms about using the engine for hours at a time. We were under no critical eyes and we had on board no disciple of Hilaire Belloc who, as a yachtsman, had such a loathing for engines in small boats that, as he averred, he would rather die of thirst lying becalmed than have one in his boat. So we worked our iron tops'l hard, but with discretion. On deck its subdued rumble can easily be tolerated, but in the cabin the noise is barely endurable for the space of a meal. So we often stopped it at meal-times and never dreamt of running it at night, or what our clocks told us was night. Off Hare Island, near the northern entrance of the Vaigat, we began really to see icebergs, spewed out by the tide from this narrow strait in their hundreds to begin their slow journey northwards across the head of Baffin Bay until halted by the winter's sea-ice. Icebergs of all shapes and sizes, some like fortresses with sheer sides, others with pinnacled towers like glistening cathedrals, all floating serenely on the stillest of blue seas.

Now that we were approaching our journey's end, where Charles and I would have to gird up our loins for action, instead of being filled with joyful anticipation, flexing our muscles, doing a little quiet limbering-up on deck, both of us went about our work like a couple of cripples. I had a gathering on one hand and could still feel my rib when breathing—an unavoidable act at most times and more than ever necessary when climbing. Charles disclosed for my inspection a

Iceberg in the Vaigat

## NORTHWARDS TO IGDLORSSUIT

79

toe which looked as if it had been frost-bitten and required immediate amputation. Naturally he took a more serious view of this than I did and wanted me to make for Umanak, a small town where, according to the *Sailing Directions*, there was a hospital. I demurred strongly to this. As the Arabs say, the camel-driver has his thoughts and the camel he has his. We were already later than we should have been, and by the time we had been to Umanak (sixty miles away) and back, and Charles had had his foot looked at and probably been told not to put it to the ground for a month, we should have wasted a good many days.

So to Charles's chagrin and with some slight misgiving on my part we held our course for Ubekjendt Island and the settlement of Igdlorssuit in Lat. 71° 30′. Ubekjendt is a name given by the Dutch whalers and means 'unknown'; Igdlorssuit is Eskimo and for that language is a comparatively short name. A brief glance at the map of these parts had served to disgust me with Eskimo names. Their length and their doubled consonants combine to make up words that no ordinary man's tongue is able to pronounce. For their repellent appearance we must, I suppose, thank Hans Egede who coined the orthography for his translation of the Bible into Eskimo. Igdlorssuit lies on the east side of Ubekjendt Island, an island that rises to over 2000 feet. In my eyes it looked rounded, featureless, dull; but Rockwell Kent, an artist and a writer, who in 1933 built a house at Igdlorssuit and lived there for a year, had viewed it with far different eyes, the eyes of an artist, a man with a soul, as opposed to a man personifying, as a French writer has put it, '*le mépris de vulgarisation, du clubalpinisme et des yahous.*' He, Rockwell Kent, thus describes Ubekjendt:

> Both by the suggestion of its name and by its position and character—its seagirt isolation, the simple grandeur of its stark snow-covered table-land and higher peaks, the dark cliff barrier that forms its eastern shore—there is the glamour of imponderable mystery about the island which dignifies it even at the gateway of a region of stupendous grandeur. Its cliffs, proclaiming inaccessibility, preclude the thought of human settlements. When, therefore, on approaching its more mountainous north-eastern end, where, just ahead, steep mountain walls rise sheer from the water's edge, the barrier ends, the shore sweeps inward in a mile-wide crescent of smooth strand and, cupped

80  MISCHIEF IN GREENLAND

by mountains, there appears a low and gently sloping verdant foreland, jewelled with painted buildings, one's spirit, in sudden awaken-
ing to a need, exults in grateful consciousness of its fulfilment.

When we rounded the northern end of the island and started down its
east coast in search of the settlement, we wondered much as to what we
should see. At the time I had not read Rockwell Kent's book and, as I
have said, the island appeared to me an uncommonly dull and barren
lump. But it was in the nature of the settlement we were mainly interested, not the island. Obviously we could not hope for igloos, for there
was no snow below the 2000-foot level. Perhaps we expected to see
semi-troglodyte dwellings of stones and earth, their blear-eyed and
smoke-grimed inhabitants, clad in furs and reeking of blubber, crawl-
ing out to greet us with cries of 'Pilletay, Pilletay' ('Give, give'), as we
read of their doing in accounts by McClintock and other early explorers
in search of the North-west Passage. It was therefore with mixed feelings that we finally brought in view a row of some twenty gaily-painted
wooden houses (Rockwell's 'jewels') straggling along the beach and
in the background what was obviously a church. However, we were
cheered when with the aid of binoculars we made out numbers of husky
dogs, kayaks, sledges, and racks of drying shark-meat. We felt that the
last item should have been blubber, but shark-meat it proved to be.

The settlement lay in no proper bay, there was merely a slight
indentation of the coast-line. In such windless waters a sheltered
anchorage seems hardly needed; anyway the island protected us from
seaward and we were surrounded by land, the nearest being the island
of Upernivik some eight miles to the east. Compared with Ubekjendt,
or indeed with any island in the world, this really was a magnificently
mountainous island. It fairly bristled with peaks, their rock spires and
snow domes at that moment aglow in the westering sun, while three
glaciers, like broad, white highways, led from the waters of the fjord
up into the mountains. These same waters, we noticed, were thickly
strewn with icebergs, several smaller specimens lying grounded in our
vicinity. We let go the anchor in five fathoms about a hundred yards
from the beach. For our first night there we deemed it prudent to set an
anchor watch. Drifting icebergs are dangerous and (who knew?) the
natives might be hostile.

CHAPTER VII

# AT IGDLORSSUIT

BEFORE LONG A BOAT-LOAD of natives came aboard. Among them, by putting two and two together and judging from what I had been told, I recognized one Bertheson, schoolmaster, pastor, and leading seal-hunter. As well as lesser fry the boat contained a tough-looking character who, I was delighted to see, wore a pair of sealskin trousers. I had understood from my friend Dr Drever that Bertheson the schoolmaster spoke some known language, implying, so far as I was concerned, that he spoke either English or American. Nothing of the kind. Eskimo or Danish—I could take my pick—were all he had to offer, so that our conversation, limited to grins and handshakes, was about as useful and intelligent as that between two apes. Most men visiting Greenland for the first time would at least take the trouble to glance at an Eskimo dictionary, and having had their interest in that language quickly quenched by the length of the words and the super-fluity of consonants, would turn to Danish as the next best thing and swot up a few phrases or words. For my part, the true-born English-man, I set out on my travels with the firm intention of speaking (if speech is necessary) in English, whether to an Eskimo, a Chinaman, or a Canoe Indian. Out of regard for their weak minds one might speak it slowly and clearly so that any fool, one might think, would under-stand, but that was as far as I was prepared to go. With some acumen the schoolmaster had brought with him an English-Danish diction-ary, fearing possibly that his own Danish was a little rusty and that we might fire at him with words too high for his understanding. With the aid of this we learnt some striking facts such as his age and the age of his wife, facts which were more trouble to elicit than they were really worth. When a sufficient number of our cigarettes had been consumed the party broke up.

I don't pretend that it is not a good thing to be able to talk to the natives in their own tongue, to glean a few facts about them and

81

82 MISCHIEF IN GREENLAND

their country at first hand even though the facts may later prove to be nonsense or lies. Indeed, in my more sombre moments I often think it a waste of time to travel unless one can talk to the natives—which, of course, is one good reason I have for preferring to travel if possible where there are none. But I would not have taken much to heart our inability on this occasion to hold a conversazione, were it not that Dr Drever had suggested that when we went up the fjord in search of mountains we should take with us two Igdlorssuit men to supply us with local knowledge, fish, and possibly seal-meat. Obviously we had now no hope of putting to them this interesting proposition, not to mention the important details of food and pay which would have to be settled. We must do without them. Such an arrangement would no doubt have provided amusement for both parties but apart from that I don't think we missed their services. Fish we could catch ourselves and in the fjords where we went there were no seals to be shot.

To show what we could do we caught some fish for breakfast before we turned in that night. They were what are called fjord cod, smaller and less firm-fleshed than their fellows of the open sea, despised by the natives but welcome to us. Although we expected to be here several days, and although one could see from the boat pretty well all that Igdlorssuit had to offer in the way of sight-seeing, we lost no time in going ashore fully armed with cameras. In fact we spent five days here, mainly on account of Charles who was now lying up nursing his foot, still convinced that only a visit to Umanak would save it. Like the rest of the Greenlanders the people of Igdlorssuit are far from being pure Eskimos, yet they and their way of life appeared to us more like the real thing. The huskies, of which each family had some twenty, the sledges lying about, the kayaks carefully stored high up out of the dogs' reach, the racks of shark-meat drying in the sun, the women sewing skins on a new-built kayak, all these led us to believe we were seeing life in the Arctic, even while we trudged along the sandy beach sweating in the sun and cursing the heat and the mosquitoes. A walk of about half a mile, the sea on one hand and on the other a gravel fan sparsely covered with grass and a few flowers (Rockwell's 'verdant foreland'), brought us to the heart of Igdlorssuit life—the store and the post-office, and the shed where barrels of sharks' liver were stored. At least the revolting stuff we watched being weighed was, I am told, shark liver, and

Igdlorssuit Eskimos or Greenlanders

Igdlorssuit—church and rack of shark meat

84 MISCHIEF IN GREENLAND

several times up the fjord we saw the fins of these creatures sticking out of the water. The store, owned by the Greenland Trading Company, buys all the sealskins and shark liver brought in and sells all that the community needs in the way of food, clothing, household goods, beer, tobacco, tools, implements, fishing gear, rifles, shotguns, ammunition, and fuel for their motor boats. Thus although their occupations have not changed and they still live, though indirectly, by their skill in sealing and fishing, yet their way of life has greatly changed from the self-sufficiency of the old days when the seal provided their clothing, boots, tents, and boats, food for men and dogs, fuel for cooking and heating, and oil for lighting.

The three or four motor boats anchored off the settlement were used for going to various islands where at this time of year seals might be found. Generally a kayak was carried on board for use in the final stages of the hunt. Hunting so wary a creature as the seal calls for no little skill and patience even with modern firearms. The only evidence of seals we saw were mere fleeting glimpses of a head poked above water and immediately submerged. The best chance of a shot is when they are hauled out on a berg or floe, or ashore on an islet. They must be shot through the head or they will roll into the water and sink or escape. In winter they are netted or harpooned at breathing holes, or stalked on the ice, the hunter behaving as much like a seal as he can and taking hours over the stalk. A few seals were still being got in July when we were there. I remember seeing a dory with two seals tied behind being towed along by a team of huskies. The beach is steep-to and the water so calm that there was no difficulty in keeping the dory afloat while the dogs walked along the beach. The seals are not the fur-seal, but the skins of these ringed and hooded seals are valuable to the fur trade. As privileged visitors and prospective buyers we penetrated to the back premises of the store where the skins were kept. We were not allowed to buy the quality skins—lovely, silvery fawn skins in prime condition which were reserved for export to Denmark—but we all invested in a few of the lower quality at prices in the region of £1, depending upon the condition. From his purchase Terry Ward knocked up a useful pair of bedroom-slippers. My thoughts were running on sealskin trousers and the figure I should cut in them at home. This novel idea never came to fruition though it seemed to me to be a

AT IGDLORSSUIT

more proper use for sealskins than the elegant coat for my sister that, as I should have anticipated, they eventually made.

Husky dogs and children, alike, swarmed in Igdlorssuit. Both seemed to be well cared for, the dogs being fed daily on shark meat. In late winter, when the fjord is finally frozen over, when hunting parties go out and when visits are paid to neighbouring settlements, the dogs earn their summer keep by pulling sledges. For the children our visit was a godsend. They played on and around *Mischief*, showed off for our benefit in a kayak, and followed us diligently on our walks. Apparently the sensible arrangement prevailed of closing the school entirely for the summer months. The children were well clad in European clothes—brightly-coloured anoraks were a favourite—as were their elders, apart from one or two old-timers and the young he-men who affected sealskin trousers. Nearly everyone wore sealskin boots. One woman on seeing me approach with a camera darted into her house and reappeared in full-dress costume, with beaded vest and beautifully embroidered white sealskin boots reaching well up the thigh. This dress, we were told, was worn on Sundays for church, but in summer, by a less sensible arrangement, the church, too, seemed to be closed. Both in manner and appearance the people struck me as being very like Sherpas, the same short, sturdy figures and Mongolian features, their brown cheeks suffused with red; cheerful, happy-go-lucky, and always ready to laugh either at us or themselves. The oldest inhabitant was a delightful character; a man like a barrel, as broad as he was long, who walked about (sealskin trousers, of course) aided by a stick, a benign smile on his leathery, wrinkled face and a short cutty pipe stuck firmly in his toothless mouth. They shopped freely at the store buying sugar, flour, jam, sweets, tinned meats and fruits, so that their normal diet seemed to be as humdrum as our own. It must be a sad change from their former regime of blubber, seal meat, and sea birds. In time one can get used to anything and no doubt they still eat enough of these natural, wholesome foods to prevent them from getting scurvy. They certainly looked healthy enough and in little need of the services of a sort of district nurse who visited them about once a fortnight in a small motor vessel from Umanak which brought also mail, stores, and passengers.

Having undertaken to collect plants for the Natural History Museum I spent most of my time botanizing around the settlement

Doryman under sail

Igdlorssuit—weighing shark liver

AT IGDLORSSUIT                                             87

where flowers might be found growing up to the 500-foot level. I now
had lumbago—'a trifling sum of misery new added to the foot of my
account'—so that I had to be careful when bending to dig out a plant
for fear of not being able to straighten up. Really, I thought, I should
be far better employed exploring the Brighton front or Cheltenham
from a bath-chair rather than Greenland; to be joined there no doubt,
in the very near future, by Charles, provided that vehicles of that kind
were procurable on easy terms. But Charles was now on the mend.
Our second-hand accounts of life's busy scene in Igdlorssuit would no
longer serve. He must see for himself. So rising from his bed of pain
he announced his intention of going ashore, and in order to save him
a long walk we rowed the dinghy to a landing place just below the
store. The populace, scenting something unusual afoot, had gathered
in strength and they were well rewarded for their pains. In yachting
cap and gum-boots, his beard a sable silver, monocle in eye and supported by an ice-axe, Charles stepped ashore like a slimmer edition of
King Edward VII landing at Cowes from the Royal Yacht. The crowd
were speechless with delight. At last, they thought, the captain of *Mischief* had condescended to visit them.

Evidently it was time for us to move. We could loiter on the way
and I hoped that by the time I had done a little mountain reconnaissance Charles would be fit to climb. When Dr Drever had first mentioned the possibilities of this Umanak fjord region and had showed
me a map, I had plumped for the Qioqe peninsula as the most promising place to begin. This peninsula, some twenty-five miles long and
a bare eight miles wide, juts out from the mainland behind the island
of Upernivik. We could not therefore see the mountains from Igdlorssuit but according to the map there were plenty of them from
5000 feet to 7000 feet high. Maps for a good portion of the west coast
have been published on a scale of a quarter inch to the mile. These
are fairly accurate but in a complicated mountain region such as the
Qioqe peninsula we found that some of the peaks marked were not
easily reconciled with those on the ground. My choice, as will be seen,
turned out to have been a poor one. It was no doubt influenced by
the fact that there lay the highest mountain of that region, probably
the highest in West Greenland, a peak of 2310 metres, or about 7500
feet. It is generally true in mountaineering, if not always in life, that

88MISCHIEF IN GREENLAND

'we needs must love the highest when we see it'. Just before sailing, however, I learnt that the peak had been climbed by an Italian party in the previous summer, but by then the Qioqe peninsula had become for me a fixed idea and we went to it with no very clear idea of what we intended doing there. Plans should certainly be flexible but this was flexible to the point of vacuity.

This Italian expedition of 1960 had been remarkable in more than one way. Most remarkable of all is the fact that the leader, Piero Ghiglioni (who was killed in a car accident later that same year), was aged 77. (A friend who sent me an account of the expedition remarked when he sent it: 'There is hope for you yet.') But Piero Ghiglioni was quite exceptional, a man who had spent a life-time climbing in all parts of the world and who seemed to have the secret of eternal youth. He and his two companions, a doctor and an Italian guide, in the course of three weeks, with the use of a motor boat chartered at Umanak, climbed this highest peak which they named Punta Italia, the highest peak on Disko Island, 6188 feet, and the highest peak on the Nagssuak peninsula, 6981 feet. Moreover all these peaks were climbed in a day from sea-level—no camps, no bivouacs—the climbing of Punta Italia taking eighteen hours. The party enjoyed the same settled weather as we did, and they had before them a clear-cut plan with three definite objectives. They did not mess about looking for a mountain to climb, as we were to do.

Before we left Igdlorssuit we heard of another curious piece of climbing news. Terry Ward, no more gifted as a linguist than the rest of us, soon acquired a knack of conversing more or less intelligibly with these Eskimo, partly by speech and partly by intuition or guess-work. I have often noticed when in foreign parts with the army that the so-called other ranks, men with no pretension to knowing any language but their own, often got on better with the local people, and learnt more of what was going on, than those who had had a supposedly better education and even some smattering of the language. Terry came back on board one day with the story that a week or two before four members of a climbing party of unknown nationality had been killed when climbing on the peninsula just north of Qioqe. We had no knowledge of any other party being in the area and to me it seemed an extraordinary story. Perhaps for once Terry's intuition had been at fault and this heavy death roll pertained to seals, sharks, or polar bears rather than men. However, when we got back to Godthaab the story was confirmed by the Commissioner of Police who was extremely upset about it. A party of nine Belgians had been climbing, four of whom, three men and a woman, had been killed, and the Commissioner had had to organize some attempt at recovering the bodies. Moreover some hard things had been said by the Belgian Minister in Copenhagen about the lack of help that had been forthcoming—as if any help could be expected for mountaineers in such a region, or as if a party of nine were not sufficient to help themselves. At present there are no restrictions on those who wish to climb in Greenland, except for scientific parties or for expeditions venturing on to the ice-cap when, I believe, a deposit has to be made against the possibility of a rescue party having to be mounted. And it is to be hoped that in so fine a field as West Greenland no restrictions upon small climbing parties will have to be made. Mountaineers are aware of the risks they run and in a place where no aid can be expected, where in case of trouble they must rely upon themselves, it behoves them to act accordingly.

CHAPTER VIII

# AMONG THE MOUNTAINS

O N THE SAME AFTERNOON, having extracted Charles from the thick of an admiring crowd, we got our anchor and sailed out. The wind soon died. After drifting on to a large iceberg and fending off with the boat-hook we started the engine. We had about forty miles to go to the anchorage I had in mind, a bay at the root of the Qioqe peninsula with the remarkable name of Kangerdlugssuakavaak. 'Kangerd' means fjord—the fjords between which our peninsula lay were called Kangerdlugssuaq and Kangerdluarssuk. Since most of the forty miles would have to be done under the engine we anchored for the night on the south side of Upernivik Island off the snout of a dying glacier. In the fjords it is difficult to find water shallow enough to anchor in without being perilously near the rocky shore. Usually the most likely place is off a glacier, or a stream that emerges from a glacier, where silt and debris have accumulated.

Early next morning a small floe got under our bowsprit and we had to move to another anchorage. I spent an hour ashore looking for plants. In West Greenland there are several hundred species of flowering plants, grasses, and ferns. In our short visit we collected only some sixty species but many of the flowers were no doubt over by the time we arrived. There are many familiar forms such as buttercups, dandelions, saxifrage, campions, poppies, harebells, willow herb; and of the larger kinds, creeping willow, dwarf birch, crowberry, and bilberry. As we motored up Kangerdluarssuk, with the Qioqe peninsula on our port hand, we met with a bitter wind blowing straight from the ice-cap. The day was unusually cloudy with cloud down to about 500 feet so that we saw nothing of the mountains but their lower cliffs, broken occasionally by steep and narrow valleys filled with ice. At its upper end the fjord widens. In the middle lies the small island of Qeqertak; in the south-east corner a massive glacier descends from the inland ice, filling that part of the fjord with big icebergs; and in the north-east corner

AMONG THE MOUNTAINS

was the bay with the long, unpronounceable name where we proposed to stay, a bay well protected from drifting ice. We dropped anchor in seven fathoms off a wide gravel fan left by a retreating glacier. Even so we found the stern touched the bottom about twenty yards from the shore. We had to lay out a kedge anchor astern to keep her lying parallel to the beach.

David was eager to set foot on a glacier, so next day he and I took a walk up the valley which runs right across the root of the peninsula to Kangerdlugssuaq fjord on the north side. In winter this valley is used as a sledge route. Rockwell Kent describes a journey made in January from Igdlorssuit to Umanak when, owing to open water, they could not sledge direct to Umanak and had to sledge up the northern fjord, haul the sledge over the peninsula by this valley, and continue down the southern fjord and along the coast to Umanak. A short walk up the gravel fan brought us on to the glacier itself which, fortunately for David, for he had on only shoes, was smooth, unbroken ice covered with gravel and flat stones. After about three miles of easy going, passing on our left the mouth of the valley whence the glacier descended, we reached the moraine on the far side of the glacier and were soon on the low divide looking down to the northern fjord. Thick mist covered the fjord while we basked in sunshine. On the evidence alone of this short excursion I began to fear that we had come to the wrong place for a climbing centre. Certainly the glacier led into the heart of the peninsula in the direction of the bigger peaks, including Punta Italia, but its ice-fall, filling the valley that we had passed, seemed to me an effective barrier. The peaks were too far to be climbed from the boat so that we should have to carry loads up the ice-fall, and besides that they looked inaccessible from the glacier head. I did, however, notice a peak of about 6500 feet which was within reach and which could be got at by way of a steep but ice-free valley less than a mile from the anchorage.

Charles, too, had been out for the day exercising his foot. When we compared notes I gathered that in his view this ice-fall was a minor obstacle. In the course of many years of climbing, mostly in the Himalaya, the times I have failed to come to grips with some peak on which I had set my heart, having been balked and forced to retreat by some ice-fall, are sad memories.

92 MISCHIEF IN GREENLAND

Most ice-falls, I admit, can be overcome with time, patience, or possibly ladders, as, for example the ice-fall leading to the West Cwm on the south side of Everest. But unless the goal beyond is all-important they are best left alone by small parties like ours, especially if loads have to be carried up them. Charles, as I have said, did not agree. He judged this ice-fall to be, so to speak, a piece of cake, and persuaded me to try it in spite of my conviction that we were wasting our time. He concluded by saying there was nothing he liked better than worrying his way through an intricate ice-fall. My reply, couched in phrases that might have shocked anyone but Charles, was that I thoroughly disliked messing about in them. However, since I had had my way over the little matter of not going to Umanak I thought that this harmless whim of his should be humoured.

Accordingly next day we started up the ice-fall. I must say Charles did his best while I studiously refrained from any discouraging remarks and even tried to show the enthusiasm I did not feel. As we got higher even a one-eyed man might have seen that there was no likelihood of finding a route up any of the big peaks beyond had we surmounted the difficulties of the ice-fall, but Charles was so engrossed in mastering it and showing that it could be mastered, that the uselessness of doing so hardly occurred to him. Nothing daunted, Charles pressed on, only a little astonished to find that after one terrace had been laboriously gained there was always another above. We lunched precariously, surrounded by crevasses and seracs in hideous confusion. Shortly afterwards, when we were still some 200 feet below what really was the top we were stopped by a series of gaping crevasses, around, through, or over which, Charles had to admit there was no way. He had had his fun, so on the way back to the boat I pointed out the 6500-foot peak I proposed we should tackle next day. The steep valley leading to it narrowed higher up to a gully packed with snow. By way of the gully we could reach a high snow shoulder and possibly the rock peak beyond. We could not see what lay between shoulder and summit but the mountain was well worth trying. In spite of the encouraging example of a so much older man, I had some misgivings about my own ability to emulate Piero Ghiglioni's feats. I asked Charles how he felt about climbing 6500 feet in the day. Many years ago, at a much higher altitude, I had climbed 6000 feet and back in

Anchorage at Upernivik glacier

Summit ridge of peak climbed on Upernivik

94          MISCHIEF IN GREENLAND

a day; and Charles, searching his memory, thought he had done as much before and could no doubt do it again.

The condemned men ate a hearty breakfast—cod steaks, if I remember right—and at 8.30 we had ourselves rowed ashore. Not the least blessing of climbing in Greenland is that one can start at a reasonable hour; no turning out in the small hours, as one must in the Alps, to cook and swallow some food, that were it food for the gods would be revolting at such a time, and then to stumble out into the cold darkness guided by the feeble light of a candle lantern. All this to avoid being be-nighted, of which in Greenland there is happily no fear. Some loose scree in the valley took a little of the shine out of us but when we reached the gully we found almost continuous beds of hard snow up which we could kick our way. We lunched just below the shoulder, having climbed about 3000 feet. We continued kicking steps until when about 500 feet below a flat snow ridge at the foot of the final rock peak we were obliged to cut steps. Charles, who was in front at the time, thought we might avoid this by making use of some old avalanche snow off to our right. When this proved delusive we came back and I took over the step-cutting, for Charles, even at this early stage, was beginning to suffer from mountaineer's foot—the inability to put one in front of the other.

At four o'clock we came out on the level ridge whence we looked straight down to the waters of the fjord and across it to the great glacier rolling down from the inland ice. A mountain prospect from a high place is enthralling but to look out over sea and mountains is, I think, even more moving—to feel at once the immensity of the one and the steadfast, unchanging nature of the other, both indifferent to man's presence and yet to many men an inspiration and a solace. However that may be, that which concerned us more than the majestic view was the formidable aspect of the rock and ice ridge which sprang upwards towards the summit almost from where we stood. There were nearly a thousand feet of it. It might improve on acquaintance, but to two tired men it looked sufficiently daunting. Charles now admitted that he had shot his bolt and while I might have gone farther I did not feel capable of looking after him as well as myself on what would evidently be the hardest part of the climb. Reluctantly, and keenly disappointed, we accepted defeat. For all that it had been a day of rare enjoyment, of strenuous endeavour in glorious surroundings and in flawless weather with only our own feebleness to blame for our failure. At 8.30 that evening, dejected and humbled, we rowed back to the boat.

Before trying this fairly long climb we had had only the one short day on the ice-fall. We preferred to attribute our failure to lack of exercise rather than to excess of years. But I did not want to sweat up that long gully again and risk another breakdown. I felt we should move to a base where we should have more scope. Before quitting the fjord, however, we wanted to take some pictures of *Mischief* under sail, mainly for the sake of the film which Terry Ward was engaged upon. The wide head of the fjord, tolerably free from icebergs, afforded a good opportunity provided we had some wind. With the first breeze we sailed to the little island of Qeqertak preparatory to sending off the dinghy with the camera party. We had, of course, first to walk round the island, for islands have the power of suggesting to those that visit them that they are treading unexplored territory. Having hoisted sail and got under way we promptly went aground. But she soon came off and we made several runs across the fjord, taking care to have the big glacier as a background when the pictures were taken.

While Charles and I had been amusing ourselves on the mountains the crew had set about giving *Mischief* a new look. At Godthaab we had not been able to find any cream-coloured paint like that on her topsides. At David's suggestion we bought instead some bright yellow paint; he thought that with black bulwarks and yellow topsides she would look pretty rakish so this new colour scheme was now adopted. All Danish ships plying to Greenland, and all the local fishing boats, are painted a standard red-lead colour, presumably to make them conspicuous when among ice. Personally I liked the new colour scheme, but when we returned to Lymington, where yachts are either glossy white or nothing, I failed to detect any gasps of admiration from frequenters of the Yard. To finish this as well as other work we stayed yet another day at this anchorage. Among other jobs the starboard topping lift needed renewal and besides working on board we spent time ashore washing both our clothes and ourselves in a fresh-water pool. Although the water came from a snow-bed not far away, thanks to the continuous sunshine it was not really cold. The weather continued

96            MISCHIEF IN GREENLAND

unbrokenly fine and even if the barometer fell the weather sensibly
ignored it and remained serenely cloudless and calm.

On July 29th we had a long day's motoring back down the fjord
and through the narrow winding channel called Inukavsait between
the tip of the peninsula and Upernivik Island. Each glacier we passed
we scanned closely as a possible way up into the mountains, but most
of them were mere ice torrents. The scenery in Inukavsait is spectacular. Gaunt cliffs tower over it on both sides and at the half-way point,
where the fjord narrows and makes a sharp bend, we appeared to be
heading for an unbroken face of rock. Beyond this, on the peninsula
side the cliffs receded and we made for a beach where a glacier stream
debouched. At 8 p.m. we anchored close inshore opposite the widest
part of a detritus fan. After supper, alarmed at the sight of a big berg
drifting past within spitting distance at the rate of about two knots,
we decided to move to a little cove on the north side of the fan. With
no winch to help we had a tussle getting the stern anchor and having
reached our new anchorage we found a berg had grounded there
leaving us no room to swing. Back at the first anchorage we set an
anchor watch, for there were many bergs about drifting up and down
with the tide. Some we recognized as old friends that we had passed
earlier in the day.

Owing to a couple of days of bad weather and a relapse in Charles's
condition—knee trouble this time—we spent nine days in this uneasy
anchorage for the sake of climbing one peak. Near the landing place
we found traces of recent visits by Eskimos and the reason for these
visits became clear when on walking upstream as far as the entrance to a
gorge we saw the cliffs were occupied by a colony of glaucus gulls. This
was the only bird colony we saw and Terry spent a lot of time on top of
the cliff and below it trying to take pictures. Apart from the gulls, a few
snow buntings and sandpipers, and rare families of ptarmigan, were the
only living things we saw on land, excepting always mosquitoes and
midges. They were particularly bad along the banks of the stream which
was also the richest collecting ground for flowers. I was nearly driven
mad and remembered with shame how at Godthaab, where some of the
Danish workmen wore head veils, I had thought them 'cissy'.

The only peak that could be reached from the boat appeared not
to be intended for climbing, at least not by Charles and me. Evidently

AMONG THE MOUNTAINS

we should have to try up the glacier, the stream from which had cut the gorge where the gulls lived. There was too much water in the gorge for us to walk up it and we had to make a long, high detour crossing a series of old moraines and boulder-strewn slopes. On this sort of ground Charles is greatly handicapped because, as a result of his adventure in Spain, he can focus only one eye at a time. Boulder-hopping is trying for a fit man with two good eyes and it is easy enough to take a bad toss. Charles had to move with caution and deliberation and he had not the turn of speed to make up time when on easy ground. Having sat down on a boulder to wait for Charles I had frequently felt the force of the Nepali saying that 'he who rests on a stone is twice glad'. Heaven knows, I myself move slowly enough nowadays but when climbing with Charles I felt how apt were the poignant lines of one Joseph Cottle, a very minor poet:

> How steep, how painful the ascent:
> It needs the evidence of close deduction
> To know that we shall ever gain the top.

When at 1 p.m. we finally reached the glacier we were thankful to find that this glacier really was a broad highway, rising very gradually—*une pente insensible*, as the French guide-books say—tolerably free from crevasses, and for the most part clean, dry ice. After going for three hours we had at last got on to névé and found the snow soft and deep, and since the col we were making for was still distant we decided to call it a day. But the excursion had not been altogether fruitless. Up a side valley I had noticed a nice-looking peak up which there seemed to be a way.

By the time we got back to the boat we had been walking for twelve hours, so the next day we remained on board. We started to paint the deck with oil and red ochre, a mixture that takes so long to dry that only half the deck can be done at a time. Charles's knee then swelled up again and another three days passed before he pronounced himself fit for action. Upon this we made up four loads and set off for the glacier accompanied by John Wayman and Michael as assistant porters. Unpractised though they were in the aggravating game of boulder-hopping they moved a lot faster than we did. We put the camp by a lake in the ablation valley alongside the glacier. It was

98 MISCHIEF IN GREENLAND

only 1200 feet up and a long way from the peak but we reckoned that a bed on warm gravel instead of on cold ice would compensate us for the extra toil. Having supped richly on pemmican and breakfasted on porridge—for we did ourselves well—we set off about eight o'clock of a dull morning. Two hours later when we turned off the main glacier into the side valley we found it to be a glacier-filled cirque, its head overhung by threatening seracs and its floor strewn with their debris. Charles viewed the scene with disfavour. His mountaineering principles are quite rightly orthodox and they teach that objective dangers such as this are to be shunned. In reality the risk was slight because our route lay up a rock buttress at the head of the cirque and once on the buttress we should be out of the line of fire. The weak point of the buttress lay up a yellow rock gully which proved steeper than it looked and very loose, so loose that we deemed it safer to climb unroped, lest the rope should dislodge something on to the man below—in this case Charles. By lunch-time we had reached easier ground on top of the buttress.

The cloud had thickened and a penetrating wind began to blow as we sat on a wet rock ledge to eat and to view the prospect ahead. It was very discouraging. The buttress that from below had appeared to lead direct to a snow slope, we now found to be cut off from it by a wide, shallow scoop of bare ice, an ice scoop that had been polished by debris falling from some ice cliffs a few hundred feet above. Below us the scoop heeled over steeply to disappear from view. For the moment the cliffs looked stable enough; the difficulty lay in the fact that we had about 150 feet of ice to cross, so that, with only our 100-foot rope, at one stage both of us would be on the ice at once and neither able to check a slip. Having canvassed all possible alternatives, and having decided that the snow beyond the scoop looked suspiciously thin, we were in two minds about going on or giving up. Manlier thoughts prevailed. While Charles belayed himself to the rocks I started cutting steps across the ice; good, large steps, too, for we should have to return the same way. Having run out all the rope I cut a stance and Charles embarked on the ice. Passing below me he cut on till he had reached the snow which, as we had feared, proved to be lying thinly on ice. However, after another rope's length we were in deeper, safer snow and moved freely across it to gain a rock ridge. This steep ridge was also

AMONG THE MOUNTAINS

very loose so we unroped again and climbed steadily up into the mist. An ice slope lying at an easy angle, up which I quickly nicked steps, led finally to the snow summit where—*longo intervallo*—I was joined by Charles. We had got our peak and by bad luck on quite the worst day we had had. Visibility extended to only a few yards and merely the fact that on all sides the slope fell away showed that we were on the top. The height by aneroid was 5800 feet. It had taken us nine hours from camp. All went well on the descent, our steps were still good, and at the top of the buttress we once more unroped. Charles has a flair for remembering a route. Without him, in spite of the odd stones we had placed to mark various pitches, I should have had difficulty in sticking to our line of ascent. At 9 p.m. we were off the rocks. I reached the tent by 11.30 p.m., but by the time I had brewed pemmican and Charles had arrived to eat it, it was one o'clock in the morning.

It was raining when we packed up and started down next day. On arriving at the beach, expecting to be wafted swiftly on board for a pint or two of tea, I was peeved to see that *Mischief* was on the move. Threatened by an iceberg the crew had had to get the anchor with all speed and move to yet another anchorage. At this place, where we had had to stay so long, we enjoyed little peace. It put me in mind of a remark in the *Admiralty Pilot* about an anchorage on the North African coast: 'Anchoring in this bight must be prompted by necessity and not by any hope of tranquillity.' We maintained an anchor watch all the time and that night at 2 a.m. in my watch a strong puff of wind caused the anchor to drag. Having started the engine and moved to a fresh spot we let go the heavy fisherman-type anchor. Partly to save ourselves labour we had trusted to the CQR pattern anchor, one which holds well in mud or sand but is not much use on a rocky bottom. A CQR anchor is relatively half the weight of a conventional pattern anchor. It is stockless, shaped like a ploughshare, and depends for its holding power upon digging itself in. CQR, I believe, stands for an abbreviated, or perhaps an American version, of the word 'secure'. In the fjords where one has to anchor, as it were, on a mountain side, where the bottom may shelve from six fathoms to twenty fathoms in as many yards, an anchor is easily dislodged.

Mountaineering is happily not yet a competitive sport. There are no medals to be won, no records to be broken. The mountains,

Glacier on Upernivik

In Inukaavsait between Qiope and Upernivik Island

AMONG THE MOUNTAINS

whether or not we overcome them, are the prize, and there are as well the rewards which each individual climber finds for himself—health, peace of mind, high endeavour, adventure, a sense of achievement, staunch companionship, and at the end of it all a store of mountain memories. It is not a competitive sport, as I have said, but at times the old Adam will out. A prime example of this, of course, was the struggle for Everest which ended in almost becoming an international affair. Similarly, on a minor scale, I could not help feeling that our activities, if such they could be called, compared ill with the achievements of that swift-moving successful Italian party of the previous year. It was now August 8th, the season was advancing, but we had still time for another foray provided Charles's legs held out. As I pointed out to him, 'stren-uousness is the immortal path and sloth is the way of death'—a truth that elicited merely a non-committal grunt. Conditions were certainly less favourable now than earlier in the summer; on the lower slopes the snow had turned to ice while higher up it was soft and wet. Upernivik Island, where we should have gone in the first place, seemed now our best bet.

Accordingly we got under way and after entering Kangerd-lugssuaq fjord we turned westwards and coasted along the north side of the island. On the way we had a look at the glacier leading up to a mountain called Sneepyramiden (7217 feet) on the peninsula north of Qioqe. It was, I think, while attempting this mountain that the Bel-gian party had met with disaster. There was evidently no way inland by that glacier which lay in a narrow gorge and was guarded by a wall of black ice only a few hundred yards from the shore. We felt no qualms about writing that off. Near the north-west corner of the island there is a group of islets and around them a vast congregation of icebergs had gathered, many of them probably aground. Going dead slow we forced a spectacular passage between two sheer-sided monsters each about 100 feet high. While Terry kept the cine-camera whirring, I kept an anxious eye on the narrow gap of water where any suspicion of a light green colour would betray the presence of a projecting tongue of ice. Threading our way through these and other concentrated dangers we anchored early in the afternoon off the first of the three big glaciers on the west side of Upernivik. Having lost our seven-lb. lead we had to do our sounding now with a home-made lead consisting of a three-foot length of iron piping filled with sand and plugged with a bit of wood. It was a cold, wet day with low clouds. In the evening, when the clouds lifted to reveal a very broken ice-fall, we decided to move on to the glacier three miles farther south directly opposite Igdlorssuit. Here, after nosing round taking soundings, we found a good berth in six fathoms only about fifty yards from the snout of the glacier.

Wasting no time in reconnaissance four of us started next morning carrying loads for a two-night camp. We made good progress, first on moraine and then on dry ice, and at 2 p.m. at a height of about 2000 feet began to look for a camp site. At first we feared that Charles and I would have to sleep on ice or, as a refinement of cruelty, on stones on top of ice. But presently we found a little hollow on the mountain side above the glacier which provided all we needed; a few minutes' work with ice-axes levelled a tent site, and at hand a snow-bed supplied us with water. A short walk up the glacier in the evening revealed a peak well within our grasp.

On that climb the finding of some yellow poppies at 3000 feet and the view from the summit were the only happy memories, for to tell the truth we had a fearful trudge. Near the summit the wide, gently sloping, uncommonly dull snowface up which we had slogged all morning narrowed to a ridge of red rock crowned with a series of rock gendarmes. One side of the ridge, as if it had been sliced off with a knife, fell sheer to the glacier 3000 feet below. The height was 6370 feet, high enough for us to see over the surrounding peaks and islands to the open sea dotted with icebergs and to the distant mountains of Disko Island. We realized now what we had missed by not coming here first and staying here, where there were glaciers on which one could move freely and many unclimbed peaks of great character. Instead of buzzing, as we had done, like elderly bees from flower to flower gathering very little honey, had we but established our camp high on Upernivik we might have drunk our fill. With these sad thoughts we turned our backs to the mountains. Next morning we carried the loads down and having stowed for good our boots and ice-axes we motored over to Igdlorssuit.

CHAPTER IX

# HOMEWARD BOUND

WE HAD ONLY TO MAKE OUR FAREWELLS and perhaps buy a few more skins, so we stayed but the night. We had had no dealings with the people of Igdlorssuit other than over the store counter for cash, but they were such a friendly, likeable lot that we were sorry to leave. Our thoughts turned often to them and we wondered what life was like there when the sun no longer rose over Upernivik, when the blue waters of the fjords turned to ice. I suppose really to grasp what life in the Arctic means one must winter there. Perhaps instead of spending the winter months in the mud of Lymington river it would be more in keeping with *Mischief*'s character, as well as a rewarding experience, if she wintered for once in Greenland ice.

We were now homeward bound, or on the first leg of our homeward journey, for we had still to call at Godthaab. Wind or no wind we made a point of hoisting sail when leaving Igdlorssuit, a gesture that no doubt was largely wasted on the natives who would only conclude from it that we were in no hurry to get anywhere. That evening we got no farther than the south end of Ubekjendt where we anchored for the night. On the next day, too, we did more motoring than sailing, finally coming to anchor at the mouth of the Vaigat in a place where we caught more cod than we could eat. On the way north we had been driven out of the Vaigat by a northerly wind and now a southerly wind did its best to stop us going south. We beat against it all day, made good about thirty miles, and anchored for the night in thick fog close to the Disko shore.

The wind died in the night. We were motoring as we passed by Qutdligssat where the coal-mine is situated. It is the strangest coal-mine—a high yellow cliff and at its foot at sea-level a wide black seam where the coal is dug. A couple of small coasters anchored close in were loading coal from lighters and hard by them lay some large icebergs aground. On this grey, sunless day, the ships, the ice, and the cliff

104    MISCHIEF IN GREENLAND

streaked with coal-dust looked forlorn and grim. The yearly output of some 8000 tons is barely enough to cover the consumption in Greenland. Soon after passing the mine we ran into dense fog. So far north as this the compass is too sluggish to steer by and we adopted the method of keeping the land close aboard. Though instinct may prompt one to keep well away from dangers it is generally a sound rule when navigating in narrow waters or in fog to keep the danger always in sight. But as visibility was less than fifty yards it was not easy to keep the shore in sight and the boat afloat at the same time, for, as we presently discovered, the coast here is not steep-to. When we finally took the ground and came to a more or less grinding halt the skipper was at the helm—a circumstance that allowed no blame to be apportioned to anyone, not even to the compass. We were merely victims of fate. Having for the moment lost touch with the shore and thinking it was time we knew where we were, I had begun closing with it and soon found it. Had we been using the lead, as we should have been, this could not have happened. The tide was ebbing and our efforts to winch her off with a kedge anchor failed. Luckily the bottom was sand but when she took on a heavy list we had to shore her up with the topmast as a leg. When she still listed we swung the boom out and very nearly made her fall over the other way. So we stopped meddling and contented ourselves with guessing how much farther the water would fall. In the space of three uneasy hours the tide began to make and by 8 p.m. we were able to haul her off. The fog having cleared we put in a couple of hours motoring before anchoring in six fathoms at the unusual distance of half a mile from the beach. Unlike the greater part of the Greenland coast, at this place, appropriately named Mudder Bay, it is a sort of Arctic Southend of shallow mud flats.

Passing out of the Vaigat we motored across Disko Bay in a flat calm. The bay is rich in magnificent and monumental icebergs. We passed some of the largest we had yet seen, their towering sides mirrored in the still water. These more than fulfilled our expectation, but the scenery of the Vaigat, what little we had seen of it, hardly began to compare in grandeur with that of the regions we had left behind. Five days out of Igdlorssuit, and still attended by fog, we reached the open sea where at last we got some wind—wind from ahead. The brief but glorious Arctic summer seemed now to be over as we beat slowly south in rain and bitter cold weather. On August 21st, another day of southerly wind and rain, when we were still 150 miles north of Godthaab, we met a great many trawlers on the Store Hellefiske bank. At one time we had twenty-five in sight. Besides the annoyance of an exasperatingly slow passage we were worried on Terry's account. He had long given up eating and complained of violent stomach pains. He attributed it to stomach ulcers which he had had before. We could do nothing for him but press on to Godthaab. So on the next day, which was calm, we put in twelve hours of motoring. However, that night we had wind enough. When I turned in at midnight, the wind being fresh from south-east, I was in two minds about reefing. Having gone below I was soon up again roused by the noise of a flogging sail. The jib outhaul had parted so I took the helm while David got the sail in. At one o'clock, the wind apparently increasing, I put my head out of the hatch to ask David how things were. According to him we were doing well. We were indeed. To my startled senses, when after struggling into oilskins I went on deck, the rain pelting down, it seemed to be blowing a gale, the boat heeling over and solid water foaming half-way up the lee rail. Without waiting to call the crew—getting into oilskins takes time—I told David to lash the tiller down while we put some rolls in the mains'l. Busy as we were with this I was not too busy to notice that the stays'l had stopped drawing. Rushing back to the tiller I found it had been lashed up instead of down. The boat had paid off, brought the wind aft, and in another moment we should have had an unholy gybe. Moreover we had not yet secured the boom so that all the rolls in it would have come adrift. Nor was that all. In our haste we had forgotten to cast off the vang, a two-and-a-half-inch rope knotted round the boom, which when wound up with the reefed sail was enough to split it. All that day the wind blew hard, but we were on course and made good more than sixty miles before the wind packed up. In the evening we got the sail down and David and I held a sewing party in the rain.

On the following night, when we were approaching Godthaab, we came within an ace of putting the ship ashore for good. It was mainly owing to my stupidity. Even now the recollection of it makes me sweat. By this time the nights were dark but on this occasion it was a clear, moonlit night, a swell running but the sea smooth. As we were unable to lay the course for the Godthaab beacon we were

106　　　　　MISCHIEF IN GREENLAND

pointing for the coast about ten miles north of it and sailing fast. I had not closely examined on the chart the nature of the coast thereabouts, nor appreciated the fact that we had less far to go to reach it than if we had been on course for Godthaab beacon. Anyway, I thought, on a clear, moonlit night the mountainous coast should be seen from several miles off. Normally when closing the land, even if it is thirty miles away, I am all anxiety, and I could not have been wholly at ease that night for I was lying down with one eye open and the other only half shut. David had been relieved at midnight but half an hour later, rather to my annoyance, he was still clumping about the deck in his heavy seaboots, either enjoying this fast midnight sail or perhaps not entirely happy about our course. Suddenly he let out a startled yell. I reached the deck with a jump to see a string of low islets half a cable's length to starboard and breakers ahead and to port. With no room to gybe I put the helm hard down. She missed stays. Next time, the breakers meanwhile appearing horribly close, with the stays'l backed she came round. Taking care to follow closely the course on which we had sailed into this perilous place, we sailed out again. It had been a near thing and might have been nearer still had not David delayed his going below. Having made a good offing we put about and at 3 a.m. picked up the Godthaab beacon.

Before closing the beacon and sailing up the fjord we hove-to to wait for daylight. When nearing the town, motoring against wind and tide, with the engine going at 1800 revolutions, we almost stood still and had to increase the revolutions to 2500 to make headway. We occupied our old berth but at the invitation of the harbour-master, who assured us there would be no ships coming in that week-end, we went alongside the quay. I had mentioned to the harbour-master that Terry Ward was unwell but we were astonished and a little embarrassed when an ambulance drove on to the quay, for Terry was not yet a stretcher case. Off he went, however, in the ambulance and we soon learnt that appendicitis was his trouble. Whether or not he would be able to sail with us was doubtful. He had to go to hospital again for further tests and await the result.

Meantime we had two interesting visitors. The Commissioner of Police, hearing we had been climbing in the Umanak region, came to tell us about the accident to the Belgian party and the uncalled-for

Entrance to Kangerdkuarssuk and mountains on Wegeners Halvo

Iceberg in the Vaigat

MISCHIEF IN GREENLAND

complaint made by the Belgian minister in Copenhagen. We then had a visit from the 'steersman', as he was called, of a Norwegian fishing vessel lying alongside. She was a 'long-liner' as opposed to a trawler, fishing with lines up to three miles long. By fishing deeper than the trawlers they can catch bigger fish and on this account 'long-lining' is considered as profitable as trawling. The catch was salted down on board and between April and November they made two voyages to these waters. This salt cod, known as 'stockfish', is exported mainly to Mediterranean and South American countries. Something went badly wrong with what might be called the harbour-master's shipping forecast. At two in the morning the Norwegian had to move to make room for a modern German stern-trawler which then moored so that we lay between her and the quay. No sooner was she fast than pandemonium broke out. Men began to jump from her deck down to ours on their way ashore, and an hour or so later, in much livelier spirits, were jumping from the quay on to our deck. Some insisted on climbing up our shrouds in order to land with a more resounding thud. By breakfast time the party was still in full swing, though the trawler, as we heard, should have sailed again at 4 a.m. A stream of men and women flowed across our deck, accordions wheezed, and drunken men danced on the quay. Charles himself is no mean beer drinker and on the previous evening had brought on board a small private stock of two dozen bottles which he had carelessly left on deck. The German trawlermen had not ignored this generous gesture, as Charles discovered immediately he came on deck. Had they realized that he was their unwitting benefactor they could hardly have given him a louder cheer when he appeared, and when he tried to discuss the question of the missing beer they merely stroked his beard. By this time, although it was a Sunday and the harbour-master's day of rest, he was down on the quay trying to shepherd the drunks on board. We had had enough too. Casting off one of the trawler's warps we backed out and returned to our anchorage.

After a final visit to the hospital Terry's fate was sealed. The doctor would not risk his going with us; he was to remain and return later in the *Umanak* where there would be a doctor to look after him. I was sorry to lose Terry and disliked having to leave one of the crew in strange hands in a foreign land. We should miss him on the way home both on account of the extra watch we should have to keep and because he alone was familiar with the main engine and the charging engine. The former would not be likely to give trouble but the charging engine was up to tricks of all kinds. I was wrong in saying Terry was the only man among us with mechanical knowledge. As we now discovered, Charles, thanks to his two years at the Military College of Science, had a wide theoretical knowledge of combustion engines as well as some practical knowledge picked up in his palmier days when he ran a vintage Rolls-Royce. He had used it less as a vehicle than as a movable residence—a rudimentary caravan, in fact—the back of it, the bedroom, as it were, being well stuffed with hay.

We sailed for home on the afternoon of August 28th with a fair wind which gave us a flying start of over 100 miles on the first day. In wet weather, with plenty of wind, we worked our way south and were in the latitude of Cape Farewell and a hundred miles west of it by September 2nd. By now the nights were long and if they were clear we witnessed every night a display of 'Northern Lights'. The wide zone where this phenomenon occurs runs in the form of an oval from Northwest Greenland across Hudson Bay, back towards Cape Farewell and across the Atlantic towards Ireland. Inside the zone activity of some kind may be seen almost every night in a clear sky. At a distance of 500 miles from the centre of the zone the frequency diminishes to some seventy nights in the year. In the zone itself, according to one's position, the lights may be seen in the south, overhead, or in the northern sky. Those we observed took the form of a pale, greenish glow varying in brightness and in form, sometimes like broad shafts, sometimes as a vast arch, or more often a shifting, shimmering curtain of light against the dark background of the sky.

At noon of September 5th, having done six knots most of the night, we had logged 135 miles in the twenty-four hours, our best day's run either outwards or homewards. Five days elapsed before we again reached the hundreds, five days of rain, fog, variable winds, marked by a few minor troubles. The mainsail had to have another big patch added to those already there, a staysail boom broke when we were running with the wind aft, and the charging engine packed up for good. Charles wrestled with it for several days, spent long hours in silent communion with it, but for all that it never went again. As usually seems

110　　MISCHIEF IN GREENLAND

to happen towards the end of each voyage, we were without light. We adjusted our time so as to have supper before dark and in the galley Charles made do with a tiny oil lamp not much better than a night-light. When homeward bound such small hardships and shortcomings may easily be tolerated; hence the phrase 'homeward-bound stitches' for sails repaired with stitches an inch long.

On the 11th the glass started falling and remained low throughout a five-day spell of wet, windy weather. We reefed down and finally changed the mainsail for the trysail, for I expected worse was to follow. But though the sea was rough—a full teapot landed in Mike's lap— the wind did not exceed Force 6. This long spell of moderately dirty weather coincided with the passage of hurricane 'Debbie' which struck the coast of Ireland and Scotland on September 16th. Between the 15th and the 16th it appears to have travelled 600 miles on a NNE course and must have passed about 200 miles east of us on the 15th. We were out of reach of any shipping forecasts and happily ignorant of any hurricane being at large in the western Atlantic. A friend in the meteorological office has kindly supplied me with a trace of Debbie's track and her brief history:

Debbie was first suspected during the period 5th–7th September in reports from the Cape Verde Islands and from a Danish steamer. On the 7th indications were that tropical storm intensity had been reached with winds up to 50 knots. During the next three days very little information was received, the storm moving into an area of little ocean traffic and out of range of reconnaissance aircraft. Observations were received from a KLM airliner on 10th September indicating that the forward speed had slowed down and that the storm was moving north-west. On the 11th reports from ships and the U.S. weather satellite Tiros III re-located the hurricane near 25° N., 45° W. with maximum winds of 75 knots. The storm moved northwards and during the 12th maximum sustained winds were estimated at 100 knots. On the 13th the storm curved north-east near 35° N., 45° W. It passed across the Azores on the night 14th–15th. Curving northward on the 15th it passed just off the west coast of Ireland early on the 16th. Gusts reached 92 knots at Ballykelly and 93 knots at Tiree and Snaefell. At least 11 deaths and many injuries were attributed to Debbie in Ireland and extensive damage occurred in Wales and Scotland.

On the 15th we sighted the first ship of the homeward run and a few days later we spoke the *Iron Age* asking to be reported at Lloyds. On the 20th we picked up the loom of the Fastnet light but it was four days later before we made our proper landfall at the Scillies. The Channel has a reputation for being unkind to yachts returning from long voyages; at least one circumnavigator has recorded that he had met there his worst weather. We had a fast, pleasant sail. Having missed the tide off Portland we anchored in Chesil Cove. Sailing inside between the Bill and the Race we carried a fair wind all the way to the Needles, cheated the ebb by going through the North channel, and anchored off Lymington river on the night of September 26th with 7000 miles on the log.

Two days later, *Mischief* having been cleaned out and stripped bare alow and aloft, the crew went their several ways. It was sad to see them go, for we were unlikely to sail again together, or even to meet again, and I owed them much. Few sign on for the second time. This, I think, is not because 'once is enough' but because so few have the time or the opportunity to make one voyage, let alone two. Though *Mischief* is hardly a luxury yacht, neither is she a 'hell-ship'. I hope that this brief account has shown that although life on board may not be ecstasy it is at least comfort. Michael had to embark on a University life, while John Wayman returned to City life tempered, one hopes, by days with the Wasps. David had to go to sea again at once to earn money against the day of his impending marriage; there was thus little hope of his being foot-loose again. Charles and I move in orbits that occasionally cross, and no doubt we shall meet again. But the cook in a small boat deserves special thanks and I should like to record both that and my gratitude to him for his long-suffering companionship upon the mountains.

# PART TWO

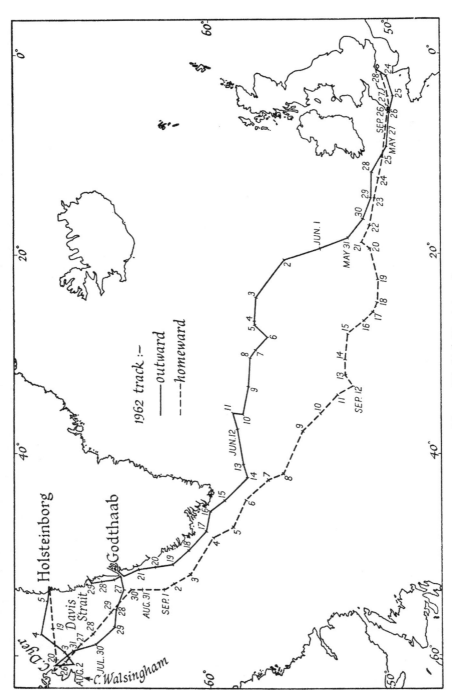

Map 2: *Mischief*'s Track in 1962

CHAPTER X

# A NEW OBJECTIVE

EPICURUS WAS OF THE OPINION that for most men rest is stagnation and activity madness. It is, I suppose, a question of degree, but if a choice had to be made between the unqualified alternatives most men would no doubt prefer the madness of activity. In my case the activity took the form of another voyage to northern waters. Keeping a boat is like keeping a dog in that both must be exercised, though in fact no spur was needed to persuade me to repeat what had been a successful experiment. The advantages that I had expected such a voyage would have over a voyage southwards had been demonstrated—the time spent at sea and that among the mountains had been less unequal, a crew had been less trouble to find, and, of course, the cost had been less. For a mountaineer Greenland has two great attractions—he will have the mountains to himself instead of sharing them with a horde, and he will find a large number of unclimbed peaks. For the yachtsman, although the east-to-west crossing of the Atlantic may be a cold, rough passage, the Davis Strait and the west Greenland coast, despite the fog, make a wonderful cruising ground; a place where he may see at close range some of the largest icebergs afloat, enjoy the finest of fjord scenery, catch unlimited fish, and possibly have better weather than if he had stayed at home. A summer's day off the Greenland coast has unrivalled charm—freshness and clarity, soft colours, and the serenity of sea, ice, and mountains under the pale, northern sky.

With a second voyage to those regions in view and having a liking for remote, desolate places I turned my attention to the Canadian coast on the west side of Davis Strait. Taken by and large the west coast of Greenland can hardly be called remote and desolate, and it is far from being uninhabited. Letters from Europe reach Godthaab in three days; few of the fjords are without either a small town or a settlement, or that at any rate are not frequently visited by Greenlanders for fishing or hunting; and off the coast the sea is thick with vessels

# MISCHIEF IN GREENLAND

of some kind—trawlers, schooners, coasters, or local fishing boats. On the other hand on the Canadian side of the straits the Cumberland Peninsula is as desolate as a man could wish, more or less uninhabited, and besides that mountainous. In fact at the start of the first Greenland voyage I had had at the back of my mind the hope that we might have time to have a quick look at the Cumberland Peninsula. Before sailing I had been in touch with the leader of a Cambridge party who were about to go there to climb. Lieut R. E. Langford, R. E., was then in residence at King's College—an unusual place to find a Sapper—and I met him there later when both parties had returned. The Cumberland Peninsula on Baffin Island in Lat. 67° N., just inside the Arctic Circle, is about the size of Switzerland and equally mountainous, though its highest mountain is only some 7000 feet. There are two passes across the peninsula formerly used by Eskimos as sledge routes. Few expeditions have been there because access by sea or by land is difficult and only recently has it become possible to reach it by air.

The Cambridge party flew there and spent six weeks in the interior, climbing seven peaks, doing some geological work, and also crossing the peninsula from north to south. It was from Langford that I first heard of Mt Raleigh, a mountain on the coast of the peninsula, seen and named by John Davis in 1585 and still unclimbed. John Davis made his first voyage in search of the North-west Passage in 1585. On August 7th, anchored in Exeter Sound on the east coast of Baffin Island, 'altogether free from the pester of ice', as the narrative says, 'we lay under a brave mount the cliffs whereof were orient as gold. This mount we named Mt Raleigh.' Nowadays when pretty well every nook and corner of the earth has been explored, only large-scale Antarctic expeditions, helped by aircraft and Snowcats, and hindered, perhaps, by the pressing needs of science, may still hope to make fresh discoveries. The individual with a taste for discovery has for the most part to content himself with following the tracks of early explorers, obtaining a vicarious thrill from making the landfalls they had made. On our last voyage we had by chance made the same landfall at Cape Desolation as Davis had when he rediscovered Greenland. This Elizabethan seaman and explorer therefore roused my interest, and since he has perhaps been overshadowed by his more famous contemporaries such as Drake, Hawkins, Raleigh, I have subjoined a short account of his

A NEW OBJECTIVE

life, a life spent for the most part on hazardous voyages in the service of exploration and of his country. Here it is necessary only to mention briefly his three voyages in search of the North-west Passage.

Davis's search for the North-west Passage was no doubt instigated by Sir Humphrey Gilbert's famous *Discourse* published in 1576. The loss of the little *Squirrel* in 1583 with Sir Humphrey and his companions must also have made a deep impression, coming so soon after he had penned the famous words with which his *Discourse* closed, words which in those brave days rang like a trumpet call: 'That he is not worthy to live at all, that for fear or danger of death, shunneth his country's service or his own honour; seeing death is inevitable and the fame of virtue immortal.' On his first voyage Davis, as we have seen, after making his landfall at Cape Desolation anchored in what he called Gilbert Sound, the present Godthaab, where he had friendly intercourse with the Eskimos. Crossing the Strait he discovered and named Capes Dyer and Walsingham, and anchored in Exeter Sound; and finally explored Cumberland Sound in the belief that it was a strait and possibly the desired passage.

In 1586 with the same ships *Sunneshine* and *Mooneshine*, and *Mermaid*, a larger vessel of 120 tons, he landed first at what is now called Old Sukkertoppen. Having again entered Cumberland Sound he sailed down the coast, explored the Labrador coast, and returned home bringing with him some salt cod and 500 sealskins. For his third and last northern voyage in 1587 he had the old *Sunneshine*, another vessel *Elizabeth*, and the clinker-built pinnace *Ellen* of twenty tons. In Gilbert Sound he made a heroic decision. To satisfy his backers by making the voyage pay, he dispatched the two bigger ships to the Labrador coast to fish while he continued his exploration in the barely seaworthy *Ellen*. He went north as far as the great cliff now called Sanderson's Hope in Lat. 72° 12′, or as he wrote, 'Sanderson his hope of a North-west Passage, no ice towards the north, but a great sea, free, large, very salt and blue, and of an unsearchable depth.' A northerly wind drove them westwards where they encountered the 'middle pack' and were forced once more into Cumberland Sound. Sailing south down the coast off Hudson Strait they met with 'a mighty race, where an island of ice was carried by the force of the current as fast as our bark could sail'. On these three voyages Davis charted long stretches

118                    MISCHIEF IN GREENLAND

of coast on both sides of the Strait and much of the Labrador coast and took regular observations for the variation of the compass. As Clements Markham wrote:

> Davis converted the Arctic regions from a confused myth into a defined area. He not only described and mapped the extensive tract explored by himself, but he clearly pointed out the way for his successors. He lighted Hudson into his strait. He lighted Baffin into his Bay. He lighted Hans Egede to the scene of his Greenland labours. His true-hearted devotion to the cause of Arctic discovery, his patient scientific research, his loyalty to his employers, his dauntless gallantry and enthusiasm, form an example which will be a beacon-light to maritime explorers for all time to come.

Of many remarks made by Chinese sages of the past one of the less pithy (but one that I like) is that of Chang Cha'o: 'If there are no famous hills then nothing need be said, but since there are they must be visited.' Mt Raleigh by its association with John Davis merits fame and as an objective it had for me other desirable features. True it was not very lofty, but lofty enough for a man of whom it might be said that years have tamed his mountain passion without clouding his reason. Besides its romantic name and romantic association it was a mountain lying upon a wild and desolate coast, a coast that would be hard to reach. Indeed when I had read all that I could about the ice conditions in summer on that coast I did not rate our chance of success highly and was prepared to be disappointed. *Mischief*'s hull has not been strengthened in any way to make her fit to shunt ice, as she would have to do if we tried to force a way through loose pack-ice. We should therefore have to wait until the ice had cleared away from the coast, and much depended upon our experiencing a favourable season. In any case our time on shore would be short. It would probably be late before we were able to get in, and although we were not likely to be prevented by ice from getting out, we wanted to be home by the end of September.

The conditions governing the movement of ice on that coast and what may therefore be expected are shown in the following extract from the *Pilot of Arctic Canada*:

A NEW OBJECTIVE

The general movement of the ice in Davis Strait and Baffin Bay is controlled mainly by the north and south-flowing currents, and its distribution at any time is largely dependent upon the strength and direction of the prevailing winds. It has been estimated that, with the exception of icebergs, not more than two-thirds of the ice in those sea areas is of local origin, and its concentration throughout the summer season is, therefore, greatly affected by the quantities which enter from the sounds at the head of Baffin Bay, Smith, Jones, and Lancaster Sounds.

Along the Greenland coast the warm north-flowing waters of the West Greenland current keep the more southerly stretches free of ice during most of the winter, and a narrowing belt of open water usually continues up the coast to north of Upernivik until about Christmas. Some time in January, as a rule, the ice becomes consolidated around Disko Island and the heavy west coast pack spreads out to meet it. From here the pack arcs south-westwards and extends as a broad belt off the entrance to Hudson Strait and along the Labrador coast. The south-west coast of Greenland remains practically ice-free until January when it is invaded by the heavy polar ice carried by the East Greenland current. This 'storis', as it is called, drifts up the coast as far as Frederikshaab or in some years even to Godthaab, blocking the approaches to the harbours of South and South-west Greenland.

On the western side of Davis Strait the cold waters of the south-flowing Canadian or Labrador current permit the formation of ice along the entire shore-line. All the fjords become covered with an ice-sheet and along Baffin Island the land-fast ice borders the coast as far south as Cape Dyer (near Exeter Sound), extending seaward about ten miles. South of Cape Dyer the belt of fast-ice is usually narrower and over long stretches may be entirely absent. Beyond the fast-ice the heavy pack moves with the great eddy circulation of Baffin Bay along the Greenland coast beyond Disko, around Melville Bay, and from there southwards along the Canadian coast. Although in winter Baffin Bay has generally a 10/10 ice cover, it is not a solid sheet but rather a cemented drifting pack in which the floes may at any time be subjected to violent rearrangement by the gales. In the western part of the bay it appears to drift south at the rate of about four miles a day even in winter.

## MISCHIEF IN GREENLAND

At the head of Baffin Bay lies the famous polynia, the 'North Water', which whalers aimed to reach as early in June as possible, threading their dangerous way through the heavy floes along the edge of the vast sheet of fast-ice in Melville Bay. The ice round this polynia breaks up early and usually by the beginning of June open water extends southwards along the western shore of Baffin Bay to the vicinity of Lancaster Sound.

Because of the atmospheric circulation in the area and of the higher temperatures and salinities introduced by the West Greenland current, the ice in this part of the Canadian Arctic is the first to disintegrate—usually in late May or early June. During June and July heavy fields of close-packed ice move down the Baffin Island coast in a solid belt which has been known to extend 125 miles eastwards from Cape Dyer.

The heaviest concentration of pack—the 'middle pack' of unhappy memory to whalers—appears to lie as a tapering north-south belt just west of the central axis of Baffin Bay. As summer progresses this zone gradually shrinks but in its southern limits, extending along the coast to beyond Cape Dyer, heavy ice may persist in some years until late August. Ice may also remain heavily packed until the end of July or even August along the entire coast of Cumberland Peninsula southwards beyond Cape Mercy, blocking the entrance to Cumberland Sound and sometimes completely filling it.

August and September are usually the most ice-free months, in fact in some years the only ice to be seen in these months may be the stream of icebergs moving south to the Labrador Sea. On occasion the early part of October may also be favourable for navigation along the Baffin Island coast but ice usually forms during the last weeks of that month. Failure to realize the relative lateness of the navigation season in those areas led the early navigators to impose a heavy handicap on themselves by their arrival off the entrance to Davis Strait in May or June in hopes of being able to complete their explorations and return home by early September at the latest.

The above source, and many others I consulted, all seemed to show that at the best we could not hope to reach the coast of Baffin Island

A NEW OBJECTIVE

before early August, and at the worst, or nearly the worst, not before early September. In an exceptionally bad ice year we might not be able to reach it at all. If we sailed, therefore, at the usual time in May we should have practically the whole of July available for climbing in West Greenland. There was a strong temptation to return to the Umanak fjord region where I knew where to go for mountains and where the people were the nearest approach to real Eskimos that we were ever likely to see. But it was rather too far north, both of Godthaab and of Exeter Sound, and we might waste a lot of time in getting there and back. I remembered that the passage south to Godthaab that last voyage had cost us twelve days. For the mountains of Southern Greenland, in the Cape Farewell region, we might well be too early if we arrived as expected by the end of June, for in that month the whole of the Julianehaab Bight may be full of ice (as it proved to be). So there remained for us the mountains of the central part of West Greenland which lie about 100 miles north of Godthaab and are in almost the same latitude as Exeter Sound and at the narrowest part of the Davis Strait.

*Mischief*, I knew, would be able and willing, so with a rough plan already formed there remained only the finding of a crew. Plans for such a venture as this are best left rough, for as the great Von Moltke said, few plans withstand contact with the enemy. In finding a crew for this voyage I had to start from scratch, no volunteers having presented themselves. There are one or two sailing clubs or associations based on London which notify their members of boat-owners in need of crew and it was by this means that I got my first victim. He did not belong to the Association concerned but happening to see their list of crews needed he introduced himself to me at a lecture I gave there. Hans Hoff was from East Germany. Too young to serve in the war, he had been working as an apprentice to a watchmaking firm when the Russian army arrived at his home. (He had some curious tales to tell of those days.) Having got out of East Germany in good time and having spent the last seven years in England he spoke excellent English. He knew something about boats and his keenness on voyaging had led him to attend both navigational and signalling classes when living in London. I had no hesitation about taking him on. The Germans are people with a strong sense of discipline. I could see Hans setting an example to the rest of the crew by springing to execute my slightest command, though to be just no such example was needed. As I was then on the way to Lymington I suggested that before he committed himself he should come down at the week-end to have a look at *Mischief*. Hans duly arrived and I showed him over the boat. There is nothing more depressing, nothing more likely to deter a man bent on making a voyage, than looking over a boat out of commission on a wet, winter's day. Below it is as cold and dank as a tomb, moisture drips from the beams, cupboards gape open, and half the floorboards are up to encourage whatever air there may be to circulate. A man would scarcely think of housing his dog there, let alone going to sea in it himself. Hans, however, was no stranger to the forlorn appearance of boats when laid up for the winter and the sturdy appearance of *Mischief* from outside impressed him more than the dismal state of things below. So Hans agreed to come and since he was a German I did not expect to be let down.

I then had given me the names of three possible candidates by Charles Evans, a climbing friend who is also himself a boat-owner. Two were unable to come but the third, Michael Rhodes, a research student at the University College of North Wales, Bangor, thought he could. The fact that Dr Charles Evans is the Principal at Bangor probably justified this optimism. When riding over from Bangor on a motor-cycle to see me he got lost on the way and arrived an hour or so late. As I was not looking for a navigator that did not really matter. He was a keen dinghy sailor with the physique of a Rugby player, evidently a man who could put a lot of weight on a rope. His particular line of research at the moment concerned blow-flies, and he astonished me by asserting that he expected to make a rich haul of blow-flies and bugs of all kinds in Greenland and Baffin Island. His presence, therefore, would lend the expedition a faint, if slightly unwholesome, aroma of science. He thought he might be able to borrow a 16-mm cine-camera, so I took him on in the role of seaman, scientist, and cameraman.

So far, with only about two months to go to the time I hoped to sail, I had two hands. I wanted three more and particularly someone who would be willing to cook. As had happened before when hard pressed, I had recourse to an advertisement in the Personal Column of *The Times*. In the past such an advertisement had always brought

## A NEW OBJECTIVE

a large number of offers, some of them serious, and even one or two acceptances. Unlike when one is hoping to sell something through that medium, when the wording cannot be too bland, it does not do to clothe projected voyages or ventures in words of much promise. It is safer to err on the other side, for there are many who answer such advertisements from force of habit or out of curiosity, as well as many who are ready to fly at anything they see. Thus the advertisement I had used for an earlier voyage merely said: 'Hands wanted for long voyage in small boat; no pay, no prospects, not much pleasure.' The advertising manager who, more than anyone, I should have thought, must have daily dealings with the lunatic fringe, was rude enough to query both the advertisement and my good faith. Even so, when it finally appeared, the response was far too hearty to be dealt with in conscientious fashion.

For the present cruise the advertisement ran: 'Cook wanted for cold voyage in small boat; five mouths to feed for five months.' This, too, was well received but it did not get me anyone. One promising candidate whom I interviewed, having agreed to come, wrote a letter and posted it the same evening to say he had changed his mind; and another, a young flautist, badly wanted to come but would not dream of cooking. But I had let myself in for a lot of trouble by omitting the words 'men only', a mistake that obliged me to write at least a dozen letters of regret to all the women who applied. My regrets were sincere, too, since some of these applicants would have filled the bill admirably had I been able to overcome my fear of having a woman on board for so long in such inescapable circumstances. 'Discord,' as yet another Chinese sage has remarked, 'is not sent down from heaven, it is brought about by women.' One of these women had crossed the Atlantic cooking for a crew of five men and from the way the letter was worded I gathered that these poor fish might consider themselves lucky to have had her with them. Shrinking hastily away from this sea-faring Amazon, I hesitated long before refusing another who wrote less stridently to say she had cruised in several yachts in the Mediterranean, cooking the meals and arranging the flowers, and that she was a cordon bleu. Flowers we should have to forgo, but my mouth watered at the thought of the meals we might have. So much for the advertisement—guineas thrown away. Roger Tufft, who had sailed in *Mischief*

## 124                    MISCHIEF IN GREENLAND

on the Crozet venture and who still corresponded with me in desultory fashion, knew what was afoot but kept me for a long time in suspense. He is a man who sits loosely in any sedentary job, his usual occupation during his brief stays in England being that of teaching. At length, however, the temptation proved too strong and he wrote to say that he would come. Moreover, failing anyone else, he offered to try his hand in the galley. He was a great acquisition. We knew each other and he was a mountaineer as well as an experienced hand; added to that he was as strong as a horse, able to carry a load or kick steps until further orders. Instead of having time to sit about on stones, as on the last Greenland trip, I should find myself always toiling in the rear. The fact that he knew the boat and the way things were done would be valuable when starting with a strange crew, and there are few men, not excluding some of the rummer birds who have sailed in *Mischief*, with whom Roger would not be able to cope.

I had still two to find and I found them, rather late in the day, and quite by chance. At a lecture in Portsmouth I met the owner—another German—of an old Baltic trading ketch then lying at Gosport. Having a morning free I went on board to have a look at her. The owner and his wife were living on board, so she was not out of commission, nor was this a wet, winter's day; but on going below I felt that even Hans might have thought twice about making a long voyage in her. In the vast, gloomy cavern, formerly the cargo hold and now the main cabin, the only place where the crew could sit or sleep was on top of what I took to be winged-out ballast—two narrow, concrete platforms about three feet high running the length of the hold. But that by the way. The point is that this tough German concrete-lover subsequently got talking in a train about boats and the sea to another young man from whom I presently had a letter inquiring about the proposed voyage.

Shaun White had a small boat of his own, knew more than a bit about engines and all things mechanical, and was above all a dedicated bird-watcher. I suppose the earnest watching of birds is a full-time occupation—all round the clock in fact if one feels strongly enough about it. Admittedly a lot of birds sleep, but owls hoot all night and there are many others which spend the night dashing themselves against lighthouses. However, young Shaun had another occupation which I discovered later from incidents and from remarks he let fall. It seemed he

## A NEW OBJECTIVE

happily combined—mainly on the shores of the Solent—the pursuits of bird-watching and beachcombing, pursuits which have much in common for both need the use of binoculars and a trained eye. When he joined *Mischief* he brought with him as a goodwill offering a number of useful articles—safety belts, inflatable jackets, a searchlight, rockets, distress signals—all articles concerned with the preservation of life at sea, for Shaun was perhaps a little apprehensive and came prepared for the worst. We learnt that all these things—and these were merely a selection—had either been found on the beach or salvaged from the sea. Indeed in the course of time we began to suspect that some of the things picked up had not been lost until Shaun found them, and could not be regarded legitimately as flotsam, jetsam, or lagan. This weakness of his reminded me of those Texan soldiers of whom Stonewall Jackson, the great Confederate general, remarked that 'the hens have to roost mighty high when the Texans are about'.

By arrangement Shaun, on his way home from a bird-watching week-end on the Isle of Wight, came to have a look at *Mischief* and thereupon decided that he would go with us. On another week-end less than a month before sailing day he visited me again, this time at the head of a small flock of fellow birdwatchers. Till then I had no idea that the disease was widespread among the young, by no means the affliction mainly of retired men, in particular Field-Marshals or eminent Bankers. Luckily none of the yacht-owners, the patrons of the yard, were about or they might have wondered what yachting was coming to. The flock or horde, suitably clad for bird-watching of the roughest kind, bowed down under rucksacks big enough for a Himalayan expedition, having boarded *Mischief* and dumped their loads on the deck, began at once to devour huge chunks of bread which they dug out from the pockets of the rucksacks. One among them, a very tall youth, who seemed to me at least seven foot long, confided that he would like to sail in *Mischief*. Roger Brown was a friend of Shaun's and about due to finish his engineering apprenticeship in Portsmouth Dockyard. Here, I thought, is the man to look after our engine. The difference in design between engines of 40,000 horse-power such as one might find at Portsmouth Dockyard and those, like *Mischief*'s, of forty horse-power may be considerable; but since the greater comprehends the less I imagined that Roger Brown's knowledge would be invaluable. He had had no sailing experience and his height would be a handicap for working in the galley, but on the understanding that he would look after the machinery and cook I took him on. On the outward passage at least, he did neither. But we had now a full complement and we should soon learn what each could do.

CHAPTER XI

# TO CAPE FAREWELL

I N THEORY, WHEN THREE OF THE CREW joined *Mischief* about ten days
before sailing, there should not have been much to do beyond rigging her, bending the sails, and stowing the gear. In the course of the
winter I had as usual overhauled the blocks, tackles, running rigging,
life-lines, and all movable gear. Having had no time to do the job alone
I had had the inside of the boat painted by the yard. The cabin looked
so white and clean one hardly dared to sit down. But invariably it takes
a great deal longer than one expects before a boat is in all respects
ready for sea. In fact we had a lot to do. I went on board on May 11th
and three of the crew joined on the 14th. Yet, hindered to some extent
by wet weather, we had to work hard to be ready by May 23rd.

This time no one fell into the river, but on my first morning on
board, when some letters were being handed from the quayside, the
whole lot dropped in the drink. Having quickly grabbed all within
reach I noticed another drifting past the stern. I was in two minds
about rescuing a buff-coloured envelope marked O.H.M.S., suggesting something to do with Income Tax, the loss of which would not be
grievous. But having fished it out with the aid of a boat-hook I found
I had won a Premium Bond prize of £25. Various sententious sayings
appropriate to this happy incident suggested themselves—appearances
are deceptive, all cats are grey in the dark, inaction is a crime, or perhaps, cast your bread upon the waters and it will return to you after
many days.

Still moderately elated by this windfall I went next day to Southampton to check the stores list with Messrs Burnyeat, the ship-chandlers who have for many years been accustomed to finding for me
things like dried skim milk, egg powder, concentrated lime juice,
alleged (wrongly, I feel sure) to be fortified with forty per cent rum;
and to packing the dry stores like sugar, flour, rice, milk, oatmeal,
macaroni, in fourteen- and seven-pound tins with press lids, and the

128          MISCHIEF IN GREENLAND

whole ten-pound cheeses in soldered tins. The application for permission to take bonded stores—cigarettes, tobacco, and drink—had gone through, but I heard the less reassuring news that our calling at Belfast on the previous voyage had not gone unnoticed. Having cleared the ship for Godthaab and then called at Belfast, which is in the United Kingdom, we should have notified the Customs authorities there so that the bonded stores could have been sealed while we were in port.

Before the crew joined I had an interesting and interested visitor, a Mr Rayer, who had served for two years as an apprentice in *Mischief* when she was a pilot-cutter. I felt he was a little critical of amateurs because as soon as he arrived he asked me when I had last had the service over the eye-splices in the shrouds removed in order to examine the state of the wire. His pilot and owner had been one William Morgan, known in the Bristol Channel in those days as Billy the Mischief, a tough character who remained at sea whatever the weather until they had picked up a ship or, failing that, had run out of bread and water. I have read somewhere that Frobisher and Hawkins when cruising in search of Spanish ships used to declare that they would continue to cruise 'as long as the beer lasted'. According to Mr Rayer, who should know, a story concerning Bristol Channel pilot-cutters that has gained wide currency is a myth. He had never seen it done or heard of it being done. It relates to their alleged method of getting the punt on board by making the painter fast to the boom and then gybing, so that in theory the punt leapt from the sea on to the deck where it could be grabbed and secured. As Mr Rayer said, there were then neither stanchions nor life-rail, so that had any bold man attempted this labour-saving method there was nothing to stop the punt from flying inboard. In his day the chain-locker used to be in what is now the galley and they did their cooking on a Dover stove at the fore end of the cabin. This stove burnt day and night and the apprentice had the job of keeping it bright. 'Always a pleasure to look at,' added Mr Rayer reflectively, looking hard at me as we stood in the galley by a rather dirty Primus stove. They used to carry two mainsails, one light and one heavy, a spinnaker, three jibs, topsail, and storm canvas. Instead of hauling out on a slipway they had legs fitted, and for scrubbing and painting, the boats were put on the hard at Ilfracombe. He said

# TO CAPE FAREWELL

129

that *Mischief* was sold out of the Pilot Service for £80, but this seems an absurdly low figure even for pre-1914 days.

All the ratlines on the shrouds needed renewing, a process which is known as 'rattling down' because, I suppose, one naturally starts at the lowest ratline and works up. Each ratline is clove-hitched round the middle shroud and the eye-splice at each end is seized to the outer shrouds. A real sailor, I imagine, a man whose every finger is a marline spike and every hair a ropeyarn, would have no trouble in turning in splices in one-and-a-half-inch rope while standing in mid-air half-way up the shrouds. If on the other hand, after guessing the right length (for each ratline is shorter than the one below), you make them up on deck, you invariably find that after the clove hitch has been put on the ratline is either too short or too long. If the job is well done it looks smart and symmetrical, if ill done it looks like the ladder Jacob might have dreamt about. While I was thus busied Shaun White rode on to the quayside on his motor-bike looking like Shock-headed Peter. He was soon followed by Hans Hoff and Roger Tufft so that next day we got down to work shipping the bowsprit, boom, and gaff, and reeving the halyards. The sheaves on the mast for the jib halyard which had given us so much trouble had been renewed. And, not before it was needed, I had had made a new mainsail which next day we bent on. Much to my relief it fitted nicely, for there had been some discrepancy between the measurements I made and those of the original sail (after allowing for stretch) as recorded by Gowen, the makers. On the last voyage we had constantly been stitching, whereas on this new sail we never once used a needle. The lee-side topping lift is the main cause of chafe, but unless we were making short tacks we took care to cast it off altogether.

Michael Rhodes then joined bringing with him the promised cine-camera and a miniature trunk of entomological gear—poison bottles, test-tubes, specimen cases, a butterfly net, and a young furnace used for extracting mites from earth samples. Shaun then left to spend the week-end at home, offering to bring back a lifebuoy, life-jackets, and a drum of paint, all the harvest of the sea. Unluckily the lifebuoy, the one thing we needed, had been eaten by his dog. In spite of the rain that fell too frequently we managed to paint the deck, bulwarks, stanchions, cockpit, and to cover the bare patches on the

## MISCHIEF IN GREENLAND

hull. The hull was to have been painted by the yard but in view of the weather it would have been time wasted. I was glad we had not had it done because after we had painted the deck with oil and red ochre, a heavy shower distributed much of this over the yellow hull, so that she looked like a pirate ship with blood running out of the scuppers.

When Roger Brown at length joined we were about ready to go. I had reserved for him the longest bunk and had had no difficulty in doing so because it is also the most inconvenient, situated so close to the deckhead that the occupant has to roll in sideways and has not the least chance of sitting up. The stores were then brought over from Southampton accompanied by a Customs officer to seal up the drink and tobacco, and by an Immigration officer to record Hans's departure. On May 23rd we cast off and motored down the river, receiving a salute of one gun from the Royal Lymington Yacht Club as we passed. I doubt if *Mischief* has ever before got away to a starting gun. Anyway this mark of recognition was much appreciated by the crew, none of whom were members of the Club. When we hoisted sail outside a fresh westerly wind obliged us to tack several times before passing the Needles and these manoeuvres were carried out without any of the hitches one might have expected on the first day at sea with a strange crew. All except Roger Brown had sailed before in some kind of craft. Soon after clearing the Needles we were overhauled by a blue-hulled pilot-cutter, very like *Mischief.* She passed close and no sooner had this excitement subsided than the crew one by one began to feel unwell. Roger and Hans decided to take their meals on deck, Shaun looked pretty wan, while poor Michael and Roger Brown were prostrate. All recovered quickly except Michael, who was sick off and on most of the way across and who even on the return voyage succumbed in rough weather. Such a state of affairs is more than discouraging, but Michael never allowed it to get him down or to prevent him from doing his work.

The wind freed us during the night. Instead of steering south we could steer west and by the following evening we had Guernsey abeam. After this little shake-up we ran at once into real yachting weather with a light north-east wind and a calm sea. The invalids had recovered but as Roger Brown showed no enthusiasm for taking over the galley, Roger Tufft came to the rescue as he had promised. He had armed himself with a Penguin cookery book and very soon began

TO CAPE FAREWELL

baking cakes and boiling duffs. We had no oven to fit on the Primus stove and he got over that by putting the cake tin or basin inside a saucepan with an asbestos mat to prevent the bottom burning. Except in port or at anchor, when the crew relieved him in turns, Roger went on cooking until we were homeward bound, and whatever the weather never failed to feed us well. When at length we turned towards home Roger Brown woke up and undertook to show what he could do in the galley. In that he was remarkably successful, the more so because by then all our luxuries and many of our necessities had been finished. But so long as there is enough rice or macaroni on board there is no difficulty about following the Chinese precept: 'A well filled stomach is indeed the great thing—all else is luxury.' Few men in any of the crews I have had could be described as delicate feeders. On this voyage we had some good trenchermen. Michael, or Mick as he was called, between his bouts of sea-sickness naturally ate prodigiously to make up for lost time. Hans, in a methodical German manner, ate his way through whatever quantity might be piled on his plate, while young Shaun's swallowing capacity seemed interminable. Both bird-watchers had a peculiar aversion to tea or coffee and insisted on drinking cocoa, a beverage that one associates with Temperance and Little Englanders and on that account holds suspect.

Our bird-watchers lost no time in following their vocation. We had on board one too many, for it seemed impossible for one of them to spot anything without his feeling obliged to draw the other's attention to it, to compare notes, or to have an identification confirmed. At first it startled me out of my wits and by the end of the voyage I had still to get used to it. A profound peace would be reigning above deck and below when suddenly a piercing yell, quivering with urgency, would ring out. Whereupon, according to which of the two was below, there would be an upheaval from the direction of Shaun's or Brown's bunk and a stampede for the door which would be wrenched back and hurled to again with equal violence. No need for alarm; we were neither on fire nor sinking; a bird had been seen. Provided both were safely below it was possible to relax; but Mick and Roger, who were also interested in birds, though less fervently, soon caught the infection, and if they were incautious enough to seek expert opinion on some bird they had seen, a double stampede would take place. In the Southern Ocean birds

132 MISCHIEF IN GREENLAND

such as albatross and giant petrels are plentiful and well worth looking at. In the Atlantic and home waters an uninstructed man might imagine birds were few and those few represented merely by gulls. Nothing of the kind. Plenty of birds of various species can be seen if they are looked for, and provided one has powerful binoculars, years of practice, and an assertive manner, they can be confidently assigned to their various species.

For a whole sunny afternoon we lay becalmed, the peace broken only by the bird-watchers or by the splash of someone diving overboard for a swim. Those who bathe in May, we are told, will soon lie in clay. I remember on the last voyage having given this piece of news to Dr Joyce as he clambered back on board after a swim in the Irish Sea, and having been quite startled by its unexpected effect. Either my solemn manner must have been convincing, or advice on the care of his health from a layman shook him. He wilted visibly and, much to David's amusement, retired below in a very thoughtful mood. Whatever the weather Roger and I poured three buckets of sea-water over ourselves before breakfast and continued doing so until the sea temperature fell to 40° F. I gave up then but Roger carried on until it fell to 34° F. when he, too, had had enough. Mick joined us only occasionally, flinching less at cold water than at having to get up a moment before it was necessary.

After the calm we had a fast sail throughout the night with a fresh north-east wind and a morning sight put us only ten miles from the Wolf Rock. Fog then came down but we ran on confidently and when the lighthouse duly loomed up about a mile away the crew began comparing me with Henry the Navigator. The wind then headed us so that we had a job to clear the Scillies, sailing past the northernmost island rather nearer than prudence demanded. The amateur navigator cannot bring it off every time. Having achieved one coup I should not so soon have attempted another. We had the broad Atlantic before us, we had made our departure from the Scillies, and we were under no obligation to sight Ireland. However, the wind being fair, I laid off a course that should have taken us within a few miles of the Fastnet rock. Had we been moving a lot faster I might have gone below with the impressive words, 'Call me when you see it'. We never did see the Fastnet rock or indeed any part whatsoever of Ireland, and Henry the Navigator had

TO CAPE FAREWELL

to fall back on the accustomed excuses—bad steering, unusual leeway, currents, poor visibility.

We were undoubtedly a little out of our reckoning but we were going strong and had logged 400 miles in the first five days at sea; and when a racing pigeon alighted on board the crew had something else to talk about than the niceties of navigation. This pigeon must have been out of his reckoning as well, for Ireland was within easy reach if he knew where it lay. Or perhaps he was not trying. As the Bengali proverb says: 'The sight of a horse makes the traveller lame,' and in my experience the sight of a ship has much the same effect on homing pigeons. Their resolution is sapped, they begin to feel weak, hungry, and thirsty, and down they come, forgetting all about their prescribed journey. On one voyage we had picked up no less than five and carried them from the Eddystone to Cadiz. This one took an even longer ride, remaining with us until we were off the Greenland coast, in spite of the fact that we passed one or two homeward-bound ships to which he could easily have transferred himself and found better accommodation. At first he looked peaky and refused to take any food. Then I remembered our lentils. Whereupon he began eating voraciously, grew fat and sleek, and had to be forcibly launched in the air before he would take any flying exercise. He took up his quarters in the engine-cum-chart-room where he showed alike his gratitude and his contempt for my navigation by defecating on the charts. The bird gave us a lot of amusement and the longer he stayed the more he became one of the family and the more we cherished him. So that although he made a proper mess we were sorry when he went.

The glass remained high and steady, the sky overcast, the wind fair. For a week we had been on the same tack on the required course of west-north-west. We had passed outside the limits of the B.B.C. shipping forecasts and had to make our own guesses about the weather. A weather forecast for the North Atlantic as far west as Long. 40° is broadcast from Portishead on W-T. Our small set out of a car could not pick that up nor could we have read it. Hans had attended a signalling class and read morse at slow speeds. He had an opportunity that evening at 10 p.m. when we spoke the *Rembrandt* and asked her to report us. Having acknowledged our message she then signalled 'P' which meant 'Your lights are out or burning

134                    MISCHIEF IN GREENLAND

badly'. In fact this was an understatement because our lights were
hung up in the forepeak where they usually remain once we are out
of home waters.

At sea, in a world comprising only six people, their personal
appearance and what they wear is commonly a subject for comment.
At Lymington Mick had had his reddish hair cropped very close; now,
when his beard of more or less the same colour had made some growth,
it became difficult to tell whether one was looking at his face or the
back of his head. Hans also had a reddish beard which developed in
course of time into a coir mat through which little could be seen but
his eyes. Roger Brown had come on board wearing a beard; now, in a
life that for him seemed to hold few other pleasures, he spent a lot of
time combing it. Roger Tufft, as one might expect, had a virile mane
like a horse-collar, while Shaun had so much hair on his head that none
could be spared for his face.

The glass began falling for the first time on June 1st. The wind
went aft and in consequence we soon had our first Chinese gybe. In
the evening we changed to twin staysails to avoid the risk of any more
gybes, and ran all night at five knots. It had been a day of incident. Our
passenger pigeon took off and disappeared from sight eastwards, and
returned after an absence of five hours. How, we wondered, did he find
us again? Then the sighting of a long-tailed skua and an unidentified
species of black petrel well-nigh drove the bird-watchers into a frenzy.
Bangers and mash, followed by a rib-binding rice pudding, brought
an eventful day to a firm finish. The wind freshened in the night and in
one two-hour watch we logged fourteen miles. By noon we had done
131 miles and on each of the next two days we ran 120 miles. We spoke
another ship, the *Jessie Stove*, a small ore-carrier, but on account of the
sea running she could not read our lamp. At one moment we would
be in view on top of a wave and the next we would drop out of sight
with the lamp obscured in the middle of a letter. I told Hans to stop
sending but to my dismay the *Jessie Stove*, now about a mile astern,
swung round and steamed after us. They evidently thought we were in
trouble or wanted something. Included in the short list of urgent and
important signals to be used by vessels in sight of one another, there
is no group of letters or letter signifying 'Buzz off'. The simplest thing
to send and the most likely to be understood was 'OK'. This had the

## TO CAPE FAREWELL

135

desired effect and she soon resumed her course, no doubt cursing us for a lot of incompetent asses.

Our pigeon seemed unsettled, possibly homesick, or remorseful on account of neglected duty. Taking off once more it fell straight into the sea. Having managed to get back on board it was sick, spewing up lentils and sea-water. Again it took off and fell in and this time it drifted helplessly astern while skua gulls gathered round to attack it. This really looked like 'curtains', but the game bird managed to get off the water and flew back to us to be received with a cheer. The pigeon was not the only one sick, for we were enjoying a rough spell. The wind rose to gale force and since by running before it we should lose a lot of ground we hove-to with the mainsail rolled right down and a double-reefed stays'l. Defying the weather Roger produced for supper, sausages, fried onions, and a noble duff. The wind began to take off in the night but in the twenty-four hours we logged only sixteen miles. This was the first wind we had had from any westerly quarter and we were already half-way across in Long. 27° W. June is supposed to be the quietest month in the North Atlantic; gales are infrequent and usually short-lived. This brief blow was followed by three quiet, sunny days. We had the Genoa up and during the calms some of us bathed overside, the sea temperature being 47° F. Unquestionably we were enjoying far more favourable conditions than those of the first voyage, warmer weather and better winds. We began counting the days to Cape Farewell.

From June 9th to the 11th we had another spell of wet, dirty weather during which we shipped a lot of water through the skylight. In spite of the windows let into it, the fitting of its cover makes the cabin a little gloomy, so that its fitting is usually put off until everything below is pretty well soaked. By now we had worked up to N. lat. 59°, only a little south of Cape Farewell, and we were about 250 miles east of it. There is no fishing bank in that area, where we now had a curious encounter with a Russian trawler from Petsamo, a White Sea port. In the police court phrase she seemed to be loitering with intent, steaming slowly and aimlessly in no particular direction. Having nothing to do she came over to have a look at us. We signalled with the lamp but got no reply. After dropping back she came up again in the afternoon and for some time we cruised in company, each having a good look at

136 MISCHIEF IN GREENLAND

the other. I should say almost a third of her company were women and by their appearance active members of the crew rather than floozies. On June 14th a fine, sunny day, we were some forty miles south of Cape Farewell with not an iceberg in sight. We altered course to north-west and before breakfast next morning we sighted high snow mountains. We were only twenty-three days out from Lymington. On the previous voyage it had taken us thirty-five days. The difference in time is actually greater because the figures are from Lymington and Belfast respectively and the distance from Belfast is some 300 miles less. As has been seen we met no contrary winds at all until we were half-way across the Atlantic, no one had complained of the cold, and on the whole it had been an enjoyable trouble-free passage.

CHAPTER XII

# TO GODTHAAB AND EVIGHEDSFJORD

CAPE FAREWELL, SO NAMED BY JOHN DAVIS, is the southern extremity of an island 2700 feet high. Surrounded as it is by high mountains it does not stand out prominently, but like most capes that mark the culminating point of large masses of land it is noted for stormy weather. In addition much ice accumulates round it, sometimes extending as far as 150 miles seaward. But the average distance is seventy miles in April, decreasing in August to thirty miles. For our part we could not have rounded it in fairer conditions. Sailing west-northwest parallel to the coast, mountains glistening all along our starboard hand, we romped along at five knots over a sparkling blue sea on a day of brilliant sunshine. And what fascination there is in the sight of this Greenland coast; how bracing the austere beauty of sea, snow mountains, and ice! In the morning we sighted only one big solitary berg and in the afternoon passed another close enough for us to take photographs. In order to have the best light we passed it on the wrong side, that is to leeward, where we had to dodge a number of bergy bits or growlers which had broken off. A German stern-trawler from Kiel altered course to have a closer look at us and greeted us with three blasts of his siren. The air temperature that day was 36° F. and the sea 42° F.

Next day we lay becalmed. It was an equally brilliant day and the few icebergs scattered about were curiously distorted by mirage. On this account, too, we could not make out whether a white bank all along the horizon to starboard was fog or ice. At the same time we were much puzzled by a low, rumbling noise. Some thought there must be a fishing boat about, others an aeroplane. True we had a bottle-nosed whale close aboard at the time but we could not hold him responsible for a noise like that. When a breeze sprang up we closed with this white bank and found it to be heavily congested pack-ice so distorted by mirage as to appear twice its height. It was this pack-ice that in spite

138       MISCHIEF IN GREENLAND

of the perfectly smooth sea maintained the low menacing growl which we had heard from miles away. In similar circumstances John Davis and his company had been confounded by the noise of the pack: 'Here we heard a mighty great roaring of the sea, as if it had been the breach of some shoare, the ayr being so foggie that we could not see one ship from the other. Then coming near to the breach, we met many islands of yce floating, and did perceive that all the roaring that we heard was caused only by the rowling of this yce together.' We sailed to within a hundred yards of the pack to take photographs before standing out to sea. From so low a viewpoint as our deck photographs of pack-ice proved singularly unimpressive. In the vicinity of the pack the sea temperature was down to 34° F.

All next day as we drifted and sailed up the coast we had the pack in sight, for apparently it filled the whole of the Julianehaab Bight as far north as Cape Desolation. Ghosting along all night we tacked once to avoid a raft of small floes covering a mile of sea. The morning broke clear and sunny and again we found ourselves surrounded by floes with just enough steerage way to avoid them. A seal lay basking on a floe but when we tried to edge close the whisper of wind failed altogether and when we started the engine he dived into the sea. In the afternoon we ran into fog. The air temperature fell to 36° F. and the moisture on the ropes froze. By evening, the fog still persisting, we found our way barred by a narrow belt of pack-ice. Although the water beyond appeared to be clear of ice we hesitated to break through and coasted westwards alongside the ice searching for an opening. For four hours we motored at four knots, dodging loose floes, and still having the more solid ice about fifty yards away on our starboard hand. At length at ten o'clock, tired of dodging stray floes and thinking I saw an opening, I turned her head towards the ice. We were nearly through when in making a tight turn to avoid a floe on the port side we suffered a frightening blow below the water-line from a tongue of ice projecting from a floe on the starboard side. Those who were below were more than a little startled. As one man they rushed on deck to see what had hit us such a sickening thud. Assuming a calm which I was far from feeling I told them we had just grazed a bit of ice, that the ship appeared not to be sinking, and that at least we were through the ice and able to resume our proper course.

## TO GODTHAAB AND EVIGHEDSFJORD

So far as Greenland waters were concerned this was our last encounter with pack-ice and had I exercised a little more patience or caution it need not have been so rude an encounter. Such a blow, I felt, could hardly have done *Mischief* any good. For the next few days I watched closely the well of the bilge, but the number of strokes needed to clear it showed no increase. (In calm water she makes very little water.) Of course, inside a boat such a noise is exaggerated. This tap on *Mischief*'s hull had sounded sufficiently like the crack of doom momentarily to scare the crew, and to leave one or two of them with a sense of insecurity that was not finally dispelled until two months later when we had had her slipped and examined the hull. What gave me most concern was our meeting here with so much ice where in the previous year there had been only icebergs. I felt that it did not augur well for our chances of reaching Baffin Island. Before sailing I had had a talk at the Meteorological Office at Bracknell and had been told that the Arctic winter had been more severe than usual, implying that in summer more ice would find its way down from the North. As against that, the sea in the south-western part of Davis Strait was reported to be unusually warm. We had undertaken to keep a weather log for the Meteorological Office, as well as ice reports and notes on the aurora we observed. Roger Tufft took this in hand, as he had on a previous voyage on behalf of the South African Meteorological Service. He had, by the way, spent three years on one of the Antarctic bases as a meteorologist. We could not, of course, transmit reports but the log we kept would ultimately be valuable for analytical purposes, especially as few British ships visit the Davis Strait and West Greenland.

We began sighting numbers of trawlers fishing on the Frederik-shaab Bank, including a very smart-looking vessel from Klaksvig in the Faeroe Islands. We were out of sight of land and managed to get sights to fix our position. All the way over Hans had been assiduous in taking sights and plotting our dead reckoning position by means of Traverse Tables. Whenever I got my sextant out he followed me on deck with his, and old and battered though it was, with the horizon mirror only half silvered, our sights generally agreed within a minute or two. Like Charles Marriott he stuck to old-fashioned, time-honoured methods, wrestling with cosines and haversines as he had been taught at his navigation classes. I have a feeling that those who teach navigation are averse to short cuts. With some justification, perhaps, they may think that without a thorough understanding of spherical trigonometry no man can hope to understand the theory of navigation, and that to practise it without understanding the theory is to be no better than a quack. Or, with more reason, they may think that if all would-be navigators took to using trouble-saving tables—for example, the American H.O. 211 that I myself prefer—the use of which any fool can master in half an hour, there would be no more need for instructors.

I was thankful to get sights that day because on the following day, June 21st, we got no sights at all and had to rely upon dead reckoning for finding the entrance to Godthaab fjord in thick weather. In navigating by dead reckoning, estimating the course and distance made good, there is as much luck as skill. Lord Kelvin, whose remarks are quoted in Lecky's *Wrinkles*, held strong views about trusting too much to dead reckoning when nearing land:

> We often hear stories of marvellous exactness with which the dead reckoning has been verified by the result. A man has steamed or sailed across the Atlantic without having got a glimpse of sun or stars the whole way, and has made land within five miles of the point aimed at. This may be done once, and may be done again, but must not be trusted to on any one occasion as probably to be done again this time. Undue trust in dead reckoning has produced more disastrous shipwrecks, I believe, than all other causes put together.
>
> I believe it would be unsafe to say that, even if the speed through the water and the steerage were reckoned with absolute accuracy in 'the account', the ship's place could in general be reasonably trusted to within fifteen or twenty miles per twenty-four hours of dead-reckoning. And, besides, neither the speed through the water nor the steerage can be safely reckoned without allowing a considerable margin of error.
>
> All things considered, a thoroughly skilled and careful navigator may reckon that, in the most favourable circumstances, he has a fair chance of being within five miles of his estimated position after a two hundred miles run on dead reckoning; but with all his skill and with all his care, he may be twenty miles off it.

All day we ran with a good following wind until evening when we had expected to sight land somewhere south of Godthaab. In thickening weather we could see nothing so we stood out to the north-west and that night we ran another fifty miles. At four in the morning, visibility being then about half a mile, we went about and pointed at where I hoped Godthaab fjord might be. After we had run about fifteen miles without seeing a thing, a brief glimpse of a cargo ship appearing and disappearing like a wraith in the mist gave us some comfort. She, too, might be in search of the Godthaab beacon. Presently the fog began to thin, and lo, right ahead lay the islands. Had we gone about a bit sooner we should have done even better, for now we were hard on the wind and had to make another board before we could enter the narrow channel between beacon and reef. A small, familiar-looking vessel outward bound proved to be our old friend *Mallemuken*. We exchanged salutes.

As we covered the twelve miles or so up the fjord the wind steadily increased and by the time we neared the leading marks off the narrow harbour entrance we had quite a tussle before we could dowse the mainsail. After threading the channel and opening up the harbour we met this fierce blast right in our teeth. Worse still, the harbour seemed to be occupied by too many ships. A corvette *Thetis* (ex-British corvette *Geranium*) took up a lot of room; a small survey vessel lay alongside her, and in our old berth, between *Thetis* and the rock wall, lay yet another. 'He who knows not whither to go is in no haste to move.' The wind had brought us to a stop anyway, so I signalled to let go the anchor; and as soon as it was down realized that we were in the way of vessels approaching or leaving the wharf. Without waiting for the harbour-master to come out to tell us to move we began winching in. Getting the anchor in a strong wind with a heavy boat like *Mischief* is no easy task. And there is a joining shackle on the cable which does not properly fit the gipsy of the winch, so that if there is much strain on the cable this link persistently slips back. After a severe struggle we got the anchor up and left it hanging ready to drop again. Approaching as near as we could to our old berth I again signalled for it to be let go. Nothing happened. The cable refused to run out and we began drifting rapidly astern before the wind. By this time our activities had aroused the interest of the officer commanding the survey vessel who

142                    MISCHIEF IN GREENLAND

shouted to us to make fast alongside him. But at that moment the anchor took charge and went down with a run. Seeing our plight the officer quickly sent over a launch with a warp. Slacking away on the anchor cable almost to its full scope we warped alongside the survey vessel and were able to draw breath. We were below discussing the few points about this appalling shambles that would bear discussing when a sailor appeared at the door and handed me a bottle of whisky. Next day when I sought out this officer to thank him both for his help and the whisky, his only comment was: 'You looked as if you needed it.' Our passage to Godthaab this time had taken only thirty days and the log registered 2200 miles. The previous year from Belfast we had logged 2650 miles and had taken forty days.

When we went ashore that evening we found that though the old harbour-master had gone the new one was of much the same type—genial (convivial, as we discovered later), and speaking the same sea-manlike American. We supped well at the Kristinemut which was full to capacity, and where I was greeted with embarrassing heartiness by the few old acquaintances who were not too drunk to recognize me. The crowding was due to the presence of the corvette and the even greater number of Danes employed on construction work. Much had been done since our last visit. The road from the harbour to the town had been surfaced, some three-storey blocks of flats had gone up, the fish wharf had been finished and a start had been made on the fish-curing factory. The noise of blasting and of pneumatic drills continued from 7 a.m. to 7 p.m., for the workmen, brought out only for the summer, work a twelve-hour day. The local Greenlander will have nothing to do with navvy work which is all done by Danish workmen.

The day after our arrival was Midsummer Day, a day marked by celebrations. Several huge bonfires were built, effigies burned, and a gala dance held in the cinema hall. On a brilliantly fine night—it might well have been called a sunny night—the bonfires seemed out of place. Except for Hans, who is very much a ladies' man and therefore given to dancing, the crew attended the dance as spectators. They got better value for their money than they expected when a drunken brawl started. The corvette, dressed over-all for the occasion, held a private dance to which some of our crew subsequently found their way. By

Evighedsfjord—at the first bend

144 MISCHIEF IN GREENLAND

the time they got there, however, the guests were beyond dancing, the earlier emphasis having been exclusively on drinking. I had occasion to visit the *Thetis* early next morning, for she was about to sail and I wanted to borrow a large-scale chart of the Sukkertoppen region. Even at that hour there were no traces of the night's disaster in the Captain's morning face as he very kindly went through his charts and made me a present of what I needed.

Evighedsfjord where we had decided to go for our climbing, is in N. lat. 65.50° a little south of Sondre Stromfjord. The chart showed only the first twenty miles of the fjord but we had also a map which included the whole fjord and the surrounding mountains. 'Evigheds' means, I believe, 'never ending', but the fjord is not that long. On sailing day, June 26th, rain fell heavily all day and there was little or no wind. We spent the morning alongside the quay watering and waiting with what patience we could muster for twelve gallons of paraffin that we needed. While waiting I went on board the *Ellen S.*, a small coaster. Her master struck me as being a man fully satisfied with his lot as well he might be. He spent the summer on the Greenland coast and in the winter returned to Denmark, where he had a wife and family, and whence he had to make only one or two short winter voyages. He was interested in birds and wild life generally, had a library of books on the subject, and a battery of guns which he made use of both ashore and afloat.

We had an uneventful passage up the coast, passing the usual numbers of trawlers fishing the banks, experiencing one rough day, and on another a fall of snow. But June 30th, when we tried to enter Evighedsfjord, was a day of incident, thanks to the mistakes we made. I had made a bad blunder the previous evening. Having taken a sight for longitude I decided that we were six miles west of our dead reckoning when in fact we were six miles east of it—a mistake on a par with reading right for left. It is a matter of comparing the angle read on the sextant with the calculated angle that would have been obtained had the ship been in the assumed position. If the angle is taken when the sun is roughly west and is found to be larger by six minutes than the calculated angle, then you are nearer the sun than you thought you were by that number of miles; in other words you are six miles west of your estimated position. Visibility was poor and we were closing the land at a fairly brisk speed on a north-easterly course. With more confidence than I usually feel under such circumstances I turned in, leaving orders to be called when we had run thirty miles. We had run little more than twenty when at 3 a.m. Hans roused me with news of an island about a quarter of a mile away. Having got the ship about on a course away from the land I re-worked the sight of the previous evening and discovered the mistake, a small matter of twelve miles.

The fog looked like staying. As there was no wind, we started the engine and motored towards the coast. An ice-breaker, the West Wind, no doubt from the American base at Thule, passed us going south. We had no clear idea where we were until in a momentary lifting of the fog we spotted a glacier which came right down to the water. On the chart the only glacier that answered to this lay in a fjord called Angmarqoq. Turning north we presently passed a group of islands which we could identify and which confirmed our position. The entrance to Evighedsfjord lay about eighteen miles farther north and the entrance could be identified by a small group of islands called Ikermiut on one of which there was a beacon. By the time we had run our distance the fog had come down thicker than ever. We had almost given up hope of sighting anything when an island crowned with a beacon loomed up close on the starboard hand. Cheered by this bit of luck, and thinking perhaps that the difficulty of navigating in fog had been overrated, I put her on course for another island six miles inside the fjord where we hoped to anchor for the night. We were attracted to it by a small settlement marked on the chart. We had not gone three miles when the vague outline of islands began to appear on either hand where no islands should have been. Either we were in the wrong fjord or in a small southern arm of Evighedsfjord. Clearly it was time to stop, so we motored over to the nearest islands and anchored between two of them in fifteen fathoms. We were very close to one island and to prevent her swinging we dropped a stern anchor with fifteen fathoms of chain attached to a warp. Hans let it go while I took a turn with the warp, which promptly broke. We lost the lot. For an hour and more we rowed about in the dinghy dragging a grapnel, but the water was too deep and we caught nothing. We had better luck fishing, and having caught three big cod we set an anchor watch and turned in, the fog being as thick as ever.

Kangamiut

Among loose floes

# TO GODTHAAB AND EVIGHEDSFJORD 147

Fresh-caught cod, by the way, are very different from the shop-soiled variety we get at home.

During the night the fog cleared. How simple everything then appeared. We were, as we suspected, in the southern arm of the fjord; either the tide had set us off course or the compass had played us a trick. With a brisk wind blowing into the fjord we set off for the settlement of Timerdlit six miles up the fjord. We did not expect to go any farther north this year and had strong hopes that Timerdlit would prove to be something like Igdlorssuit, a place with huskies and kayaks, with a stronger flavour of Greenland than Godthaab. Having rounded the island we began to beat up to the settlement lying on the mainland inside the island. As the channel between was barely a cable wide it would have been easier and quicker to motor, but we were being closely followed and watched by a small local fishing boat. By our skilful handling of *Mischief* under sail in confined waters we hoped to astonish the natives, just as earlier explorers accomplished the same end, though with less trouble, by removing their false teeth or their glass eyes if they were fortunate enough to be so equipped. More than once we had to warn our escort to get out of the way as we prepared to go about. We must have gone about at least ten times in that narrow channel. At last, the patience of both parties nearly exhausted, the Greenlanders pointed out the anchorage and we came to rest off Timerdlit, a place comprising one deserted frame hut and the concrete base of what may have once been a store.

The Greenlanders' boat, full of fine fish, came alongside and we at once bought a big halibut for a packet of cigarettes. No words were needed for this transaction and beyond learning that they came from Kangamiut, an island at the northern entrance to the fjord, we got no further information. They wore store clothes—not a pair of sealskin trousers or boots among them—and we realized sadly that so far south as this we should look in vain for huskies, sledges, kayaks, or anything associated with the old Eskimo way of life. We spent the afternoon roaming the hills behind the deserted settlement. The collection of bones, offal, and bits of skin in and around the frame house not only showed that it had been recently lived in but afforded a fruitful field for Mick to begin collecting blow-flies. I began my usual collection of plants. We came upon several graves, remains of old stone huts, and a

148 MISCHIEF IN GREENLAND

stone erection about the size and shape of an old straw skep whose use we could not fathom. In the evening a survey vessel, a strongly-built wooden vessel of lovely lines, anchored near by. Her skipper and the chief surveyor paid us a visit.

She sailed early in the morning and later we passed her anchored close in while the survey party toiled up a 4000-foot mountain to occupy a station. For the first fifteen miles the fjord is wide and the mountains lie well back. (The Eskimo name for Evighedsfjord is Kang-erdlugssuatsiaq.) It then makes a right-angle bend at a point where two great glaciers descend from what is known as the Sukkertoppen ice-cap, a field of ice covering some 900 square miles between Evigheds-fjord and Sondre Stromfjord and quite separate from the main inland ice. Beyond the bend the fjord narrows to a canyon, its abrupt black walls broken only by some desperately steep and narrow clefts filled with ice, looking like mere ice torrents. After another fifteen miles it bends sharply north and continues for another twenty miles, but at the bend there is a wide bay and there we decided to stay. This bay called Kangiussaq lies immediately below the highest peak in the area, a peak of 6995 feet called Agssaussat. It had been swathed in cloud as we motored up the fjord but as we neared the anchorage the clouds rolled away. As the sun illumined its summit snows and the black crags and pinnacles of its western face, it looked a formidable mountain. But mountains have more than one face and when it came to climbing Ags-saussat (which means, by the way, 'Big with child') we found a simple way up. Late that evening we anchored in fifteen fathoms about a hun-dred yards from the beach. Even in that depth, when the boat dropped back on her anchor, there were only five fathoms under her.

CHAPTER XIII

# CLIMBING IN EVIGHEDSFJORD

◆

THE LESSON I HAD LEARNT the previous year on our first attempt to climb a peak had sunk in. It never occurred to me to try to climb Agssaussat from the boat. Roger and I started at the very reasonable hour of 11 a.m. to find a way up the glacier. The ice stopped short of the beach by a hundred yards and about a mile beyond this point it rose in a steep ice-fall. Once above that we imagined we should find it all plain sailing and from a camp up there we could strike at Agssaussat and possibly another peak. After some preliminary boulder-hopping we took to the ice where the going was good. At the foot of the ice-fall a snow-filled gully between the glacier and the confining rock wall offered an easy way of gaining height to within a couple of hundred feet of the top of the ice-fall where the gully petered out. Both the ice above and the rock on our left were unclimbable but to our right a shelf traversed the ice-fall to the far side. We followed this and without having to cut more than a few steps we gained the rocks on the far side whence we soon reached the flat glacier above the ice-fall. It was a good route but liable to change. Melting was going on rapidly and the gap between ice and rock which we had easily stepped over would soon widen. At 2200 feet we found a camp site on a bit of rough moraine and by four o'clock we were back on board. Mick had shot a long-tailed duck. Having no means of roasting it and no apple sauce, we curried it, brutal though that may seem. We curried it, I might add, with full honours, for we had some of the essential trimmings—coconut, dates, raisins, and lemon. Mick, too, has mastered the difficult art of cooking dry rice without which the spiciest curry is but a mockery, so that altogether it was a memorable meal.

As he was ferrying the loads ashore next morning Roger Brown, who was to be one of the carrying party, dropped his camera in the sea and retired on board to spend the day drying it. His load had to be divided among us, and Mick, who was to have come merely as

149

150           MISCHIEF IN GREENLAND

camera-man, had to carry a load as well. In the snow gully we roped up and had lunch at the top of it before shepherding the novices across the ice traverse. All went well and by 3 p.m. we had the tent up. Roger went down with Mick and Shaun to see them safely off the ice. With Mick busy, as it were 'on location', they took so long that I went down to satisfy myself they were all right.

All next day we were confined to the tent by rain and sleet. We read and played chess. The tent began leaking along the seams, pools gathered on the floor, and as I was unable to keep well afloat owing to a punctured air-mattress, we resorted to stabbing holes in the floor to drain off the water. At last towards evening the rain stopped, the clouds began to thin, and little by little between the cloud rifts we pieced together the south-east ridge of Agssaussat clear to the summit. There appeared to be no difficulties. Next day after a lot of snow plodding and a little rock scrambling we reached the summit in just over four hours. It was a hot, cloudless day. Against the dazzling brilliance of the surrounding snow-fields the fjord looked like a strip of dark green jade and the sky a wan blue. Nearly 7000 feet below we could make out *Mischief*, a mere speck, like 'a tall anchoring bark diminished to her cock'. As we neared our camp at 3 p.m. the firm *névé* over which we had sped in the morning had turned to watery slush in which we waded to our knees. The sun temperature was 92° F. and in the shade 76° F.

The weather was equally fine and hot next day when we climbed a peak of 6125 feet close to camp. Some intricate route-finding at the start up rock and snow made it an interesting climb, and the snow slope by which we gained the summit ridge was so steep that we had to dig our hands in to keep in balance. On the way down, when this slope would be wet and unsafe, we avoided it by traversing the mountain and rejoining the glacier well above camp. There were no other peaks within reach of this camp so that afternoon we packed up and went down. Carrying heavy loads, we cautiously crossed the ice traverse using crampons, and having reached the top of the snow gully we uncautiously unroped. For here Roger slipped and began rolling down, missing the gaping maw of a crevasse by inches. A fall in the gully would have been harmless for it flattened out at the bottom, but the crevasse demanded respect and we had

Evighedsfjord—crossing the ice-fall

152        MISCHIEF IN GREENLAND

already three times skirted and peered into this obvious receptacle for falling bodies.

The crew had already fitted a new cranse iron, oiled the wire rigging, and rove a new lacing for the mainsail, but we spent another day here to continue work on the boat and to collect plants and bugs. The tropical weather continued and in the course of a botanical excursion to a near-by glacier valley I suffered severely in the cause of science. Instead of following the beach I embarked on a bush-crawl through thickets of alder and dwarf birch, attended by a private cloud of mosquitoes and streaming with sweat. In order to obtain some respite while I had lunch I lit a fire and sat in the smoke, and having stamped the fire out began the return journey by the easier way of the beach. When half-way home I noticed that my fire, far from being stamped out, had taken hold. By evening the whole hillside up to about 500 feet was burning and a great pillar of smoke hung over the fjord. The fire would certainly discourage a great number of mosquitoes and could harm no one, nevertheless I felt slightly guilty as anyone must who is responsible for starting a holocaust. The crew advised that next time before going ashore I should be searched for matches. Three days later, from the top of another mountain many miles away, we could still see the smoke of this infernal fire.

Our next anchorage was down the fjord beyond the big bend in a land-locked bay called Tasiussaq. We discovered a reef across the entrance where we had only five fathoms of water as we sounded our way in before anchoring in six fathoms about 100 yards from the shore. We dined off cod kedgeree and we had the hope that by coming to this bay we might be able to vary our cod diet with salmon. These hopes grew when we came to explore the wide valley at the head of the bay through which meandered a clear, blue stream some twenty yards wide. At one or two of its pools we noticed stakes and a day later a party of Greenlanders arrived to camp on the beach and to net salmon. In a short time they had caught two sacks full. We bought some of these and later, when Roger and I were climbing, the crew caught six. They used a fine nylon net which Shaun had bought in Godthaab for netting birds. It was an expensive net and only his greed for salmon overcame his scruples about allowing it to be used for fishing. Boiled salmon with mussel sauce made another

## CLIMBING IN EVIGHEDSFJORD

memorable meal to be recorded with gratitude. The stomach has a long memory.

Viewed from afar this verdant valley appeared to offer pleasant walking. In fact the going was deplorably bad. In the flat bottom where the vegetation was rich, one had to leap from moss hag to moss hag, while the slopes above, though bare, were seamed with little gullies. The alder bushes attained a height of ten feet, dwarf willow and juniper abounded, and willow herb grew profusely in great patches of pink. Birds were more numerous here. Besides snow buntings and red polls we saw a sea eagle, several merganser duck, and coveys of ptarmigan. Roger and I had our eyes on a snow-peak about six miles away for which we should have to take a camp up the valley. Before doing that we had a day on a near-by rock peak, 'Amaussuaq', of 4620 feet. The name means 'Like a hand' and four pointed towers standing on the summit ridge make the name apt enough. Leaving the boat at nine o'clock we had an hour of boulder-hopping before reaching the foot of a snow-gully. From the col at the top of the gully, easy rock climbing brought us to the summit by one o'clock. For the descent we found a gully on the other side of the mountain which gave us a thousand feet of glissading down to the main valley.

With Hans and Shaun assisting to carry we started the long slog up the valley. The going, I repeat, was bad—all bog and bother, as Jorrocks would have called it—the day blazing hot, and each of us had our personal swarm of mosquitoes and black flies. I had brought some tubes of a repellent called 'Dusk' which was fairly effective if applied at frequent intervals to face and hands. We made little height till we had crossed the river—where Shaun fell in—and began climbing up a side valley leading to a col. Halts became longer and more frequent. All of us had had enough when we camped just below the col near a patch of snow. Having dumped our loads Roger and I walked up to the col. We were profoundly shocked by the sight of two very deep gorges lying between us and our mountain. The height of the col was 1300 feet and the bottoms of the gorges were at almost sea-level where they drained into a neighbouring fjord. After taking some food Hans and Shaun had to face the long, hot walk home; but Roger and I, lying in the tent, were on no bed of roses. The sun beat fiercely upon the tent from which all ventilation had

Evighedsfjord from half way up first peak

CLIMBING IN EVIGHEDSFJORD

been excluded for fear of mosquitoes. The few mosquitoes that were inside, and that had survived our first onslaught, took their siesta on the roof of the tent finding it too hot to start worrying us. We lay there stifling, sweating, unsleeping, not far from the point of having heat stroke.

With the probability of a long day in front of us we left the tent by 7 a.m. and sat for some time on the col examining our mountain. That was our mistake. The longer we sat and looked the weaker became our resolve. We had some doubts about whether or not an ice wall which guarded the whole length of the main ridge could be breached; and then the ridge itself impressed us unfavourably, a good mile or more of snow which long before midday would be like wet cotton wool. Besides that were the two gorges, looking deeper than ever in the clear morning light. We were ready to welcome any change of plan provided it meant less effort. We decided to go for a peak which was actually slightly higher but more accessible. We should have to drop into the far gorge but only in order to follow up it to the glacier whence its stream originated. This glacier happily proved to be dry ice and remarkably unbroken considering the steep angle at which it rose. With the aid of crampons we gained height quickly. So far we had seen only the top of the peak; there might or might not be a route up. But had we brought with us our map we should have noted that near the summit there was a sign indicating a trigonometrical beacon, a fact that would have reassured us about there being a route and might well have stopped us from bothering to climb the mountain.

When the whole face of the mountain at length came in sight we saw on one side of it an inviting gully. The finding of a bit of a rusty tin showed us we were not the first comers and at the top of the gully on a shoulder of the mountain we found a cairn with a plate cemented into the rock engraved 'Trig. No. 1'. The summit lay 700 feet above. We felt the survey party deserved full marks for having found the only easy route, a route which lay hidden from sight until one was right under the face of the mountain. The height proved to be 6250 feet and even there, on the snow, we were followed by mosquitoes. Thanks to a sequence of snow-beds we shot down the gully at a great rate and soon we were trudging down the glacier with the melt streams pouring off in increasing volume every minute.

156        MISCHIEF IN GREENLAND

In a lake between the moraine and the glacier these combined melt streams caused a most curious effect. At a point in the middle of the lake the water was spouting up with a whoosh like an oil gusher, and surrounding the turbulent spot was a growing mound of gravel deposited by the spouting water.

We reached the tent by five o'clock, much too soon for comfort, for once more we had to lie sealed up in the tent half-naked and sweating. Roger, bless him, produced a tin of deliciously cold Mandarin orange slices—we had nothing of the kind on board—and then we brewed a lot of tea, thus raising the temperature even higher. Some of our bodily needs being met we fell to reviewing the events of the day. At first we felt we had shown a commendable lack of spirit. Roger had surprisingly lagged behind and had been off colour and had we stuck to our first objective we should, I believe, have had only the satisfaction of having tried. But that, of course, is what matters, and matters far more than climbing a peak. In fact by slinking off to bag an easy peak we had lowered rather than raised our self-respect. Was our moral fibre slackening? If so it needed stiffening. So when the evening became cooler I set about preparing the stiffest brew of pemmican we had yet had. Pemmican as thick as this, I noticed, my scientific interest fully aroused, does not bubble when it boils. This hell-broth of mine merely heaved slightly, shivering like a quicksand, while at long intervals a globule of imprisoned air expired on the surface with a melancholy sigh.

We packed up and started down next morning expecting any moment to meet Mick and Roger Brown who were coming up to help with the loads. Mick we shortly saw but no Roger Brown. Once again he and his camera had fallen into a stream. Shaun, too, we heard, had soaked his camera in the same way, and I remembered that at various times he had thrown overboard a mop and the gash-bucket. Are bird-watchers prone to this sort of thing? Are they unsteady on their feet or is it that their eyes are always in the air looking for birds instead of on the ground? To most of us Shaun's camera appeared to be ruined beyond hope and we told him so. But he took it all to pieces, dried it, and successfully re-assembled it. In fact with him and Hans, the apprentice watch-maker, there were few jobs on board, however finicking, which could not be tackled. One small job, however, that defeated

## CLIMBING IN EVIGHEDSFJORD

them all were my teeth which I broke by sitting on them. Mick as a practical scientist took this job in hand. He tried first with Aerolite glue and when that failed reinforced the glue with a cunningly made steel pin. This lasted only twenty-four hours and I was lucky to find later in Holsteinborg a dentist's mechanic. A mouth without molars is like a mill without stones.

On July 15th we intended sailing for Godthaab, calling at Kangamiut on the way. It was full early to be thinking of Baffin Island, but for all we knew the season might be an open one and the earlier we got there the better. At Godthaab we hoped we might obtain a report on ice conditions in that area. As we were about to sail that evening a Kangamiut boat came into the bay and presently they came alongside to ask for some oil. We gave them diesel oil but apparently they wanted paraffin which we could not spare. Instead we gave them a tow. For two hours we beat down the fjord, until the Greenlanders, tired of our slow progress and getting uncommonly wet, cast off the line and made for the beach. The wind then died and we enjoyed a wonderfully clear, still evening as we took our last look at the mountains, their familiar outlines reflected in the quiet water. Kangamiut itself lies on an island surrounded by many others. The intricate approach terminates in a long, narrow strip of water almost like a dock. Although it was midnight when we arrived two local men boarded us and helped us to moor with an anchor from the bow and a warp to the shore.

The steep rocky hillside overlooking the harbour is lined with rows of gaily painted little wooden houses where live the 300-odd Greenlanders of Kangamiut. They depend mainly upon fishing and there is a curing factory for salting down the cod and halibut. The salmon in the streams up the fjords are now being exploited. We were told that fifty tons had been caught the previous autumn; these were sent to Sukkertoppen for freezing. We spent the morning at the house of the manager appointed by the Greenland Trading Company, a man responsible not only for trade but for the general welfare of Kangamiut and its inhabitants. He had spent fourteen years in Greenland both on the east coast and the west and had enjoyed it. One of his tasks had been the moving of the entire Eskimo community of Thule, where the American base is, to a place seventy miles farther north where they could pursue their normal life hunting seals, walrus, and polar bear, free from the

158                    MISCHIEF IN GREENLAND

distractions of jet planes and Coca-Cola. The manager showed us his
collection of Eskimo curios collected over the years, soapstone and
ivory carvings and implements of all kinds. Naturally we were on the
look-out for such things, particularly carvings, but nowadays they are
virtually unobtainable by the casual visitor. Few are made and those
few are bespoke by the residents. While we were there an old man came
into the house to offer us a beautifully made model kayak complete in
every detail. He asked £5, might have accepted less, but found among
us no takers. In the afternoon the manager paid us a visit bringing with
him his clerk who very kindly cut my hair. We were sitting down to
tea when we felt *Mischief* bump on the bottom, a hint perhaps that she
was impatient to be off. We found she had dragged inshore. We were
sorting this out when a big naval picket boat arrived from nowhere,
dropped anchor too close to us, and then drifted across our warp. So,
taking the hint, we bade the manager a hasty farewell, got our lines in,
and sailed out.

Going down the coast we experienced the usual calms, light
breezes, and, of course, fog. Whenever the fog came down the temperature dropped to 36° or 37° F. On the morning of the July 19th,
after being becalmed all night, we were sailing close inshore in foggy
weather. The sun shone pleasantly overhead but visibility was less than
200 yards. We were steering southeast for the beacon at the entrance to
Godthaab fjord which we reckoned to be about five miles away when
suddenly an island loomed up close ahead. After clearing it by gybing
we went back on course and soon sighted more islets on the port hand.
What they were we had little idea for the whole coast hereabouts is
thick with islands, islets, and skerries. An hour later yet more islands
appeared ahead but this time when we altered course to clear them we
found ourselves hemmed in. Whichever way we turned islets appeared
to cluster like peas on a plate. For the next hour we were dodging them
as if they were ice floes, following a likely looking lead until it closed
and then gybing or going about to try another. Fortunately the sun
shone strongly overhead enabling us to judge pretty well by the colour
of the water where shoal patches lay; but this did not altogether spare
us some frightening moments when on looking over the side we saw
the bottom very close beneath us. At length we reached open water—
open so far as the fog permitted us to see—and we hove-to to await

Evighedsfjord—on shore at the first anchorage

Mountains in Evighedsfjord

160 MISCHIEF IN GREENLAND

a clearing. From the number and density of this group of islands we judged we had crossed the mouth of the fjord and sailed right in among the fifty or more on the south side. With a little more luck, we thought, we might have sighted the beacon, for in the course of the morning we must have sailed past nearly every one of the fifty. For some time we had been hearing the noise of an engine and presently a small fishing boat loomed up out of the mist. When hailed he came alongside and proved to be a Faeroe Island fishing boat. Asked where the beacon was, they told us east-south-east and barely a mile, whereupon we let draw and soon found it. As was generally the way, as we drew inland up the fjord we ran into clear weather while the fog lay in a heavy bank out to sea.

This final visit of ours to Godthaab extended to seven days, partly owing to delay in the matter of obtaining an ice report. A Canadian who looked after the maintenance of the Catalina seaplanes run by East Canada Airways proved most helpful. When a signal to the big air base at Sondre Stromfjord produced no results he got in touch direct with the air-strip on Cape Dyer. Cape Dyer is one of the two big easternmost capes of Baffin Island, the other being Cape Walsingham forty miles to the south. Exeter Sound and Exeter Bay lie a few miles south of Cape Dyer. In 1955 Cape Dyer had been chosen for the siting of a link in the Distant Early Warning chain stretching across the Canadian Arctic and an air-strip had been built there. Besides this matter of an ice report the Canadian helped us to find in Godthaab a new solenoid starter for our engine and presented us, rather prodigally, with five gallons of oil. We carried on board, a relic of Cape Town days, a five-gallon drum of fish oil for use as storm oil. This had become almost solid so I asked the Canadian if he could let us have some used engine oil. He told us they dumped used oil and sent our drum back filled with new engine oil.

The *Mallemuken* (what a lot of time she spent in Godthaab!) had a new commander and a new crew neither of whom had paid us any attention. The day after our arrival two of us had a bucket bath on deck. Later, on the quay, I met a petty officer from her crew who asked me if we had enjoyed our bath; I told him we preferred hot showers when we could get them and that afternoon we made free with the shower bath in *Mallemuken*. As the Faeroe Islanders had done us a

CLIMBING IN EVIGHEDSFJORD 161

good turn in giving us the bearing of the beacon I thought to give them a bottle of gin. Rowing over to the fish wharf where they were lying I had a look over their boat which was little bigger than *Mischief*. They come out early in the summer doing the 1200 miles in eighteen days relying entirely upon their engine. The three of them berthed in a tiny cabin forward where there were actually five bunks, the two spare bunks being occupied by a couple of Greenlanders whom they took on for the summer's fishing. They had five big reels of nylon line ranged along the bulwarks and used as a lure artificial sand-eels. One of them said he once had fourteen cod on at a time. The catch is put in ice and sold at Faeringhaven, a fishing port about twenty miles south of Godthaab. Their galley had the beauty of simplicity. It was merely a cupboard, like a small wardrobe without any drawers, standing on deck aft, and inside it a small gas-ring supplied from a gas cylinder standing outside. There was no going inside this galley. To see how things were going the cook had merely to open the doors; nor could he stir and sniff at his pots as most of us like to do unless he lay down on the deck. In September these hardy souls return to the Faeroe Islands. They pressed on me some cod and a Kingfish, a big red job which made prime eating.

We did some work on the boat. Painted half the deck—which was duly rained on—turned all the halyards end for end, and mulled over the idea of hauling her out to look at the bottom. At Godthaab there is no convenient wall for a boat to be leant against. The harbour-master recommended a little creek near the anchorage where a big trading schooner was at that time hauled out and lying on her side—careened in fact. We had a look at the place but what with the boulders lying about and the difficulty of keeping *Mischief* upright, we thought that more harm than good might result. Finally we went alongside the quay to fill up with water, fuel, and paraffin, for we had no clear idea of what we should do if unable to reach Exeter Sound, or where our next port of call, if any, might be. Against this contingency, and through the influence of our Canadian friend, I changed some Danish money into dollars at the Kristinemut. Our standing there should have been high enough as it was, for we ate there every night, ringing the changes on whale steaks, salmon steaks, beefsteaks, and smörgenbrod and shrimps.

162        MISCHIEF IN GREENLAND

At last on July 25th we got a report from Cape Dyer. The main item of it, 'heavily congested pack-ice two to five miles from the coast', was not very encouraging, but we thought we might as well go and see for ourselves. On the following morning we had a final shopping round-up, taking on board among other things no less than twenty-six massive loaves of rye bread. Later that day we entertained two guests, very fortunately for us at different times. Mick had been paying daily visits to the dentist. She—most of the dentists in Greenland appear to be women—having expressed a wish to see over *Mischief*, we invited her to lunch. Having seen this visitor ashore I went along to say good-bye to the harbour-master. It must have been a holiday because I found him in the go-down along with a few choice friends and on the floor in front of them two open cases of Carlsberg lager. The cases were nearly empty but this evidence was hardly needed to tell one that the party had been in progress for some time. Having helped them to finish the beer I began making my farewells. But that would not do. The harbour-master himself must come and see us off. So they staggered across the quay and lowered him down the ladder rung by rung into a waiting boat. It was a much bigger boat than our dinghy, and a good thing too, for throughout the short passage the harbour-master insisted on standing up to sing while he surveyed his watery domain with uncomprehending eyes. Having got him safely over the rail and down into the cabin we gave him a stiff go of rum to calm him, whereupon he signified that his boat's crew must have the same treatment. Getting him off proved to be a more difficult task than that of getting him on board. After a few groping, tentative efforts at cocking his leg over the rail he gave up and collapsed on the deck. So we pushed him under the rail and into the welcoming arms of his boat's crew amid loud cries of 'Bon voyage'. By then it was five o'clock so we got our anchor and sailed out.

CHAPTER XIV

# FIRST ATTEMPT ON EXETER SOUND

A FAIR WIND TOOK US QUICKLY down the fjord. Approaching the islands we ran into fog and took care to keep them in sight one after another as we sailed by so that we made sure of passing the beacon. That done we pointed her head due west, the nearest we could get to north-west which was the course for Cape Dyer. After three days' sailing hard on the wind, and sometimes having to tack, we were disappointed when a noon sight put us in lat. 64° 20´, or only some twenty miles north of the latitude of Godthaab. We attributed this poor result to leeway, because out in the middle of Davis Strait there should not have been any south-going current. We were surprised, too, to find that the sea temperature had risen from 40° F. to 44° F., but that could be accounted for by our being north of that branch of the Greenland current which turns westwards just south of what is called the Davis Strait Ridge between N. lat. 63° and 64°. Our first sunny, fogless day was more than welcome, for the weather for the first three days had been thick, raw, and wet, making the ropes and sails perpetually sodden. The next day, too, was so fine and sunny that some of us bathed on deck, the air and the sea temperature being the same at 44° F. There were several big icebergs about and also some bottle-nosed whales.

That night we ran fifty miles north-west, passing at midnight in fog within a hundred yards of a big berg. We reckoned we had Cape Walsingham abeam about forty miles away but on account of fog we could get no sights to verify this. By now it was clear we were in the Labrador current amidst the south-going stream of icebergs. Bergy bits and scattered floes became more numerous and that morning we passed a berg which we estimated to be a quarter-mile long. Not many minutes after this monster had disappeared in the fog we heard a thunderous roar like an avalanche which went on for an appreciable time.

Evidently a part of it had broken off and capsized. I fully expected a miniature tidal wave would follow us but nothing happened. Until

164  MISCHIEF IN GREENLAND

early afternoon we worked our way north through loose floes and belts of scattered pack-ice when we emerged into what appeared to be open water—open, that is to say, for about a half-mile which was the limit of visibility. A seal rolling about and playing on one of these floes seemed quite unalarmed and watched us with interest as we sailed by only fifty yards away. The wind continued fair so we held on northwards with the intention of reaching the latitude of Cape Dyer before turning in towards Exeter Sound. By now the sea temperature had dropped to 34° F. and the air to 40° F. These are not low temperatures for that region and we had nothing to complain about, but the all-pervading fog and damp made us feel extremely cold. Winter woollies and extra sweaters were now the wear and on deck oilskins had to be worn over-all. All that day we had not the least hint of sun, the sky having an unbroken leaden hue almost as dark as the sea. We began to find the constantly thick weather a little discouraging. But, as Sancho Panza used to say, all ills are good when attended by food, and that night we ate a rich risotto and screwed it down with a monumental plum duff— Michael Rhodes *fecit*.

At ten o'clock that night we had to heave-to, the sea being so cluttered with bergy bits. With a wind we could have steered round them but when the wind dropped, rather than start motoring, we just let her lie while the ice drifted by. Generally the floes drifted clear and only once did we have to poke an intruder out from under the bobstay. Of course if the sea had been rough we should not have viewed our small but dangerous neighbours with such complacency. Next day, August 1st, we continued motoring towards the land. At last, later in the morning, the fog cleared and we got sights which put us in Lat. 66° 26′ N. and Long. 60° 15′ West, about forty miles from the coast and a little south of Cape Dyer. Early in the afternoon we sighted high land and after examining it through binoculars we could make out a radio mast and some buildings. Although we were aware of the air-strip on Cape Dyer, the reality was a nasty sight for men like ourselves who liked to think that they were closing a wild, desolate coast, unspoilt by man or traces of man. Even nastier, however, was the sight of a vague unbroken line of white close inshore. It might be fog but we feared almost certainly it was ice. Early that evening we reached the edge of this pack-ice, for so it proved to be. We were then ten to fifteen miles

## FIRST ATTEMPT ON EXETER SOUND

from the coast and from the masthead we could not see how far the ice reached for behind it lay a bank of fog. We motored slowly into the loose pack at the ice edge, more for the sake of taking photographs than with any intention of trying to force our way through.

This ice, of course, was no more than what we had expected to find. We had no call to be either surprised or disappointed, the question was what we should now do. Under the circumstances, with no promising leads in sight and ignorant of how thick the belt might be, we should have been foolish to enter the ice in the hope of barging a way through. We were not in a fjord but in the open sea where any wind or rough weather would start all this ice moving and heaving up and down. And merely 'getting through' might not be enough. For all we knew Exeter Sound itself might be jammed with ice. In the seasons of 1955 and 1956 when steamers were unloading stores in Exeter Bay for the building of the Cape Dyer establishment operations were much hampered by ice. On August 7th, 1956, the ice was so heavy that ice-breaker assistance was needed to break the ice in the anchorage so that unloading could continue. In summer the pack-ice moves freely, the ice groups and regroups, leads open and shut, according to the strength and direction of the wind. We might, therefore, hang about, Micawber-like, hoping something favourable would happen. Alternatively we could go back to Greenland and wait there in much more comfortable circumstances. We had still a month in hand and to our inexperienced eyes the solid belt of ice in front of us seemed hardly likely to disperse in much less than that. We decided to compromise by going down the coast as far south as Angijak Island south of Cape Walsingham. If the ice proved to be continuous and no openings presented themselves we would retire to Holsteinborg. Southwards seemed our best bet, for north of Cape Dyer the coast trends to the west, so that ice drifting down from the north would tend to bank up against the land.

All that night we sailed south. The helmsman, Roger Brown, reported killer whales but whether they were seen is another matter. Roger Brown had such a propensity for seeing this voracious kind of whale that he himself earned the name of 'Killer'. Hans, by the way, had long answered to the name of 'Uncle'; not that he was rich but that his manner was a little avuncular, fussy, and prone to giving advice to the younger members of the crew who, indeed, sometimes, stood in

166 MISCHIEF IN GREENLAND

want of it. At midnight fog came down again and remained with us throughout the whole of as vile, wet, and foggy a day as we had yet experienced. The sea temperature was 34° F. and the air 36° F. In the evening we had to turn west to avoid ice and after resuming our southerly course we met more pack-ice at midnight. We hove-to for the night in a position estimated to be thirty miles east of Cape Walsingham.

On a drizzly morning with a fresh easterly wind and no ice in sight we let draw and continued southwards. What, we wondered, had happened to all the ice we had seen at midnight? The glass remained steady, but off that coast, whether it went up or down, the weather remained consistently thick and wet. Later we again sighted the familiar line of white stretching away both ahead of us and to starboard. Again we made a board of five miles out to the east before turning south and once more we saw ice ahead of us. Hereabouts, forty miles off the coast, there seemed to be more ice than around Cape Dyer. So at noon we gave up and set a course for Holsteinborg 180 miles away across the narrowest part of Davis Strait. In the evening, when we saw another great raft of pack-ice covering several miles of sea, we rashly concluded that we had seen the last of it. About two in the morning Roger Brown called me to say we were among floes. I went up and took the helm for we were sailing fast in smooth water under all plain sail. That it was foggy goes without saying. At first I thought these floes were merely a few stragglers and that we should soon be clear, though the smoothness of the sea might have warned me that there was pack-ice in the vicinity. In fact if the sea suddenly becomes smooth it is a pretty sure hint that there is pack-ice to windward. If loose floes are scattered over a wide area any wind tends to regroup them and as the wind rises they collect in belts running in a direction at right angles to the wind. As we were sailing with the wind just forward of the beam we were likely to become more involved, as we very soon did.

At first it was fun dodging the floes but, sailing as fast as we were, this presently became too hazardous. All hands were called to get the mainsail off and we jogged along under stays'l alone. We had erred in not turning back on first meeting ice, for by now it was all round us and we were forced to follow the most open lead in whatever direction it might take us. Although the sea was smooth a perceptible swell added to the difficulty. At one moment we would appear to be

# FIRST ATTEMPT ON EXETER SOUND

following an open lead and suddenly floes would heave in sight on top of the swell. After two hours of it we had got nowhere and were still unable to see in what direction to steer to find open water. Then the lead we were following narrowed and began to close ahead of us. We downed the stays'l to lessen the impending impact and at the same time noticed with alarm a big tabular floe, much bigger than *Mischief*, making straight at us. It was undercut all along the water-line where even in that murky light the ice shone balefully blue, and as it came towards us, travelling faster than we were, it brushed aside the smaller floes in its path. This big, blue bastard, as we immediately christened it, seemed bent on our destruction. For one or two confused minutes we were hemmed in and to my heated imagination seemed to be lifted up and riding on ice. Then, having started the engine, we began slowly making headway. The floes thinned, the sea became rough, and at last we were in open water. Hard by lay a big iceberg, as white and fresh-looking as if it had just broken off a glacier. Under its lee we hoisted sail and resumed our course. By the time we had brewed coffee and turned in, leaving the helmsman to carry on, it was five o'clock. I suppose an experienced ice navigator, instead of taking fright at the approach of this threatening monster, would have moored his ship to it and allowed it to clear a path for him through the raft of floes.

This ice, we thought, must have been the tail-end of what is known as the 'middle-pack', the great tongue of loosely packed ice that stretches down west of the centre axis of Davis Strait from Baffin Bay to beyond Cape Dyer. We reckoned we were about eighty miles from the Canadian coast when we encountered it. The old whalers trying to reach the 'north water' in June or early July often got into serious trouble in this 'middle pack'. In the year 1830, out of the fleet of ninety-one British whalers, nineteen were lost and at one time there were 1000 men on the ice, men whose ships had already been nipped and sunk or whose ships were beset. It was known in whaling history as 'Baffin Fair'. On such occasions, thanks to the presence of so many ships, few lives were lost, but some terrible scenes took place. Once a ship was nipped and making water fast so that she looked like sinking, the men would remove themselves and their gear to the ice, the rum casks were broached, and all discipline came to an end. And apparently it became a custom or tradition that a ship so nipped should be set on fire.

Iceberg in Exeter Sound

## FIRST ATTEMPT ON EXETER SOUND

By the evening of August 5th, a lovely, calm evening, we were once more off the Greenland coast about twenty miles north of Holsteinborg. It was a Sunday. Two Portuguese schooners lay idle side by side, enjoying like us the sunny, peaceful calm. What a contrast, we thought to the Canadian coast—no ice, no fog (for the moment), and a benign sun. The sea temperature having risen to 44° F. we felt we were in tropical waters. Like most Greenland ports the approach to Holsteinborg is guarded or obstructed, according to the point of view, by islands and rocks. If one is confident enough to use them one has usually a choice of two or three channels. We were cautious and generally followed the course prescribed as suitable for large vessels. The sea-mark to pick up when approaching Holsteinborg from the north or west is Qagssit, one of a small group of low-lying islands with a beacon on it. Having given that a wide berth one steers for Anatsusok, one of a cluster of islands off the harbour entrance on which is a beacon and a light, taking care at the same time to avoid Jacob's Skaer, a rock only two feet high. It is also worth noting that three miles south-east of Qagssit is a rock with less than six feet of water over it on which the sea rarely breaks. On this H.M.S. *Valorous* struck in 1875—a long time ago, but no doubt the rock is still there. Early next morning, keeping a wary eye on the diminutive Jacob's Skaer and other dangers, we downed sail and motored through the harbour entrance. The main harbour looked so small and so full of shipping of various kinds that we went on to have a look at the inner harbour. This was large enough and completely empty, for it is cut off from the town, so back we went to the busy main harbour. A friendly police boat (one of three similar boats that were newly arrived at Godthaab from Denmark when we were last there) warned us that in a vacant hole we were making for there lurked a submerged rock. We had to go right in close to a floating jetty where the smaller fishing boats lay, where we dropped anchor and laid out a warp to the shore. We were barely clear of the fairway; I felt that sooner or later one of the many fishing boats which were constantly coming and going would fail to notice *Mischief*'s long bowsprit. Luckily it was a period of neap tides. Had it been springs we should have been on the bottom at low water.

Holsteinborg is an important fishing port, with a curing factory and a cannery for shrimps. Having a small shipyard and slipway it is

170    MISCHIEF IN GREENLAND

one of the few places on the coast where ships can be repaired and even built. That evening the assistant manager of the yard paid us a visit. He told us that except for the manager and himself the men in the yard were Greenlanders and mostly competent workmen. Apparently we were not quite the first yacht to visit Holsteinborg. An Italian—a rich man, I imagine—had for several seasons kept his motor-yacht there, laying her up in the yard for the winter, and in summer, after flying out with his crew, cruising on the coast. That summer he had taken a climbing party to the Devil's Thumb, a 1800-foot-high rock pillar, a well-known landmark, up in Lat. 74° 30′. The yacht had two 300-horse-power engines and a skipper, lent by the Greenland Trading Company, who knew the coast. It is worth recalling that a few of our Victorian yachtsmen, generally wealthy men, preferred the Arctic to the Mediterranean for summer cruises. Of course, in those days yachts were something more than what we now understand by the term and they were generally crewed by professionals. There was Lord Dufferin, for example, who sailed to Jan Mayen and Spitsbergen, and Leigh Smith, who made five Arctic voyages, two as far as Franz Joseph Land. On the last of these in 1873 the *Eira*, a 360-ton steam-yacht, strengthened for ice, was nipped in the ice and sunk. The crew wintered there successfully and next summer, in four of the yacht's boats, sailed 450 miles to Nova Zembla where they were picked up.

Besides the number of small boats engaged in fishing we were impressed by several well-kept, well-equipped fishing boats of about thirty tons, with wireless, echo-sounders, life-saving rafts, and some with a harpoon gun mounted in the bows. These were apparently built in Denmark at a cost of about £15,000 and shipped out to Greenland to be taken over on easy terms by local fishermen. There are some fifteen hundred people in Holsteinborg and we reckoned that every man, woman, and child must have owned a team of huskies. (In Godthaab dogs are absolutely forbidden.) The place fairly crawled with dogs, especially around the harbour, the wharves, and the fish factory where there were fish offal, scraps of whale or reindeer meat to be picked up, and oil barrels to lick. Some swam about the harbour in search of food. Around many of the houses there were dogs which were obviously fed, but the majority, we were told, were not fed in summer and had to fend for themselves. We had noticed on the way in a pack of huskies

## FIRST ATTEMPT ON EXETER SOUND

confined on a small island where it seemed impossible that they could eke out an existence, but we were assured that these, too, were not fed and were parked there to be out of the way. There were almost as many children running loose as there were dogs, clambering over *Mischief* and rowing about the harbour in our dinghy. When they were being unusually trying I sometimes regretted that the harsher methods of dog management had not been applied to the children.

There was no place here corresponding to the Kristinemut, nowhere for the sea-weary mariner to go to wash the salt out of his mouth except a rather dreary coffee bar. Beer could be bought only over the counter at the general store and, as we soon learnt, could not be bought at all until a fresh consignment arrived. When in harbour we liked to have our evening meal ashore and Mick heard from a friendly Dane that we might be able to muscle in, as it were, at a hostel where some seventy Danish technicians and workmen had their meals. Just as at Godthaab a lot of constructional work was in hand, new houses being built, roads made, and drains laid. Accordingly, on our first evening we repaired to the hostel. As George Robey used to sing: 'My word, it was fine; they were just going to dine; my reception gave me quite a shock.' They were all so delighted to see us, or so we imagined as we slid modestly into some vacant seats at the foot of a long table. A very good meal we had, too, conversing brightly with our neighbours, behaving with decorum, and finally paying our bill. Next morning I went up to the hostel to warn them that we should be dining with them again that evening. I was confronted, however, by the manageress, a large, square-rigged Danish woman, strikingly masculine in face and figure, who at once gave me a curt 'no' and with whom I felt no inclination to argue.

Some further slight embarrassment awaited me later that morning when I set out to find the dentist. At the quay a drunken Greenlander attached himself to me and refused to be shaken off. Every passer-by had to be stopped and told who his distinguished friend was, and presently they were being told, too, where I was bound for, the drunk having discovered my destination when I asked a Dane where the dentist lived. At the door of the dentist's waiting-room I tried to shut him out but he followed me in and introduced me loudly to each member of the small suffering assembly. The noise he made brought the dentist

172          MISCHIEF IN GREENLAND

herself into the room. Hastily explaining the matter and thrusting my broken teeth into her hand I withdrew before she had time to ask who my drunken companion was. But I had not yet done with him. I had to go to his house where, in a neat room with a polished wood floor, he made me sit while he cranked up an ancient gramophone and turned his wireless on at full bore. This brought in his wife who after viewing with distaste her polished floor, followed him with a floor-cloth as he walked about wiping away the marks left by his muddy gum-boots. Finally, seeing no end to it, she made him sit down while she hauled his boots off and threw them out. He had not brought me to his house purely out of affection. Presently he went out of the room and returned with his wife's full regalia—high, embroidered boots, shirt, collar, the lot—which he offered to me for £30. Upon my declining this bargain he asked for a 2/- tip for having shown me the dentist's house!

The drunk's house was perched perilously on a rock above the road and the floating jetty, a wooden staircase giving access to the road. It must have been one of the first houses built, for now they extend inland as much as a mile from the harbour. The floating jetty always presented a busy scene, particularly if a boat came in with a load of whale meat or reindeer meat. This would be cut up into large hunks, weighed, and sold on the spot to a crowd of eager buyers. Behind Holsteinborg and its adjacent coast there is a stretch of broken, hilly country of nearly a hundred miles between the coast and the inland ice, a piece of country well stocked with reindeer. Hunting, we were told, is permitted for two months in the year, August and February. When we tired of watching the activity on the jetty we used to walk round to the other side of the harbour where cargo was landed from lighters and where the larger fishing boats landed their catch for the curing factory. The shore gang handling cargoes consisted of women. At the curing factory the cod were hauled up in baskets to be gutted by one gang of men and filleted at adjacent tables by another. Inside the factory were high stacks of alternate layers of salt and fish which in the curing process have to be moved and restacked with, I suppose, as much expert knowledge as would be required for curing tobacco or maturing Stilton cheese.

With a slipway at hand it seemed a mistake not to have *Mischief* slipped, to satisfy ourselves that our two slight accidents in the ice had

FIRST ATTEMPT ON EXETER SOUND 173

not started a plank. The assistant manager said they were too busy. Three ships in turn had been on the slip since our arrival, one of them a survey ship which had hit a rock—an occupational hazard of survey ships on that coast. He suggested we might save time and money by putting her against the wall near the floating jetty where, he said, there were nine feet of water at high tide. We agreed to try and at midday, high tide being soon after, the yard launch came to tow us in. We had already taken some soundings and I was doubtful that there would be enough water for us. Sure enough, when a few yards out from the wall we took the ground. The yard men waited a bit for the tide to rise though to us it seemed already at a stand. They then gave us another violent pluck and succeeded in putting us yet more firmly aground. At my earnest request they then tried to pull her off. She would not budge and there we were, out of reach of the wall, with no visible means of support when the tide ebbed. Happily our friend at the yard, a man of action, saw what had happened. Hailing the launch over, he sent them back with the big wire hawser attached to the slipway winch. It did occur to us that when the electric winch took the strain our samson post together with half our deck might be torn out. But this alarming thought had hardly time to sink in before the wire tightened and we slid off into deep water.

The assistant manager would not be beaten. Night tides, he said, are always higher than day tides, so we must try again at midnight when he would send the launch and his gang to help. That night tides are always higher is a fallacy; it depends on the declination of the moon. It may so happen that for weeks together the night tides are higher; but if this is so, at another period of the year the reverse will be the case. Anyhow before midnight I rowed the head boatman across to where there was a slightly dilapidated tide gauge on which I had marked the height reached by the morning tide. Having pointed out the present level and asked him whether he thought the tide could make two feet in the next half-hour, I found he agreed with me that it was no go. So we gave the boatmen a glass of rum apiece for their trouble and sent them home. The head boatman, a man with a most villainous countenance, downed his at one gulp. As Michael Finsbury said: 'I have never seen a man drink faster; it restored one's confidence in the human race.'

174 MISCHIEF IN GREENLAND

At the shipyard next morning they agreed that we should have to wait for spring tides; they added that in four or five days' time they would be able to take us on the slip. Holsteinborg, amusing and interesting though it was, had no beer and too many dogs, urchins, and mosquitoes. Moreover it was very hot: 80° F. in the sun and 65° F. in the shade. We decided to retire to the country for a few days, to Nordre Isortok, the next fjord to the north only fifteen miles away.

CHAPTER XV

# MOUNT RALEIGH

THE PASSAGE TO ISORTOK, a matter of a few hours, took us the best part of three days. In the evening when we were rounding the Qagssit group of islands the wind piped up from south and began to blow with some vigour. At midnight, when we thought we were still south of Nordre Isortok by a few miles, we reefed and hove-to on the starboard tack, the wind then blowing about Force 6. We must have been fore-reaching fast because at three in the morning some islands showed up. They may well have been the islands at the mouth of our fjord and had we been bolder we might have run in for shelter. Instead we took fright, let draw, gybed to the other tack and stood away from the land. At the same time the outhaul and lacing at the peak of the gaff began to go. The mainsail, therefore, had to come down and a fine job we had. The new peak halyard of two-and-a-half-inch rope that had recently been fitted stubbornly refused to render through the blocks. Once the mainsail was down we could not heave-to. The boat ran off rapidly to the north until the staysail, too, had been taken in when we lay-a-try under bare poles.

We soon renewed the gaff lacing and outhaul but there was now no hope of beating back to Isortok for the wind had increased; nor could we have found it because it was raining hard as well. Throughout a long day, sea and sky one grey wetness, we lay, rolling heavily and drifting to the north-west. Poor Mick was sea-sick all the time. Early next day, the third since we had left Holsteinborg, the wind began to take off. When the rain cleared we found we had two trawlers in company. Close aboard a whale swam around the ship, sometimes turning over on its back. From its white flukes and white belly we identified it as a Piked whale or Lesser Rorqual, not more than thirty feet in length. In the course of the day we recovered the thirty or more miles we had been blown northwards and by evening were off the entrance of our fjord. On our small-scale chart the entrance

175

looked fearfully intricate, as though islets had been scattered over it from a giant pepper-pot. In reality, in daylight and good visibility, the passage proved simple enough. Nordre Isortok is thirty-five miles long. We contented ourselves with a mere twelve miles, anchoring late that night at the head of a short arm called Isortuarssuk. We noticed two Greenlander boats anchored and the light of a camp fire on shore. It was an unusual fjord in that the water shoaled gradually. When we let go in four fathoms we were a good half-mile from the shore and between us and the shore some huge boulders showed above water. By mere chance we had entered at low water. At high water all the boulders were covered so that we might easily have anchored among them and found ourselves sitting on top of one when the tide ebbed. There are no tide tables for these parts—or at least we had none—and one can only tell what the tide is doing by watching closely the water-level along the rocks of the fjord.

I cannot say I enjoyed our visit to Isortok. It had begun badly and continued as it had begun. In retrospect it seems to have been a case of one damned thing after another. The mountains in the neighbourhood are less than 3000 feet. Roger rushed up one alone the first day while I made a botanical excursion up the valley. There were few flowers and few mosquitoes but myriads of little black flies like midges. Having set out without any 'Dusk' ointment I soon found myself being driven demented. A gentle wind blew up the valley; I found that by facing about and walking into it the midges hovering round one were blown away; but those tactics could not be persisted in if I meant to walk up the valley. To stop to collect flowers, taking off the rucksack and getting out the press, was out of the question; even the sight of something as rare as a black tulip could hardly have induced me to stop. I was determined to get as far as a big lake three miles up the valley, a lake shut in by high rock walls with red screes running down to it, not unlike the Wastwater screes. By then I had had enough. The slight wind had now dropped so that no relief could be expected on the homeward journey. Instead I fled violently uphill on to a ridge on the south side of the valley, hoping to escape from my tormentors. Quite useless. At a height of a thousand feet the midges were equally at home. In Kipling's story 'The Vortex' a man takes refuge from a swarm of angry bees by hurling himself into the village pond. Nearing home,

MOUNT RALEIGH

when a deep pool presented itself, I undressed hastily and jumped in. It was too cold to stay there long and to dress meant standing still. So, snatching up my clothes and boots, I sped naked along the beach towards the dinghy. The next day my face had swelled so much I could hardly see.

After supper that night it began to rain and a wind blew down the fjord raising quite a sea. At first, as we felt an occasional shudder, we thought the anchor was snubbing and let out more chain. Whereupon she began to bump on the bottom in no uncertain way. On taking a sounding over the stern we got only six feet of water. With the tide beginning to ebb we worked hard to get her off but the anchor merely came home and the engine failed to move her. For the next hour she continued to bump and at every bump we winced involuntarily. As she finally settled she heeled at an alarming angle and remained like that until three in the morning. At five we floated again and when we got the anchor in we saw why she had dragged, the cable having taken a turn round the fluke of the anchor.

It continued stormy throughout the day. Nevertheless we went out in the dinghy trying vainly to catch some cod, watching enviously the Greenlanders on shore as they plucked salmon from the nets they had laid off the mouth of a stream. When the weather improved next day I finished painting the half of the deck we had left undone. While kneeling on the deck painting, difficult though it may seem, I managed to lose overside a favourite pipe. On top of that the mainspring of our chronometer watch chose this time to break. Watchmaker Hans could do nothing about that, but we could get on without it so long as we could obtain time signals. Where, when, and upon whom, I wondered, would misfortune strike next? So far no day at this anchorage had been without its minor accident.

Meantime the question of catching salmon was under urgent consideration. We searched the ship for empty bottles and jars to act as floats for Shaun's net and a large party went ashore at low tide to set it—as close to the Greenlanders' nets as we could manage without being accused of poaching. Having laid it out, moored it to two boulders, and fastened weights to the bottom, we watched the floats ride jauntily on the water as the tide began to make. For a few hours we had no more to do but lament the absence of green peas and new potatoes.

## MISCHIEF IN GREENLAND

Nevertheless, when the Greenlanders came to cadge flour we thought it only prudent to take some salmon in exchange. How wise we were. In our net there was not even a piece of seaweed while on the same tide the Greenlanders gathered their usual harvest of fish. Some of the salmon they salted down in barrels and some they smoked in a flue made of stones and sods. For fuel there was abundant dwarf willow and heath. They presented us with a smoked salmon, the most delicious thing we had eaten in Greenland. As well as fishing, the party were out after reindeer, or caribou. We saw fresh tracks and Shaun said he had actually seen one.

Having been away quite long enough we set out for Holsteinborg. In the afternoon when we were approaching Qagssit, the wind fair, the sea smooth, and visibility excellent, I decided to try the inner passage instead of taking the longer and safer way round. The tide setting strongly to the north took us near the shore, but in the fjords one becomes so accustomed to sailing within a stone's throw of the rocks that I thought we had room enough to weather a small projecting point. We weathered it all right though not in a very seamanlike fashion. We bumped once on a rock and slid off again before the panic party called up from below had had time to lower the mainsail. Now that spring tides were running our old berth was useless so we tied up by the shipyard quay with four boats inside us and our bowsprit almost tickling the rail of our old acquaintance *Mallemuken*. She was also waiting to go on the slip. She had discovered the whereabouts of a sunken rock by the infallible method of hitting it and had sustained considerable damage to her bottom plates. In fact the damage was beyond the ability of the yard to repair; she had to be patched up for returning to Denmark. Lying outside the harbour was the survey vessel we had met at Timerdlit. For her the working season was over and she was about to sail for Denmark to be laid up for the winter. That evening we went on board her where a large party had gathered. Her skipper showed me some extraordinary traces recorded by his echo-sounding machine; they resembled the greatly magnified teeth of a cross-cut saw. At one point the trace showed that the bottom rose from a depth of 300 metres to a depth of five metres in what was virtually a vertical line. He thought that with experience, by watching the configuration of the land, one could tell whether the

Camp below Mt. Raleigh

Mt. Raleigh from Totnes Roads, Exeter Sound

180 MISCHIEF IN GREENLAND

water would be deep or shallow; and that while it was generally safe to go between the coast and a string of islets, it was seldom safe to go between the islets themselves.

A British trawler came in that night to land two injured men and left early before we had time to visit her. A Portuguese trawler, too, lay outside with engine trouble; we were impressed by the smartness of the uniform her officers wore and by the behaviour of her men. An even more interesting visitor was the good ship *Umanak* with 40,000 bottles, or possibly cases, of beer. The news spread like wildfire and there were some ugly scenes at the General Store where we took care to be in good time to buy beer and also some fruit that she had brought. Except for lemons this was the only bit of fruit we had during the voyage.

Yet another arrival was the Portuguese hospital ship *Gil Eanes*. She carries six doctors, has the equipment to deal with any injury or illness, and is responsible for the health and well-being of the 6000-odd men in the Portuguese schooner and trawler fleets fishing on the Grand Banks and in Davis Strait. As well as taking off sick men from schooners in the open sea, she supplies them with fresh water, diesel oil, and galley coal. Having met one of her doctors, who said he had a Hull trawler man in his care, we went on board to see him and were shown all over her. The Hull man expected to be landed and flown home; he spoke highly of the skill and kindness of the Portuguese. She had several large wards, X-ray room, operating theatre with a lift down to it, and a large, competent staff. The *Gil Eanes* extends a helping hand to any sick or injured fisherman irrespective of nationality.

The *Mallemuken* was at length hauled out and behind her another small survey vessel which was to be laid up for the winter in the yard. On the first attempt, the stern of *Mallemuken* being in the way, the survey vessel could not be hauled high enough to move her sideways off the slip. So they let her down and put her on the cradle askew so that next time her bow came up clear of Mallemuken's stern. It was now our turn. The fact that *Mischief* had reclined on her side for a few hours in Isortok and had bumped on a rock on the way back, made us the more set on examining her hull. When she was hauled out that evening we were relieved to find that except for loss of paint her hull showed no sign of damage. This fact surprised both me and the crew, whose apprehensions, if they had had any, were thus set at rest. Quite a crowd gathered to see *Mischief* out of the water, the local boat-fanciers expressing admiration for her shapely, workmanlike lines.

By 9 a.m. we were back in the water and devoted the rest of the morning to shopping and to taking our last photographs before starting for Exeter Sound. There is one small building in Holsteinborg worthy of a photograph, a small, simple church with blue walls and red roof, with a golden weather-vane on its miniature steeple. It is reputed to be the original Moravian Mission church and has the date 1732 on the weather-vane. It has been superseded by a much bigger church and appeared now to be used as a sort of crèche. Outside it, in the form of an arch, are two enormous jawbones from a whale.

Until we were off Qagssit we had no wind, then with a nice breeze from south freshening all the time we went fast and bang on course. During the night, when I was on watch, I found we were encompassed by about a dozen trawlers. Trawlers at night, I always think, are as dangerous to meet as trams are to a motorist, for they follow an unswerving course. If any avoiding action is called for it is seldom taken by the trawler. At four o'clock I was roused by *Mischief*'s unusual motion, trembling all over like a weight-lifter making a prodigious effort. I found she was doing about 'twelve knots and a Chinaman' under whole mainsail and Genoa with a Force 6 wind. We usually take the Genoa in at night, for we do not like our sleep disturbed. Should one decide to leave it up, however tranquil the appearance of sky and sea, one can be fairly certain of having to turn out to take it down, such is the perversity of the weather at sea. We took it down and put two rolls in the mainsail. In the morning it was overcast, wet, and still blowing hard, and by midday we had reeled off 100 miles. That evening when we were only about sixty miles off Cape Dyer the weather thickened and we met several icebergs. The sea temperature went down to 36° F., twelve degrees lower than at Holsteinborg. At night the wind died, leaving us rolling heavily and surrounded by fog.

In the morning a fresh breeze dispersed the fog and we sailed fast all day in a rough sea until at 5 p.m. we once more sighted Cape Dyer. As we drew in towards the land south of the cape we smoothed our water and as yet there was no sign of any ice apart from a few scattered bergs. Our delight at finding the coast clear was no less than our astonishment that so much ice could vanish in so short a time. It was now

182 MISCHIEF IN GREENLAND

August 20th so that in a short three weeks the solid belt of ice along the coast had completely dispersed and disintegrated. Even with Cape Dyer as a point of reference we found the coast south of it puzzling, nor could we see any likely anchorage. When it became dark, as it did now by ten o'clock, we let her drift, the wind having died away.

The morning broke fine and sunny. It almost seemed that so close to the land or in the absence of ice the fog had no encouragement to form. Having identified Cape Walsingham to the south and the wide mouth of Exeter Sound before us, we sailed in. When the wind failed we motored for fifteen miles to Davis's Totnes Roads and to an anchorage off the mouth of a small valley. Three tall icebergs lay grounded half a mile from the shore. About three miles up the valley we could see a glacier and overlooking it the cliffs of what I had already assumed to be Mount Raleigh. Strong sunlight playing on the cliffs, as well as a little imagination, were needed to make them appear 'orient as gold'; but these were the only striking cliffs in view and from farther out in the fjord this mountain alone had filled the observer's eye.

After spreading the sails to dry we lost no time in setting foot on a shore that for so long had occupied most of our thoughts, a shore that so recently had seemed utterly unapproachable. We walked along to the mouth of the valley where the river fed by the glacier tumbled over a waterfall into the sea. A more barren, lifeless place it would be difficult to find. Yet in Davis's day there had been life enough, as witness the adventure his party had immediately they landed here:

> So soon as we were come to an anker in Totnes rode under Mount Raleigh we espied four white beares at the foot of the mount: we supposing them to be goats or wolves, manned our boats and went towards them; but when we came near the shore we found them to be white beares of a monstrous bignesse. We being desirous of fresh victuall and the sport began to assault them, and I being on land, one of them came downe the hill right against me: my piece was charged with hailshot and a bullet: I discharged my piece and shot him in the necke; he roared a little and tooke the water straight making small account of his hurt. Then we followed him with our boat and killed him with boare speares, and two more that night.

MOUNT RALEIGH                                                  183

The 7th we went on shore to another beare which lay all night upon an island under Mount Raleigh (this island was about a mile from our anchorage) and when we came up to him he lay fast asleep. Then I shot being charged with two bullets and strooke him in the head. Whereupon we all ran upon him with boare speares. The breadth of his forefoot from one side to the other was 14 inches. They were very fat, so as we were constrained to cast the fat away. We saw a raven upon Mt Raleigh. The coast is very mountainous, altogether without wood, grass, or earth, and is onely huge mountaines of stone; but the bravest stone that ever we saw. The aire was very moderate in this country.

The 8th we departed from Mount Raleigh, coasting along the shoare which lieth south-south-west and east-north-east.

We had with us a Canadian map of the area on a scale of 1: 500,000. There have been cases of 'explorers' of the present day penetrating into 'unknown' country and complaining that the maps were misleading. For obvious reasons the surveying of mountainous regions is not regarded as a matter of urgency and when it is at last done the survey need not be rigorous. For a region such as the Cumberland Peninsula, difficult to approach either by land or sea, uninhabited and apparently of no economic value, it is a wonder that there is any map at all. The map in question is therefore, as might be expected, not in a very advanced state; glaciers are shown, cliffs are marked, a few heights are given in round figures, and lakes, rivers, and the coast line are delineated with some degree of accuracy. The only named mountain is Mt Raleigh. No height is given and its position is marked with a very small dot. One felt that whoever put it there might have had doubts and half-hoped that it might be overlooked. However, there was no mistake about it for Roger, too, had a map on which the same dot appeared. What troubled us was to see that the Mt Raleigh of the map lay on the opposite side of the glacier to what we assumed to be Mt Raleigh. It looked as if we should have to climb both.

Roger and I overhauled our climbing gear with unexpected pleasure. When we had last stowed away boots, axes, rope, crampons, tent, and cooking-pots neither of us had confidently believed that we should need them again that summer. Accompanied by three of the crew we

Approaching the anchorage in Exeter Sound; Mt. Raleigh on right

Looking across to cliffs of Mt. Raleigh from cliffs of 'false' Raleigh

set out next morning to put a camp somewhere near the glacier. In spite of its cliffs Mt Raleigh did not appear to be formidable. From a point short of the glacier snout the cliffs could be avoided and the long summit ridge looked flat and featureless. We moved up the left bank of the stream over rough boulder-strewn slopes and presently came to a large lake. Skirting the shore of the lake we gained little height until we reached a steep rock dyke through which the stream had cut a gorge; above the dyke lay a smaller lake reaching almost to the glacier snout. We camped by the shore of the lake at a height of 400 feet. Surprisingly enough—for in most accounts of travel in the Canadian Arctic they are noticed with fervour—there were hardly any mosquitoes or black flies. The vegetation was sparse and the little there was seemed similar to that of West Greenland.

Leaving camp next morning at 8.45 we climbed the moderately steep slopes above it and gained the summit ridge at a height of 3000 feet. By then we were enveloped in cloud and snow fell gently but persistently. As we plodded along the broad ridge, sometimes on rock and sometimes on snow, with the cliffs falling steeply on our left, Roger, deceived by the bad visibility, surprised me by announcing that we had reached the summit. To me such news was very welcome but after years of climbing experience, with failures more numerous than successes, I regarded it with suspicion. We had still some way to go. We ate a remarkably joyless lunch sitting on a wet rock with our feet in the snow. At long length the ridge rose abruptly and we toiled up a wide stony glacis to what was undoubtedly the summit. The height by aneroid was 5700 feet. From here we should have looked out to the 'false' Mt Raleigh on the other side of the glacier but the cloud was now thicker than ever. Having built a massive cairn we started down.

Success must have gone to our heads. From the stony slope we got on to snow and after rattling along for half an hour we began to suspect that things were not as they ought to have been. When the ridge we were following narrowed and ended in a snow dome we realized we were all adrift. In spite of the falling snow our steps, which we now retraced, were fortunately still visible, and towards three o'clock we were relieved when our cairn loomed up out of the mist. This time, by keeping close to the edge of the cliffs on our right, we made no mistake. No mistake, at least, until we forsook the long certainty of

186                    MISCHIEF IN GREENLAND

the ridge to plunge down a steep gully which we thought would take us more swiftly home. The rock was steep and loose and the snow down which we had expected to glissade turned out to be hard ice. Twice I took a toss—for I was getting tired—cutting my hands and losing my axe which we found again only after a long search. We reached the tent at six o'clock. It had been raining in the valley so the inside of it was a bit wet; but we had climbed one Mt Raleigh and I went to sleep wondering whether I should have the strength to climb another one next day.

Our luck was in. The day broke fine, sunny, and windless. We went up the glacier. We wanted to explore it and we thought it likely that from the col at its head there would be a ridge leading on to the 'false' Mt Raleigh. A snow-ridge led down to the col from the mountain we had already climbed—in fact we had talked of descending by it—and we expected to find a similar ridge on the opposite side of the col though we could not see it from the camp. We found excellent going on the glacier and gained height quickly, the cliffs of the 'false' Mt Raleigh now in full view on our left and bearing a remarkable resemblance to the opposing cliffs. When we were at a height of about 1700 feet, still short of the col, we could see that the cliffs continued unbroken beyond the col and that the ridge we had expected to find did not exist. We were now almost directly below the summit of 'false' Mt Raleigh, so quitting the glacier we tackled the cliffs. These proved to be not nearly so steep as they appeared. Helped by some snow-gullies we climbed quickly and by lunch-time were only a thousand feet below the top. Lunch was far more enjoyable on that day as we sat on a sun-warmed rock, the glacier far below our feet, and confronted by the massive bulk of Mt Raleigh with cloud shadows drifting across its snow-sprinkled cliffs.

The snow of the previous day lay thick on the rocks but we were soon just under the summit which was guarded by a steep wall of ice. We outflanked this and walked over hard snow to the top. The height by aneroid was 5200 feet. The respective heights of the two mountains do not really matter, nevertheless we were pleased to find that what we took to be Davis's Mt Raleigh had the advantage by 500 feet. From the top, where we built another cairn, we could see over the whole tip of the Cumberland Peninsula, from Cape Walsingham to the south and

MOUNT RALEIGH                                          187

to a fjord to the west of Cape Dyer. From a mountaineer's point of view
this eastern extremity of the peninsula is uninviting, the mountains
uniformly rounded and uninteresting. Mt Raleigh itself, apart from its
southern face of cliffs, has not much character, and might be thought
hardly worthy of its illustrious name or of the great seaman-explorer
who named it. Nevertheless, it is a mountain that I for one shall always
hold dear. We got off our mountain by way of a long and easy glacier
which terminated at the lake on the opposite side to our camp. Walking round the muddy shore we were back at the tent by 5 p.m., our
mission accomplished. From his sack Roger produced another tin of
'Mandarin' oranges.

On the way down next morning Shaun met us below the gorge
and gave us the news. They had shot a duck but caught no fish. A fox
and an Arctic hare had been seen and a great number of caribou heads.
Shaun himself had a particularly fine specimen which had to be sawn
in half before we could find a home for it behind the engine. They had
found the remains of old Eskimo settlements and a couple of fairly
modern traps. At present the nearest Eskimo settlement is on Padlop-
ing Island forty miles north of Cape Dyer where in 1955 the population
was thirty-one. For supper that night we had stewed duck and a chocolate pudding fit for a glass case.

CHAPTER XVI

# HOMEWARD BOUND

WE HAD DONE WHAT WE SET OUT TO DO, our stores were getting low, and it was time to turn for home. Cape Farewell was nearly 800 miles away, a distance that we expected might take a couple of weeks in view of the variable winds and calms of the Davis Strait. Once to the east of the cape we looked forward confidently to being blown swiftly across the Atlantic by strong westerly winds. As well as being without the use of the chronometer watch, we no longer had the benefit of our wireless set, a valve having broken. Apart from being unable to get time signals, the lack of it hardly mattered. In some ways, I think, we were better without it. If one is going to be at sea for a few weeks in a sailing vessel one might as well do it properly and realize to the full the self-sufficiency of one's own small world by abstaining from communication with the shore or from news of whatever may be happening there. As Belloc well said: 'In venturing in sail upon strange coasts we are seeking first experiences. Trying to feel as felt the earlier man in a happier time. To see the world as they saw it.'

As for having the correct time to the nearest second I think we tended to make too much fuss. In mid-ocean it is nice to know where you are within some miles but I would not put it stronger than that. Ten, twenty, or thirty miles makes no difference out there; and to a watchful eye there are often signs indicative of the presence of land when yet a day's sail or more away, in time enough to begin taking appropriate precautions. Mick's watch was reputedly reliable. Before leaving the coast we checked it by taking a sight, working it out by the time of this watch, comparing the longitude so found with the known longitude, and thus finding the error of the watch. The rough rating of the watch was known and a few days later, in an attempt to check it, we took equal altitude sights either side of noon. That is to say one takes a sight about a quarter hour before noon and, without altering the sextant, takes the time when the sun is at the same altitude on its

## HOMEWARD BOUND

downward path after noon. The mean of these times should be apparent noon at the ship. It is rough and ready but provided the ship is nearly stationary there need not be a very large error. Lecky damns it as a method 'very alluring to people who either suffer from want of energy, or have been insufficiently grounded in first principles'. We need not have bothered. On board there was a small transistor set of Shaun's which as soon as we got within 500 miles of home waters would give us time signals, the news, or any other unpleasantness we might want to hear. Slocum, by the way, sailed round the world, making very exact landfalls, with no more elaborate timepiece than an alarm clock which he got cheap for a dollar because it had only one hand. He had to boil it, too, before it went to his satisfaction. But Slocum was reputedly highly skilled in the working of what were called 'Lunars', a method of finding the longitude without benefit of a chronometer by taking altitudes of sun and moon and the angle between the two bodies.

We sailed out of Exeter Sound on August 26th, a wonderfully fine, clear day and very cold. The sea temperature was 39° F. and the air 40° F. From a long way out to sea Mt Raleigh stood out boldly from among its neighbours like a true mountain. We had little if any doubt left that this is Davis's mountain and that the map is in error. That night and for the next fortnight, whenever the sky was clear, we observed magnificent auroral displays. The last faint occurrence we noted was when we were in as low a latitude as 52° N. On account of the name Northern Lights one imagines them always to be looked for in the northern sky; now, when we first saw them, owing to our own northern latitude, they appeared in the southern sky. On several occasions when for half an hour or so, generally before midnight, the display was at its maximum intensity, the sight was so extraordinary that the man on watch took the undoubted risk of waking up the crew to look at it. Usually a faint curtain or glow would be visible throughout the hours of darkness, but very often round about midnight the smouldering glow would flare up, brilliant bands of pale green light stabbing the zenith or forming a bright, shimmering arch across the sky. The displays were certainly brighter, more prolonged, and more frequent than any we had seen the previous voyage.

We made a mistake in being too intent upon getting to the east rather than the south, for on the fifth day out we found ourselves once

190 MISCHIEF IN GREENLAND

more approaching the Greenland coast north of Cape Farewell. It was a day of fog and the wind was such that when we were at last forced to put about we could do no better than steer a little south of west. Just before dark we sighted an iceberg, a peril that had to be taken more seriously now that the nights were really dark. The nights were long too; three times on the way home we advanced the ship's time by an hour in order to finish our supper in daylight or at the worst by dusk. There were limits to this useful expedient or we should have found ourselves having breakfast in the dark. We had stupidly run out of petrol for the charging engine, the battery was flat, and we had only six slow-burning carriage candles for lighting both the cabin and the galley for the rest of the voyage. Roger Brown had by now taken over the galley. He brought to it some fresh ideas and managed very well in spite of having to cook in semi-darkness and with the scantier ingredients of a depleted larder.

We fully realized we had made a mistake by allowing ourselves to be pushed so far eastwards when we met with the adverse Greenland current and re-entered waters where there were still enough icebergs about to give us some anxious nights. We got our first fair wind when we were in the latitude of the cape but still 100 miles west of it. We were doing six knots, we had sighted an iceberg at dusk, and in my watch from two to four, when visibility was remarkably bad, I was at times on the point of shortening sail or even heaving-to. The thought that icebergs were few and the sea very wide was reinforced by the urge of not wasting a fair wind. In the twenty-four hours we ran 123 miles, the best day we were to have until coming up Channel. A lurid red dawn ushered in a day of drizzling rain. We were still too near the land for comfort and had to gybe and steer south in order to give Cape Farewell a wide enough berth. We were twelve days out when we finally passed the longitude of the cape, and were 140 miles south of it when we saw our last iceberg. Hereabouts we fell in with a large school of pilot whales, ponderous creatures about twenty feet long which played round the ship as nimbly as porpoises for several hours. Those of us who had any film left wasted it prodigally on this unusual sight. Among the school were a great many babies. While the elders surfaced with a slow and dignified whoosh, the little chap following hard behind came out of the water like a cork out of a bottle.

Pilot whales off Cape Farewell

Holsteinborg—original Moravian church *circa* 1732

192          MISCHIEF IN GREENLAND

The brave westerlies we had so confidently hoped for failed us almost entirely. A rousing blow from north-east, when for twenty-four hours we were close reefed, was merely the prelude to a long spell of light easterly winds, a spell that with one brief break continued until we were off the Irish coast. A vast anti-cyclonic system seemed to have spread over the North Atlantic. Had we been in the tropics the barograph could hardly have traced a straighter line, or the weather remained so damnably settled. As one warm, sunny day of light contrary winds succeeded another we grew first ungrateful and then cross. It was strange to have the crew eagerly watching the barometer in the hope that it would fall. Some entries in my diary show what it was like:

Sept. 11th. Fine morning, wind still NE. Quite maddening having to sail SE or south instead of east.

Sept. 12th. Bad windless night with boom slamming. Very fine and warm. Bathed. Sea temperature 52° F. Barometer 30.2. Strange that we should be longing for a fall. Portuguese trawler with two headsails up going east very slowly. Faster than us, however.

Sept. 13th. Very light wind at night, only 9 miles done. Weak aurora: Barometer high and steady. Cut out porridge to conserve water not knowing how long this weather may last. Another Portuguese trawler with stacks of dories on deck. Masts had a cluster of short yards (for launching dories?).

Sept. 14th. No wind in night. Glassy calm at 2 a.m. Motored for 5 hours. Wind from WNW later but veering.

Sept 15th. Wind east again. Wonderful fine weather. Last night full moon, cloudless sky, flat sea. About 850 miles to Bishop Rock. Shaun began to get time signals on his transistor set. Mick's watch 1 minute 30 seconds slow. Quite a big error for 20 days. More wind at night but doing no better than south.

Sept. 16th. Wind very fresh from east and sea rough. Steering west of south so hove-to on port tack. Remained hove-to all night rather than lose easting.

HOMEWARD BOUND

Sept. 17th. Sky overcast. Wind force 5 to 6, reached 7 at times during the night. Sea very rough and an occasional douche through skylight. Glass falling. Maddening not being able to sail, and drifting to west. Drizzle with wind veering south-east and falling. Fried rice and sausage.

I suppose that when homeward bound any delay is particularly irksome to the crew, although we ourselves, with no wives and families waiting expectantly, had no good reason for haste. Perhaps a week of easterly winds in September in the North Atlantic outraged our sense of the rule of right and the eternal fitness of things. In a sailing vessel patience is very necessary but patience, as Dr Johnson observed, is a virtue easily fatigued by exercise. Our five months at sea had not been long enough to rid us of the urge to save time, an urge that seems to be the inevitable curse of a mechanical age whether men are on the road or at sea. In the old days of sail they spent days or weeks at anchor waiting for a fair wind or lying helplessly becalmed and accepted it as part of the game. It was a case of 'It is inevitable, therefore it can be approved,' as Lord Curzon used to say. For all that, I find it hard to believe that such delays were submitted to cheerfully with neither grumbling nor complaint. John Davis, for example, with no least hint of the annoyance he must have felt, merely states that on his first voyage he had to shelter in Falmouth for five days and wait twelve days in the Scillies for a fair wind; and that on a later voyage to the Magellan Straits they lay becalmed on the line for twenty-seven days. It is, I think, fair comment that in accounts of early voyages—in Hakluyt's *Voyages*, for example—too little is said about the long haul across the ocean. The bare facts are stated and no more. For the early voyagers the ocean crossing, whether of the North or South Atlantic, or of the Pacific, was merely a means to an end, an unavoidable necessity hardly worth recording; the detailed description of how the ships fared and what the voyagers felt, and thought, and saw, begins only when they reach another continent or fall upon some strange coast. Whereas nowadays, partly because accounts of voyages are mostly written by amateur sailors and because there are no longer unknown continents or strange coasts, the voyage itself is the end, the ocean crossing is the only romantic part of the enterprise, and

194    MISCHIEF IN GREENLAND

the behaviour of the ship and the reactions of the crew make up the whole of the story.

After we had made a little more westing Shaun's transistor set was able to pick up the shipping forecasts. We were still a few hundred miles west of the westernmost areas of Sole and Shannon which the forecasts embrace, but on the fragile basis of the weather prevailing hundreds of miles away to the east our two meteorologists, Roger Tufft and Roger Brown, began compiling synoptic charts. By this means they endeavoured to explain to us our predicament. The data, of course, was slender, but from the little there was we got no comfort. However, on the 19th and 20th the anti-cyclone weakened its grip. We enjoyed two days of north-westerly winds accompanied by rain in which we knocked off 200 miles and an additional bonus of fourteen miles from a current. The sea temperature suddenly rose to 59° F. The wind then flew round to south-east, the barometer climbed to 30.4, and we learnt that another anti-cyclone lay centred over the Irish Sea. Meanwhile everything but the voyage seemed to be coming to an end—no jam, marmalade, coffee, dates, raisins, egg powder, or chocolate. In another momentary panic, for fear of a water shortage, we again knocked off porridge.

Before leaving Exeter Sound we had made a book on the number of days the passage would take. Whoever had taken the shortest number of twenty-eight days was already out of the running, and we began to fear that even the longest guess of thirty-six days would be badly out. But at last, on September 24th, when we were fifty miles south-west of the Fastnet Rock, a spell of thick, westerly weather set in and blew us home in five days at the rate of 100 miles a day. Passing Round Island, our first landfall, on the evening of the 26th, we had a fast run up-Channel to the Start, scattering in our wake quantities of old clothes, tins, and junk as we hastily began clearing up below. On the way over we had sighted no ships but the two Portuguese trawlers and had not been able to report our whereabouts. Better late than never; so when passing Prawle Point, where there is a signal station, we called them up with our lamp but got no response.

Our last night at sea was stormy. The wind backed to southeast and freshened to Force 7. It was raining hard and no shore lights were visible. Sailing as we were, reefed down and close-hauled in a rough sea, I feared that what with leeway and current we might in the course of the night find ourselves caught up in the Portland Race. We held on, sailing as close as we could to the wind, and at midnight were reassured when a small coaster passed close inside us. Between rain squalls at dawn we were lucky enough to get a brief glimpse of Anvil Point light while it was still lit. Taking a bearing and roughly guessing our distance off we set a course for the Needles. Although the wind had taken off, the weather was thicker than before. By nine o'clock we had seen nothing. An ocean-going tug came suddenly out of the murk astern and passed us close on a more southerly course. If he was bound for the Needles Channel, I thought, we must be wrong. Just before we lost sight of him however he altered course and a minute later we, too, saw dead ahead of us a pillar buoy—the Fairway buoy for the Needles Channel. Soon after, the Needles themselves loomed up through the rain. With a strong tide under us we entered Lymington river and by ten-thirty of a miserably wet morning the voyage was over.

It had taken us thirty-four days, only a day better than Davis's ships *Sunneshine* of fifty tons and *Mooneshine* of thirty-five tons, which returned to Dartmouth from Exeter Sound in thirty-five days. In his day almost every voyage undertaken had been a romantic adventure. As we read the accounts of them they distil for us the essence of romance—the gay pursuit of a perilous quest. In more humdrum times, by following in the track of John Davis, we had sought and at times slightly savoured this elusive essence.

APPENDIX I

# John Davis

JOHN DAVIS WAS BORN AT SANDRIDGE between Totnes and Dartmouth in about 1550. In the same neighbourhood was the home of John and Humphrey Gilbert, some years older than Davis, and of their younger brother Adrian who was about the same age. The half-brothers Carew and Walter Raleigh also lived there and were younger than Davis. All these must have been known to each other as boys and Adrian Gilbert and Walter Raleigh were life-long friends of Davis. Davis must have gone to sea early for he is not heard of again until 1579 when he was already a sea captain of known conduct and sufficiently prosperous to marry a Faith Fulford in 1582.

In 1576 Sir Humphrey Gilbert published his famous *Discourse* concerning the North-west Passage, adducing arguments in its favour which seem fantastic to us now but were no doubt convincing enough at the time. Davis had certainly studied this *Discourse*, and the loss of the little *Squirrel* with Humphrey Gilbert and his company must have made a deep impression coming so soon after the penning of the famous words with which the *Discourse* ends. These words have been quoted in a previous chapter. No doubt they inspired Davis to do and to dare, as they inspired lesser men.

Adrian Gilbert and Davis were already deep in plans for a northern voyage and in 1584 Sir Walter Raleigh (now knighted) persuaded the Queen to grant a charter in the names of himself, Adrian Gilbert, and John Davis for the search and discovery of a North-west Passage to China. Raleigh, too, induced William Sanderson, a wealthy London merchant married to a niece of Raleigh's, to back the venture. On this first voyage in 1585 Davis, as we have seen, after making his landfall at Cape Desolation, thus re-discovering Greenland, anchored in Godthaab fjord which he called Gilbert's Sound. There he had friendly meetings with the Eskimos. He then crossed his Strait to anchor in Exeter Sound, discovering and naming Capes Dyer and Walsingham,

# JOHN DAVIS

and finally explored Cumberland Sound in the belief that this might be the much sought North-west Passage.

In 1586 he sailed again with *Sunneshine* and *Mooneshine* as before, and *Mermaid*, a larger vessel of 120 tons. He landed first at old Sukkertoppen. Having crossed the Strait he again explored Cumberland Sound, satisfying himself that it was not a strait. Sailing south he passed the mouth of Hudson Strait and explored the Labrador coast whence he returned home bringing with him some salt cod and 500 sealskins.

On his third voyage in 1587, still backed whole-heartedly by Sanderson, he had the old *Sunneshine*, another vessel *Elizabeth*, and a clinker-built pinnace *Helen* of only twenty tons. Having reached once more Gilbert Sound, Davis made a decision which shows us his inflexible determination. He owed it to his backers to make this voyage pay, so he dispatched his two bigger ships to fish the Grand Banks while he pushed north in the barely seaworthy *Helen*. He went as far as 72° 12′ north, to the great cliff he named 'Sanderson his Hope', seeing 'no ice towards the north, but a great sea, free, large, very salt and blue, and of an unsearchable depth'. A north wind drove them westwards until they encountered the 'middle pack' and were once more forced south to Cumberland Sound. Continuing south down the coast, off Hudson Strait they met with 'a mighty race, where an island of ice was carried by the force of the current as fast as our bark could sail'. On this voyage Davis had charted long stretches of coast on both sides of his Strait and much of the Labrador coast. Summing up these three voyages his biographer, Sir Clements Markham, wrote:

> Davis converted the Arctic regions from a confused myth into a defined area. He not only described and mapped the extensive tract explored by himself, but he clearly pointed out the work cut out for his successors. He lighted Hudson into his strait. He lighted Baffin into his Bay. He lighted Hans Egede to the scene of his Greenland labours.

During the three following years Davis like all other seamen was engaged in the war against Spain. His command against the Armada seems disproportionate to his ability and experience, a vessel of twenty

198          MISCHIEF IN GREENLAND

tons called *Black Dog* which acted as tender to the Lord Admiral in *Ark Royal*. She had a crew of ten men and an armament of three sakers. In those days, as in more recent times, interest and high connexions probably weighed more heavily than merit. With the Armada defeated, Davis himself fitted out a ship called *Drake* and joined the Earl of Cumberland's squadron, then cruising off the Azores for prizes and plunder. The squadron captured thirteen prizes. Davis continued this cruising until 1591, harassing the Queen's enemy, destroying his commerce, and profiting to a modest extent on his own account.

In fact as a result of these activities he was in a position to fit out an expedition more to his liking, nothing less than the passage of the Magellan Straits with a view to discovering the North-west Passage from the Pacific side. Unfortunately he was persuaded to join forces with Cavendish, the man who had completed in 1588 the third navigation of the globe. They sailed in 1591, the squadron comprising *Leicester*, *Roebuck*, *Desire* (in which Cavendish had sailed round the world), and *Dainty* owned jointly by Adrian Gilbert and Davis. Davis also contributed a large sum of money and at the pressing request of Cavendish took command of *Desire* instead of his own ship *Dainty*. The venture ended in disaster for all concerned.

Having reached the Straits in April 1592 Cavendish, discouraged by the cold and by continuous gales, proposed continuing the voyage by way of the Cape of Good Hope. When no one would agree to this he decided to return to Brazil to refresh before making a second attempt. After leaving the Straits the fleet got separated. Davis supposing they had gone to Port Desire, the usual rendezvous, went there to wait for them. Cavendish, in fact, with *Leicester* and *Roebuck*, had gone straight to Brazil and thence to England, he himself dying on the way. By August, when he had refitted as best he could, Davis, concluding that Cavendish had already returned to the Straits without calling at Port Desire, set out a second time to join him there. On the way he discovered what are now the Falkland Islands. After many buffetings, and having already been twice driven back, the *Desire* on October 9th passed into the Pacific. But a furious gale broke, sank their consort the little *Black Pinnace*, and drove them back again. By consummate seamanship *Desire* just managed to weather Cape Pillar and by the end of October they once more reached Port Desire. After refitting, they revictualled the ship for the voyage home with 14,000 dried and salted penguins, and sailed on December 22nd. The meat had been imperfectly dried, and soon a loathsome worm infested the whole ship—'there was nothing they did not devour, only iron excepted'. Scurvy broke out and when the noisome, worm-ridden *Desire* struggled into Berehaven in June 1593 only sixteen of the crew remained alive and of these only five could stand.

Davis had lost £1100 in this venture and returned a ruined and disappointed man to find that his wife, by whom he had had four children, had deserted him. He returned to his patrimony at Sandridge where he lived with his children and where he spent the next two years writing his *Seaman's Secrets*, dedicated to Lord Howard of Effingham and published in 1594: 'A brief account of such practices, as in my several voyages, I have from experience collected; those things that are needfully required in a sufficient seaman; because by certain questions demanded and answered I have not omitted anything that appertaineth to the secrets of navigation, whereby if there may grow any increase of knowledge or ease in practice it is the thing which I chiefly desire.' He also perfected at about this time the 'back-staff' or 'Davis Quadrant', an instrument that was a great improvement on the cross-staff and came into general use. And in 1595, harking back to his earlier voyages, he published an appeal to the Privy Council to show that 'there is from England a short and speedy passage to India by northerly navigation'.

In 1598 he sailed as chief pilot in a Dutch expedition to the East Indies. At Sumatra the two ships *Lion* and *Lioness* were nearly seized by treachery on the part of the Sultan, treachery largely averted by Davis who after a desperate fight on the poop of *Lion* finally drove the Malays out of the ship. Some sixty-four Dutch sailors were killed including one of the captains. The ships returned in July 1600.

In 1601 he sailed again as chief pilot on the first voyage made by the newly formed East India Company with a fleet of five ships commanded by James Lancaster in *Red Dragon*. Davis sailed in this ship and for his services he was to receive £500 if the voyage yielded two for one, £1000 if three for one, and £2000 if five for one. After a hazardous and adventurous voyage the ships returned home in 1603 laden with pepper and spices.

Davis remained a year at home before sailing on his last voyage. It had been a sad home-coming. The great Queen was dead. Adrian Gilbert, his half-brother and life-long friend, had died, and Sir Walter Raleigh, another constant friend, was already in confinement. He prepared a second edition of his *Seaman's Secrets* and before sailing became engaged to a Judith Havard, the marriage to be deferred until his return. He made a will by which his estate was to be divided between his children and his betrothed.

He went as chief pilot in a private venture to the East Indies undertaken by Sir Edward Michelborne with the ships *Tiger* of 240 tons and *Tiger's Whelp*, a pinnace. For Davis the voyage ended on the east coast of Malaya where the *Tiger* fell in with a Japanese junk, or rather a captured junk in the hands of ninety Japanese pirates. They lay alongside each other apparently on friendly terms, Michelborne hoping to obtain information regarding trade with China and the pirates resolving to seize the *Tiger* or die in the attempt, for their junk was unseaworthy. At sunset the storm broke. All the Englishmen who were in the junk at the time were killed and in the course of a fierce fight on the *Tiger* Davis met his death on December 27th, 1605. Michelborne and his men finally overcame the pirates and Davis was buried at sea near the island of Bintang.

In his life John Davis had shown himself to be a thorough seaman, a scientific observer, an admirable organizer, loyal and faithful to his men, his friends, and his employers, and above all a man of daring enterprise. He fought in war against the Spaniards and in peace against treachery and pirates. His character is thus summed up by Sir Clements Markham:

No part of his fame rests on his war services. He was essentially a man of peace. It was by the calm and collected way in which he faced, and encouraged others to face, the most terrible hardships and sufferings; by his ever-ready presence of mind and consummate seamanship in moments of danger, that he showed the stuff he was made of. The enemies against which he made war were the ice of the frigid zone, the storms of the far south, the pestilence of the tropics, and the evil designs of false companions. It was the mission of his life to study the forces of nature, and to mould and direct them for the good of his Queen and countrymen. If, as regards worldly success and his own fortunes, the life of Davis was, in some sort, a failure, in all that is worth living for, in valuable public services well performed, and in the acquisition of immortal fame, it was a success. With all his faults, John Davis, the great discoverer and scientific seaman, the consummate pilot, takes rank among the foremost sea-worthies of the glorious reign of Queen Elizabeth.

APPENDIX II

# Bird Migration in the North Atlantic

*Extracted from Shaun White's log*

| Wilson's Petrel | N Atlantic (16-19°W) | May | 1 |
| | | Sep | over 1000 |
| Leach's Petrel | N Atlantic (16-19°W) | Sep | 4 |
| Storm Petrel | N Atlantic (16-19°W) | May | 23 |
| | | Sep | 116 |
| Manx Shearwater | English Channel | May | 300 |
| | Atlantic | May | 10 |
| Great Shearwater | N Atlantic | May | 700 |
| | Davis Strait | May | 1500 |
| | N Atlantic | Sept | 1000's |
| Sooty Shearwater | N Atlantic | Sept | 70 |
| Harlequin | Davis Strait | July | 1 |
| King Eider | W Coast Greenland | Jun-Jul | 22 |
| White-fronted Goose | Isortok fjord | Aug | 21 |
| | Baffin Island | Aug | 10 |
| | N Atlantic | Sept | Heard calling at night |
| Sea Eagle | Evighedsfjord | July | 2 |
| | Holsteinborg | Aug | 1 |
| | Davis Strait | Aug | 1 |
| Gyr Falcon | N Atlantic | Jun | 1 |
| Turnstone | off Baffin Island | Aug | 2 on board |
| | N Atlantic | Sep | 100 |
| | off Fastnet | Sep | 2 |

## BIRD MIGRATION IN THE NORTH ATLANTIC

| Curlew | off Baffin Island | Aug | 2 flying, heard calling at night |
|---|---|---|---|
| Purple Sandpiper | Davis Strait | Jul | 22 |
| | N Atlantic | Sep | 5 |
| White-rumped Sandpiper | Exeter Sound | Aug | Many on shore |
| | Davis Strait | Aug | 22 |
| | N Atlantic | Sep | 1 tried to land |
| Sanderling | Exeter Sound | Aug | Many on shore |
| | Davis Strait | Aug | 1000's flying south |
| Grey Phalarope | Davis Strait | Aug | 1000's flying south |
| Red-necked Phalarope | Davis Strait | Aug | 140 flying south |
| | N Atlantic | Sep | 380 |
| Arctic Skua | N Atlantic | May | 6 |
| | Davis Strait | Jul | 2500 |
| | N Atlantic | Sep | 750 flying east |
| Great Skua | N Atlantic | Sep | 8 |
| | Channel Approaches | Sep | 10 |
| Pomarine Skua | N Atlantic | May | 25 |
| | Channel Approaches | Jun | 140 |
| Long-tailed Skua | N Atlantic | May | 20 |
| | Davis Strait | Jun | 2000 |
| Great Black-backed Gull | N Atlantic | Jun | 1 |
| | Davis Strait | Jul | 1 |
| | N Atlantic | Sep | 2 |
| Kittiwake | Davis Strait | Jul | 2500 southwards |
| | N Atlantic | Sep | 1100 eastwards |
| Arctic Tern | N Atlantic | May | 220 northwards |
| | Davis Strait | Aug | 40 southwards |
| | N Atlantic | Sep | 500 southwards |

| Brünnich's Guillemot | Cape Farewell | Jun | 200 |
|---|---|---|---|
| | Exter Sound | Aug | 300 |
| | off Baffin Island | Aug | 1000's on the sea |
| Puffin | Cape Farewell | Jun | 2 |
| | Baffin Island | Aug | 200 southwards |
| | N Atlantic | Sep | 15 |
| Greenland Wheatear | Davis Strait | Jul | 5 southwards |
| | N Atlantic | Sep | 2 on board (ringed) |
| American Water Pipit | Davis Strait | Aug | 12 southwards |
| Redpoll | N Atlantic | Sep | 12 flying SE |
| Lapland Bunting | Davis Strait | Sep | 18 southwards |
| | N Atlantic | Sep | 16 southwards |
| Snow Bunting | N Atlantic | Jun | 6 northwards |
| | Davis Strait | Aug | 20 flying SE |
| | N Atlantic | Sep | 32 flying SE |

APPENDIX III

# Zoology in the Arctic

## *M. G. Rhodes*

'THE COAST IS VERY MOUNTAINOUS, altogether without wood, grass or earth and is onely huge mountaines of stone.' Even though John Davis is exaggerating in his description of Exeter Sound he is no less accurate than the popular idea of snow, ice, and polar bears. In the Arctic a system of many animals and plants has arisen, based on the short summers. In the winters the animals that can migrate do so: in the summers the plants must cram a complete year's growth into a few weeks.

Early in the reading-up stage, well before *Mischief* sailed, I realized that I would have to be discerning, to specialize, that I could not haphazardly and magpie-like collect creatures from all the groups of animals. I must choose a limited field and concentrate on that. Very late in the reading-up stage I still had not chosen. My own particular field was no help, for we were not going to be in one place long enough to do any ecological work, to look at the relationship between one creature and another or between the creatures and the land they lived in. Even less was I going to be able to do any experimental ecology, to interfere with either the creatures or the country and watch the effect. No, the only thing to do was to collect, and to collect preferably in a way that had not been used before and to concentrate on creatures that had been ignored before.

At about the time of the First World War, an Italian called Antonio Berlese with long drooping whiskers, made a piece of apparatus with which he was able to collect some of the smaller insects and mites living in hundreds in the soil. The principle of the device was that the creatures were encouraged to walk out of their turf or soil by slowly drying it from above. As the animals in the upper surface found the climate too dry they moved down; this dried; they moved lower; this

205

206  MISCHIEF IN GREENLAND

dried lower still until eventually they fell out from the bottom of the turf into a funnel and were collected in a jar beneath. In this way a handful of moss, leaves and earth might produce several hundred creatures of many different kinds. At about the time of the Second World War Dr J. T. Salmon designed a very convenient collapsible field model of Berlese's apparatus. It was robust and acted very quickly, rapid drying being achieved by a tank of boiling water, and yet it collapsed into a small bag. With the aid of one of these extractors borrowed from the British Museum I decided to collect what I could of the Collembolans and soil mites. Very few samples of soil from Baffinland had been extracted by Berlese's method, even though Greenland had been well covered. Moreover, these creatures are small and therefore easily stored once collected. They need no complicated preserving, being quite happy almost indefinitely in a tube of 70 per cent alcohol.

Collembolans, commonly called 'springtails', are small wingless insects, the largest being only a few millimetres long, while the smallest can barely be seen without a lens. Looking a little like tiny, malformed earwigs they can be seen on the underside of most stones as small white creatures that jump when disturbed. It is by this jumping escape mechanism that they earned their popular name. It is produced by the sudden contraction of the muscles of an organ called the furcula, a forked limb on the underside of the body near the tail end. Normally it is tucked close to the creature's underside, pointing forwards and held in place by a small catch-like 'hamula', but, as danger approaches, the catch is undone and the muscles contract, pulling the furcula hard downwards and backwards against the ground and propelling the Collembolan upwards and forwards out of peril. The soil mites, like the springtails, are small and not usually seen unless looked for carefully. Many mites, close relatives of the ticks, have become parasitic, taking their food from another living animal. The soil mites, however, are free-living, foraging for vegetable and fungal food. They are plump, slow-moving creatures, generally brown in colour. With eight legs and no wings they are more closely related to the spiders than to the insects.

It was these fellows, the springtails and the soil mites, that I would collect. They have an increased ecological importance in arctic areas for it is they that aerate and turn over the soil in the way that earthworms do in warmer places, for there are no earthworms in Greenland or Baffin. Also, a study of them may indicate the origins of the animals of Greenland; whether they came from Europe or North America. Such relatively immobile creatures as these cannot cross oceans as birds do. To colonize one area from another will take a long time and can probably only take place over land. A study of the distribution of the various species over several countries may indicate which areas have been joined by land bridges in the past. For example, there are about forty-six species of Collembolans found in Greenland, of which over half occur in America and Europe as well, a further quarter are common to Greenland and Europe but not to America, while one tenth of the forty-six are found in Greenland and America but not in Europe. The explanation of this is probably that once all three countries were connected as one single land mass with the same species occurring over the whole area. It is these species, having survived the various ice-ages, that now provide over half Greenland's Collembolans. But what of the other half? Possibly the American species entered Greenland via the Canadian Islands and Ellesmere Island during the last interglacial period, the warm time about a million years ago between the two most recent ice-ages, or in the postglacial period afterwards. However, there is no such simple explanation for the fantastic journey that the European species have made. Perhaps the solution may lie in the further study of the species of Greenland and Baffin?

Thus, equipped with a little background knowledge of the creatures and the extractor, I gathered polythene bags of earth, moss and litter from the various parts of Greenland and Canada that we visited. A large part of the spare bunk in the galley was annexed from an angry cook and the collapsible 'Berlese' put together. I primed it with boiling water and lit its own internal heating lamp. Over the next six hours the heat slowly dried out the damp litter and earth, so forcing the creatures to drop into a small tube of alcohol beneath. When no more creatures were left to drive out and the soil was at its driest and crumbliest the cook had his revenge. A gentle jolt was sufficient to fill the tube with soil above the collection of mites. Just how to keep the rest of the crew from jarring the nearly dried litter was to be an ever-recurring problem. It was finally solved by starting extractions just before turning in at night and stopping them in that haze between bunk and breakfast before anybody moved fast enough to jar anything. Each extraction, and about forty samples were extracted, produced fifty or more creatures. Some two thousand animals stored in forty small glass coffins of alcohol in two tobacco tins! Apart from the usual mites and springtails other creatures sometimes appeared: once a spider and once some long white grubs, flea larvae, from a deserted lapland bunting's nest.

However, these are creatures of academic interest. Of much greater human importance are the mosquitoes. They plague the Arctic, sometimes causing workers outdoors to wear face veils and the walker to contemplate jumping into the nearest stream to rid himself of the pests.

'Man survives the polar winter by protecting himself from frost, the summer only by anti-mosquito measures,' said somebody. Someone else remarked, 'The rapidity with which a susceptible person can become worked up into an emotional state bordering on dementia... has to be seen to be believed.' One tends to couple mentally mosquitoes with heat, jungle and malaria but the Arctic has many more than the tropics, although they do not act as carriers of disease. Unlike the Collembolans, the mosquitoes are some of the most highly evolved of the insects. They are classified in the most advanced order of the insects, the Dipterans, which includes all the two-winged insects as opposed to the four-winged such as the bees, moths, beetles, and so on. In the Dipterans the hind pair of wings has been modified through evolution into a small pair of arms bearing knobs at their ends, the 'halteres'. In flight these 'arms' beat up and down extremely fast, sufficiently so for them to act in the same way as the wheel spinning in a gyroscopic compass and to resist any effort to alter the plane in which they are moving. Thus, when the insect turns right or left, up or down, or is thrown off course by a gust of wind, sufficient forces are set up to excite sensory cells at the base of the halteres and so to relay information to the insect's brain.

In addition to the mosquitoes there is another even more tiresome group of flies common in the Arctic, the blackflies or Simulids. They are again Dipterans but smaller and more heavily built than the mosquitoes; they rest with their wings folded over their backs in a typical delta shape, or walk over their victim on three pairs of legs banded as black and white as zebra crossings.

## ZOOLOGY IN THE ARCTIC

Both mosquitoes and blackflies are blood feeders, driving sharp tube-like mouth parts into the victim to draw up a meal. Exactly what causes the discomfort of the bite is not known but it is probably either a toxin produced in the salivary gland of the insect, or alternatively an enzyme produced by fungi or yeasts that live inside pouches of the creature's oesophagus. Conditions are such in parts of Northern Canada that an arm exposed from wrist to elbow may be bitten two hundred and eighty times in one minute. Be it toxin or enzyme, it is extremely uncomfortable and may even be serious. Eyelids swell and ears thicken after mosquitoes have been about. On the worst afternoons clouds of flies hovered about us in sufficient quantities to find their way constantly into eyes and ears. The blackflies are more persistent than the mosquitoes: they creep inside cuff and collar until reduced angrily to a blood-stained smudge. Smearing insect repellent over face, neck and hands gave us a reasonable degree of protection but the only complete defence was the mental immunity produced by a philosophical attitude.

The life cycle of the mosquito is divided into four stages: the female lays her eggs on or near the surface of some suitable water, probably one of the boggy pools with which the tundra is covered. From these hatch the larvae that can be seen wiggling down from the surface of any water-butt during an English summer. As a rule they feed on minute algae in the water and breathe through a respiratory tube in their tails by which they hang from the surface. The third stage is the pupae, a large-headed, small-bodied creature that can jerk about in the water and from which emerges the adult mosquito. It has been normally accepted that this newly emerged mosquito must have a blood meal to provide her with a source of protein before her eggs will successfully develop. It seems quite impossible to the casual visitor in the Arctic that more than a small percentage of mosquitoes can ever achieve such a meal: there are just not enough animals to satisfy the needs of all of them. Yet the mosquitoes obviously do lay many fully developed eggs. However, there is evidence that the mosquitoes visit flowers for either nectar or pollen, and pollen is an extremely rich source of protein. It has also been shown that sometimes the wing muscles of female mosquitoes bearing fully developed eggs have been reabsorbed by the creatures, perhaps to provide the protein necessary for the development of their eggs.

AFTERWORD

# Bill Tilman: An Inspiration

## *Annie Hill*

FOR ANYONE WHO HAS READ about H. W. Tilman, he might seem an unlikely inspiration for a young feminist and pacifist. Admittedly, I was given *Mischief in Patagonia* to read by someone who admired him without reservation, but I have read other books, equally recommended, without acquiring a life-long hero.

Bill Tilman, as I always think of him, appealed to me at many levels. I am an avid reader and believe that people often give away more in their writing than they do face to face. My father brought me up to appreciate understatement and dry humour; indeed, my family had the rather unhappy conviction that to state a satisfaction in one's own successes meant that one was 'big-headed'. Self-deprecating comments were the order of the day. So when I read Tilman's writing, I understood that it was impossible for him openly to communicate his pride and pleasure in his undertakings; one had to read between the lines.

I have owned (and lost) all of his sailing books over the years and also read the mountaineering/travel ones with great pleasure, despite neither having climbed a mountain nor been to many of the places he writes about. The climbing books give a more positive picture of his companions, leading me to the conclusion that he was happier being part of a team. Perhaps the role of leader necessarily separated him from his shipmates, particularly when they were a lot younger than he. After all, Tilman took up sailing when most people would have been considering settling down in their armchair, slippered feet on a footstool, to watch endless sport on the television.

I've read most of the sailing books several times; his predictable quotes and repeated aphorisms can sometimes irritate, but we all have our ways of deflecting questions or criticism. Re-reading the books seemed to give me more insight into the man: he was so much a product of his time and caste that it's foolish to judge him by today's standards. Tilman expected a lot from people, but no more than he demanded from himself, a trait probably inherited from his time as a soldier. He was, apparently, devoid of empathy, but again, this was not considered a virtue in the men of his time and would certainly have been discouraged in a soldier: Tilman, due to circumstances beyond his control, was a soldier for a good portion of his adult life. (The fact that he left the army after both Wars, as quickly as he reasonably could, has always reassured me that while he may have gone above and beyond the call of duty, soldiering was an unfortunate necessity rather than a chosen profession.) His misogynist persona was one I could accept as a not-unusual male affectation and I'm not sure that I am completely convinced by his apologists who point to his good relationship with his sister and nieces as proof that deep down inside he was fond of women. Conceivably he was uncomfortable around women until he got to know them, but his comments anent 'Grace Darling' in *Mischief in Patagonia*, seem to me to be far from tongue-in-cheek. For much of his life he was in a completely male environment and I suspect he simply did not know how to treat women, particularly when they were acting out of the accepted female role. However, I don't think it matters: perhaps we should admire his honesty in this respect, rather than insisting he was misunderstood.

I came to sailing almost by accident, meeting and marrying a man who had apparently thought of little else during his life. From a very sheltered, lower middle-class, comfort-loving home, it was a shock to discover how very uncomfortable and frightening a small boat could be. Sailing across the Atlantic and back at the age of 20, in a twenty-eight-foot James Wharram-designed catamaran, was, at times, shatteringly miserable and occasionally terrifying. To this day I can only attribute my setting out on this adventure to my complete ignorance.

Subsequent boats became increasingly less uncomfortable, although even by the standards of the day they were considered fairly Spartan. It was always a struggle for me to follow my husband's dreams and sail to the far-flung places he wanted to explore, far from the sunny skies and palm trees of most people's sailing fantasies. Tilman's books were a guide and a solace to me, but they also helped immensely

# BILL TILMAN: AN INSPIRATION

by drawing a picture that made the objective seem worth the fear and occasional tribulation. His quiet heroism and the stoic acceptance of the dangers, difficulties and discomfort by (most of) his crew were inspiring and reassuring. These boys had never sailed before, and while they had actually gone looking for adventure, surely they too, were often scared and wondered why they had signed on for this particular voyage? Tilman rarely praised his crew: he obviously expected that if one had agreed to do something, one was honour-bound to finish the task. It was typical of his upbringing and also reflected my father's approach to life (although wild horses wouldn't have dragged him on board a leaky boat for more than an afternoon), so that I too stuck to the voyage having agreed to take it on. When I wanted to ask my skipper to turn round and head for warm seas and sunshine, I reminded myself that without challenges, we don't grow and develop—not that I could imagine, for a moment, that Tilman would have expressed such a concept! As we sailed in the chill of the Davis Strait or tried to take sun sights in the foggy approaches to South Orkney, I would go back to Tilman's books for encouragement. He did these things, I would think, and in a damp, heavy boat, with untried crew and often unreliable gear. How easy it was for me, by comparison, in my dry, handy little ship, sailing with my skipper of many years.

When I read the books of Erling Tambs or Peter Pye, their tales were of sailing to places long lost. Nearly everywhere had been invaded by the realities of the twentieth century by the time I started voyaging, but when we went North or South the places that Tilman described didn't seem to have changed at all. They were as he described them and I felt that I was seeing exactly what he had seen, experiencing his experiences. I wouldn't have been surprised to turn a headland and see a yellow pilot cutter at anchor, the dinghy being rowed ashore. And while the Skipper would no doubt have huffed and puffed about being crowded out by another yacht—and worse, a yacht with a woman aboard—he would probably have invited us over for a glass of whisky and a yarn.

Of course, that never happened: Tilman disappeared not long after we returned from our first Atlantic crossing, so I never had the chance to meet him. But he lives on in his books, and his quiet acceptance of discomfort and the way in which he coped with dangerous situations

## MISCHIEF IN GREENLAND

were an example that I appreciated. His obvious joy in the beauty of the wild and empty places he visited resonated with mine. His personal quirks, his misplaced thriftiness and his occasionally questionable decisions meant that he was a real person rather than a super-hero. I have heard people question his pilotage, but remember only too clearly how incredibly difficult it was to fix our position while sailing into Nuuk. Our sights had been fairly good but, even after locating the correct headland, the harbour is approached through a maze of islands and skerries, which from offshore are indistinguishable from the bluffs and cliffs behind them. Somewhere there was a passage, but where? Greenland charts are generally devoid of soundings and details and one mountain looks very much like another. Interpreting charts is a skill that can't be learnt in a few weeks, and often there was no-one on board to help Tilman work out what he was looking at. Try doing this sort of pilotage yourself, before muttering that Tilman wasn't all he could have been. That he made mistakes was only to be expected.

He might have signed on better engineers too, or thrown a bit more money at his engine, but he obviously disliked the thing and, for good reason, distrusted it. In these days where the machinery seems to be given more precedence than the sails, I'm not surprised that people criticise Tilman for this, but it is an attitude that I well understand. An engine is a necessary evil in places like Greenland, but Tilman undoubtedly had a great romantic streak and I'm sure wished he could have sailed without it. To him, the object of the exercise was sailing to remote places, and I suspect he felt that using the engine was 'cheating'. Maybe its unreliability restored the element of unpredictability that makes an adventure rewarding. I dare say the attitude was irresponsible, but it's one with which I empathise. The fact that Tilman was not a perfect Outward Bound leader, to me, made him far more human. Over the years, I have met a surprising number of voyagers who have done great things while having only the haziest idea how their engine works and being in most respects extraordinarily impractical people. To me, this makes their feats the more admirable: how much braver to wander out into the unknown with hope rather than supreme competence!

Tilman was a Great British Amateur and it was that spirit that took him both to the mountains and to sea. To me, sponsorship takes away from attainment—a view I realise is held by very few—and thus I admire Tilman because his enterprises were 'planned on the back of an envelope' and funded by a small private income (something that is available to any of us, who is prepared to live minimally while earning a merely reasonable wage). Would Tilman have dreamt, I wonder, of describing *Mischief* as an 'expedition boat', without which, apparently, no-one can sail in high latitudes? I have always taken great satisfaction in being self-funded and independent and know how challenging this can be. To refit and outfit a large boat that requires crew was not easy: indeed, I suspect it was often the hardest part of Tilman's voyages. That they accomplished so much redounds to his credit and following in *Mischief's* wake, however trivially, enabled me to realise just what a success so many of them were.

You have to sail in fog and ice, with an underpowered boat, no GPS, no forecasts and minimal information, to get a real understanding of Tilman's achievements. Moreover, he was so often the first and it's a lot easier to do something when someone else has already shown the way. I am sure that I'm not alone in saying that Bill Tilman has enriched my life in many ways and my chance encounters, over the years, with people who actually knew him have always been a highlight for me.

At the end of the day, I don't think we choose our heroes. Bill Tilman inspired me, not so much because of what he chose to do, but because of the way in which he did it: quietly, without fanfare, understated, but with a profound sense of joy in his ventures and with a deep appreciation of the sublime beauty of remote places. The fact that he came home and wrote about them to share with others is the greatest of gifts. His books are classics that should be in print as long as men and women climb mountains and sail the seas.

# H. W. TILMAN

## *The Collected Edition*

For the first time since their original appearance, all fifteen books by H. W. Tilman are being published as single volumes, with all their original photographs, maps and charts. Forewords and afterwords by those who knew him, or who can bring their own experience and knowledge to bear, complement his own understated writing to give us a fuller picture of the man and his achievements. A sixteenth volume is the 1980 biography by J. R. L. Anderson, *High Mountains and Cold Seas*. The books will appear in pairs, one each from his climbing and sailing eras, in order of original publication, at quarterly intervals from September 2015:

| | |
|---|---|
| *Sep 2015* | Snow on the Equator |
| | Mischief in Patagonia |
| *Dec 2015* | The Ascent of Nanda Devi |
| | Mischief Among the Penguins |
| *Mar 2016* | When Men and Mountains Meet |
| | Mischief in Greenland |
| *Jun 2016* | Mount Everest 1938 |
| | Mostly Mischief |
| *Sep 2016* | Two Mountains and a River |
| | Mischief Goes South |
| *Dec 2016* | China to Chitral |
| | In Mischief's Wake |
| *Mar 2017* | Nepal Himalaya |
| | Ice With Everything |
| *Jun 2017* | Triumph and Tribulation |
| | High Mountains and Cold Seas |

www.tilmanbooks.com